ı the title poem of his most recent
ɔllection of poetry, *The Sunset Makɩ*
•onald Justice says, "As if...but eveɩ
ıing there is that." For Justice, Howaɩ
Jemerov, and others of their generatioɩ
ıings are understood through a kind
ropositional likening more than they aɩ
nderstood either as discrete entities or as
eductions from a traditional body of
ıought.

In this innovative study, Wyatt Prunty
ⱱaluates figure and form in contempo-
ıry poetry, especially the powers of simile
nd simile-like structures. Examining
orks by Nemerov, Wilbur, Bowers,
ſecht, Justice, Cunningham, Bishop,
an Duyn, Hollander, Pack, Kennedy,
mmons, Creeley, Wright, and others,
runty argues that doubts about lan-
ıuage, the tradition, and theistic assump-
ⱱons embedded in the tradition have
ırned simile-like patterns into major
ıodes of thought. From Lowell's early
ıterest in the "similitudo" and the
phantasm" of Gilson, to Husserl's
phantasies" and Heidegger's interest in
militude, to the use made by contempo-
ıry poets of simile, he contends that
mile-like patterns such as those created
y metaphor with slippage, mimicry,
ⱱnaphea, conjunctions, anacoluthon,
nd chiasmus, have proven to be more
ustworthy than such figures of equiva-
ⱱnce as symbol and allegory. By likening
ıings, poets have converted doubt from a
redicament of mind to a way of thinking
s simile and simile-like occurrences have
rovided poetry with variational thought
nd constitutive power.

A provocative and original analysis of
gure and form in contemporary poetry,
allen From the Symboled World will
ıake an important contribution to the
:udy of modern poetry and literature as
ⱱell as to linguistics and literary criticism
nd analysis.

About the Author

Wyatt Prunty is the author of three
volumes of poetry—*Balance as Belief;
What Women Know, What Men Believe;*
and *The Times Between*. He is Carlton
Professor of English at The University of
the South.

"Fallen from the Symboled World"

"Fallen from the Symboled World"

Precedents for the New Formalism

Wyatt Prunty

New York *Oxford*
OXFORD UNIVERSITY PRESS   1990

Oxford University Press

Oxford   New York   Toronto
Delhi   Bombay   Calcutta   Madras   Karachi
Petaling Jaya   Singapore   Hong Kong   Tokyo
Nairobi   Dar es Salaam   Cape Town
Melbourne   Auckland

and associated companies in
Berlin   Ibadan

Library of Congress Cataloging-in-Publication Data
Prunty, Wyatt.
   "Fallen from the symboled world" : precedents for the new
formalism / Wyatt Prunty.
   p.   cm.   Includes index.
ISBN 0-19-505786-4
1. American poetry—20th century—History and criticism.   I. Title.
PS325.P78   1990   811'.54'09—dc 19   89-31082   CIP

Sections of the following chapters have been previously published in different form:
Chapter one in *Agenda* 18 (Spring 1981).
Chapter two in *Sewanee Review* 93 (Winter 1985).

9 8 7 6 5 4 3 2 1

Printed in the United States of America
on acid-free paper

for Heather and Ian

Contents

"Fallen from the Symboled World"

Introduction

This is a book whose chapters might well be read in reverse order. Evidence and conviction tend toward tautology anyway. Like the Janus of doorways, bridges, and gates, or the two-faced royalties on cards, sequence is encountered in terms of before and after, passed or played. But before and after are silences that we sound by filling what Martin Heidegger would call the threshold of similitude. Discoveries are made by likening, not by causal reasoning applied to sequence, which, although unavoidable, is a demonstration of relations we already apprehend.

What Heidegger means by "the will as venture" contemporary poets have done by applying tropes to experience. They have pivoted on their own perspectives, freeing themselves from what, in the same sentence, Heidegger calls "the will to power." One way to think about what Heidegger means when he distinguishes between these two shapes for the will is to recall the old distinction between power, which is renewable, and force, which is self-exhausting. Ventured, the will renews itself by uncovering relations; thus, to Heidegger's way of thinking, venture is where real power is found. When, instead, the will is intent on possessing power, it actually resorts to force and loses itself in a retentiveness that denies the time in which it wills. Some tropes equate and thus are retentive; others only liken and thus venture relation.

As they have moved away from the tenets of modernism, poets writing since World War II have achieved a distance between their poetry and that of their immediate predecessors similar to Roman Jakobson's differentiation between romanticism and realism. For Jakobson metaphor prevails with romanticism, whereas metonymy characterizes realism. Of course, the gap between modern and contemporary poets is different and occupies its own ter-

3

ritory. It does not rest along the borders of romanticism and realism. In fact, these two "isms" still thrive among the diverse offerings
of contemporary poetry.

To further complicate things, in many ways much of contemporary poetry also retains modernist features. One hallmark of modernism, experimentation, continues happily, though perhaps with
fewer permanent discoveries. Discontinuity, alienation, and despair, all of which we associate with modernism, are descriptions
still applicable to poetry today. The reliability, even the reality, of
the objective world is still questioned. Disillusionment and in-
wardness continue to characterize much contemporary poetry. In
a way that is different yet still manages to repeat the older generation's maneuver, poets today question the tradition much the way
their modernist elders questioned history and the society that history recorded. And contemporary poetry is not set apart by its
verse, whether formal or free. The choice between formal and free
verse is an option that began with modernist rather than contemporary poets.

The shift that distinguishes contemporary from modern poetry
is not an exchange of romanticism for realism or metaphor for
metonymy but the replacement of symbol and allegory with simile-
like tropes. It is an exchange of the presuppositions behind symbol
and allegory for a more skeptical understanding that, other than
by taking doubt as its starting point, has no presuppositions and
thus builds relation from the ground up. Simile, metonymy, synecdoche, mimicry, and metaphor that is characterized by slippage
avoid the overhead of symbol and allegory, whose economies are
restricted by the requirements of equivalence. Doubt destroys equivalence, but it leaves the less extensional tropes free to bend and
deflect experience as they constitute relation through likening.

By "less extensional" I mean those tropes that are more connotative than denotative, tropes that liken things rather than urge
correspondence or equivalence. When Allen Tate wrote the rem-
iniscence "On the Death of Ransom" for the *Sewanee Review*
(82, no. 4 [1974]), he observed that the New Critical term *tension,* as it was associated with him, owed its origin to *extension* and *intension.* Describing tension as "a pseudo-erudite pun,"
Tate explained that by removing the prefixes of the two philosophical terms he arrived at something "derived from both, and

containing both." Tate linked intension with connotation or, in John Crowe Ransom's parlance, *texture*, and he matched extension with denotation—"or Ransom's *structure*—provided, of course, that the objects denoted are in an acceptable syntactical relation." What I wish to discuss are the reasons why younger poets following the generation of T. S. Eliot, Tate, Ransom, Yvor Winters, and others so often opted for the connotative half of what tension represented and avoided the denotative half. Avoiding the denotation and equivalence made possible by symbol and allegory, the younger generation of poets chose more associational modes. Yet they frequently, and sometimes curiously, turned to realism. The factualness we expect from realism, which in itself can create a sense of denotation and precision, somehow joined with the connotative powers of less extensional tropes, those that offered intension at the expense of the previously equally valued extension. The generation of poets who came into maturity after World War II employed doubt and similitude, and these were compatible with the connotative intension and texture. Whether or not these poets thought about what they were doing in quite these terms, their decisions nevertheless tended to divide tension and to rely on simile-like structures in order to pursue the connotative half of what that term was intended to represent.

The habitat for trope is language. The most dynamic and revolutionary source for the poetry of any period is language. Those contemporary poets who are most skilled verbally have access to the greatest range of similitude for their writing, but we tend to dismiss this in favor of another kind of evidence—in recent years, such episodes as the emergence of the Black Mountain school, confessionalism, prose poetry, concrete poetry, or, to use a term that tries to inflate its own tires at seventy miles an hour, language poetry. Names for literary schools and movements are frequently misleading. The most current of such road signs has been confusingly dubbed the New Formalism, suggesting, first, that the use of poetic form has not been continuous but today is new and, second, that the current formalist effort owes part of its existence to the New Criticism.

There is no real basis for associating these two schools. Nevertheless, what urges comparison is the idea, suggested by the similarity in names, that somehow today's formalists are arid throwbacks to yesterday's critics, among us by abstraction rather than the living blood of poetry. The vagueness of thought that leads to this association matches that used when people link free verse with progressive politics and formal verse with those readers of the Constitution who are strict constructionists. Robert Bly's description of John Crowe Ransom and Allen Tate, driving from town to town looking for a jail, comes to mind, as does Diane Wakoski's recent attack on John Hollander for reminding us of the ways we mistake literary fashion for something permanent. (At the time of this writing, the two most recent instances of what seems to have become a mental tic are provided by Carol Muske in the 8 January 1989 *New York Times Book Review* and Greg Kuzma in *Northwest Review* 26, no. 3 [1988].) Ransom, Tate, Hollander, and others are offenders against meliorism. The censorship here usually runs: How can one be so calculating and self-serving as to write a poem that only rhymes and meters? The implication is that since one uses verse, one only writes verse. Unpacked, this line of reasoning, denigrating in one direction and self-flattering in the other, is embarrassing. In both profiles—free and supposedly progressive or formal and supposedly repressive—poetry is not really the issue. The polarization that results from associating poetry and politics in order to flatter one type of poet and criticize another is no more convincing than the skewed analogies on which it rests. It is unfortunate that so far the New Formalists have accepted a name that promises something new at the same time it suggests their tenets are old, that they are only the latest installment of a traditional and thus conservative aesthetic. Doing so obscures the really substantive question for contemporary poetry, which has to do with what tropes poets believe they can use.

What seems salvageable about the label New Formalism is that it provokes reconsideration. This means reading the work of more established but equally formal contemporary poets. Formalism is neither new nor renewed. Our understanding of very recent poetry should begin with a broader view, one that starts with the tropes that appear in the work of poets such as Howard Nemerov, Mona Van Duyn, Anthony Hecht, Robert Pack, Donald Justice, John Hollander, Richard Wilbur, Elizabeth Bishop, X. J. Kennedy, J. V. Cunningham, Edgar Bowers, Robert Pinsky, and numerous others. The work of these poets, which is the focus of my thinking here about contemporary poetry, teaches us that what actually matters most today, or probably any day, is not formal questions so much as the related issue of which modes of thought poets believe they can use, especially as those modes appear in tropes. The use of form, evident in all of these poets, is an important but secondary matter. Form may force poets to be ingenious and this may lead to discoveries, and a formal device such as rhyme may be constitutive to the degree it clusters words, but tropes are the primary means for making discoveries. Summarizing the current use of form by certain younger poets with a label such as New Formalism seems the best that we can do—for now. A more accurate name, however, would direct our attention to the modes of thought, the means for figuration, used in poetry by a large and distinguished group of contemporary poets, ranging in age from thirty to seventy. And this, of course, would carry with it a consideration of the presuppositions that influence poets in selecting not only their means for writing poems but also their subject matter.

As I suggested earlier, our understanding of what contemporary poets have been doing inclines toward stories that recount and predict movements, offering us sequence (beginning, middle, end), but this approach generalizes our understanding. In many ways the changes that have occurred in poetry over the last forty years have been the result of an increased skepticism about meaning. As Howard Nemerov says of himself in "The Loon's Cry," we are "fallen from / The symboled world." But language is often self-sealing; articulating doubt can be the first step back to knowing. What we hold off becomes near; what we hold near becomes distant. Trope is where we do both of these. It allows us to pivot on any situation, and by doing so we apply torsions to ourselves and to our surroundings in order to uncover new relations. This is a process more basic and pervasive than any single literary movement is apt to recognize.

In 1986 Harper and Row published the anthology *Strong Measures: Contemporary American Poetry in Traditional Forms,* which was graced with a foreword by Richard Wilbur. The anthology's purpose, as defined in its introduction by editors Philip Dacey and David Jauss, was not to place formal verse above free verse but to make the case that today the "strongest poetry" is "written . . .

when all options, formal and free, are open to the poet." I have no quarrel with this peacemaking argument, but while Dacey and Jauss are busy mediating between two movements and the various ways forms, designed either for freedom or restraint, have been successfully employed by contemporary poets, they overlook a much more fundamental issue. Their discussion of forms—how poets disguise, graft, and truncate them—proceeds at a remove from the real issue for contemporary poetry: trope. Here, as elsewhere, the debate over free versus formal verse is marred by a kind of literal-mindedness that often unites with the oppositional reasoning of those who see themselves as revolutionaries or counterrevolutionaries battling one establishment or another. This kind of reasoning has been applied to physical matters, leaving unexamined the likening process provided by poetic language, which is the real justification for poetry. I have in mind the simile-like figures employed by Nemerov, Hecht, Wilbur, Van Duyn, Hollander, Pack, Bishop, Justice, and others. But first are the changes Robert Lowell initiated.

Several of the traits that characterize Robert Lowell's later poetry exemplify important modes for likening employed by his generation. Sometimes they also demonstrate the constraints that accompanied a younger generation's break with the modernists. Because of Lowell's early success as a young modernist and later success with poetry that diverged from modernist norms, his career is representative of a substantial segment of a younger generation of poets who distanced themselves from the tenets of their modernist elders. For Lowell, change in his writing was the result of various changes in his life that occurred around the time he was completing *The Mills of the Kavanaughs* (1951): mental difficulties, divorce, the death of his parents, the outcome of World War II—and the aggregate of all of these, namely, his loss of religious faith and departure from the Catholic church. The consensus is that in Lowell's poetry a major change occurred with the publication of *Life Studies* (1959). Actually that change was evident years before, between the first appearance of "The Mills of the Kavanaughs" as the lead piece in the *Kenyon Review* (1951) and several months later, when it appeared in much revised form (purged of most of its allusions to Catholicism and relying on causal reasoning and narration for its convincingness) as the title poem in *The Mills of the Kavanaughs.*

There is something particularly important about the change in Lowell's work. Lowell's revised understanding of his poetry now seems to have been representative of a general increase in skepticism during the fifties and sixties about institutions and traditional structures of meaning. The confessional mode and the realistic detail used to substantiate that mode found maturity in *Life Studies.* And the latter influenced poets and critics alike. Agreement about Lowell's career and the accuracy of his skeptical view of things has been general. But agreement is static. Poetry never rests with consensus. Thinking again about the reasons Lowell made changes in his poetry can help us evaluate the rate of exchange used by a group of younger poets intent on their new currency. Along with the valuation of Lowell's much-examined career, the implicit question of consensus itself, about Lowell and others of his generation, can be addressed in an indirect way—not so much to revise the basic facts as to reconsider why certain modes of thought used by poets writing after World War II were preferred to those used by the modernists, why similitude tended to replace equivalence, and what the gains and losses were in this exchange.

Comparing certain modes of thought that appear in Lowell's poetry with phenomenological methods provides some insight into the factualness that characterizes Lowell's later poetry, its success by realism. A phenomenologist might ask, To what extent does realism actually contribute new knowledge, and to what extent does it appeal to the preconceptions held by readers who are thus able to re-cognize as *real* the things described by the poems they read? That is, To what extent can realism itself lead to one more exercise in consensus? This question is certainly not settled by a consideration of Lowell. But because of his position he offers a good place to start asking it. In order to think about what might be the implications of some aspects of contemporary poetic thought, I compare the systematic minimalism of Edmund Husserl's method in his *Cartesian Meditations: An Introduction to Phenomenology* with the factualism of Lowell's method, which began with the second version of "The Mills of the Kavanaughs." I only intend for my borrowings from Husserl to operate suggestively. Trying to match too precisely the similarities between Lowell's poetic ruminations and Husserl's philosophical questioning would mean ignoring the gap between two very different ways of thinking. My purpose is not to urge conclusive equations but to think about the way doubt in its more recent manifestations inhibits some modes of thought while it encourages others.

Because of the skepticism of Lowell's later poetry, its central concern became authority. On what could Lowell base the truth claims for his poetry? The personalism of confession? Restricting much of the poet's intellectual experience to personalism, which often resulted in a use of imagery that in its minimalism shared a great deal with phenomenological methods? The example of Lowell dramatizes the difficulties faced by a generation of poets skeptical about the tradition's ability to represent truth. This distinguished them from their modernist elders. Both generations inherited the Cartesian predicament. But for the younger poets writing in the wake of World War II, the terms seemed to have narrowed even more. Yet this led to its own paradox. Employing certain tropes, doubt could mean *more* as well as *less*.

Degrees of constriction that accompanied doubt are what we see so clearly today. The late modern, or postmodern, poets sound sadly belated even as we try to identify just where their generation fits. Certainly part of their situation is that doubt seems to have denied poets the ability to accept hierarchical structures embedded in the tradition. Individual talents have rebelled, as a kind of personalized realism has replaced certain modernist modes. But this has not been a solely negative result. As with simile-like structures, personalism remains relational. An individual is a father, mother, son, daughter, and so forth. By likening the self to others, an individual balances the differing/subjective/autobiographical self with the likening/objective/biographical self. Generations that rebel always exist relationally to what has gone before, as they do to what will follow. They exist more as turns, therefore, than they do as breaks with the past, or the future. Lineage is crooked but not discontinuous. Thus while the apparent magnification of doubt did lead to a kind of minimalist realism among many poets writing after World War II, it also had a very positive aspect, the objectivity of experience—a modernist ideal that also was Husserl's goal, even as in all three cases the grounding for objective experience remained radically subjective.

In the middle of section eight of his "First Meditation" of *Cartesian Meditations,* a section he calls *"The* ego cogito *as transcendental subjectivity,"* Husserl addresses his wish to have the "reflective Ego's abstention from position-takings." His idea of a "phenomenological epoché," or of having means for "parenthesizing" the "Objective world," is not intended to exclude the world but to "gain possession of something," and that something is one's "pure living, with all the pure subjective processes making this up, and everything meant in them." The epoché is a "radical and universal method by which" Husserl says he can "apprehend [him]self purely: as Ego, and with [his] own pure conscious life, in and by which the entire Objective world exists for [him] and is precisely as it is for [him]." The similarity between the state Husserl describes and the way the imagination works in poetry rests with the ways both processes are intended to objectify experience that nevertheless begins within subjective terms.

In his introduction to *Phenomenology and Existentialism,* Robert C. Solomon summarizes Husserl's project as "purity of description," a method for objectivity. Experience is bracketed, or parenthesized, for the sake of clarity. According to Solomon, Husserl is after two things: the "essences that are the key to [his] analysis of necessary truth" and "the object described by phenomenology . . . the phenomenon, or intentional object of experience." In Lowell's influential case, the problem of consciousness and the object of consciousness enjoyed similar venue. Lowell's poetic imagination worked similarly to the three-part ego described by Husserl in *Cartesian Meditations.* Husserl's division requires experiencing, transcendental, and eidetic egos, whereas Lowell's falls into the categories of experiencing, remembering, and imagining selves. Husserl's process ends with a fine-tuned consciousness; Lowell's, with a realistic poem. Among Lowell's contemporaries, the substitution for impersonalism and the tradition with personalism and experience seems in large part the result of increased skepticism about language and the tradition on the part of a group of poets who followed the modernists. Lowell and many others of his generation used their poetry to achieve a kind of realism that would bracket their experience. On some influential occasions this was done in ways that were similar to Husserl's proposed phenomenological practices. Doubt influenced both philosophy and poetry. But doubt did not mean negation, finally. At the same time personalism was prospering in the hands of one group of poets, another group was using figuration to play variations on experience. Doubt meant the play of possibility, what in *Ideas* Husserl calls the *"as if."* For contemporary poets what occurred was the reliance on certain rhetorical patterns and various simile-like tropes that likened the objects of experience at the same time they separated them for analysis. The imaginative play made possible by likening provided poets a means for apprehending what Husserl would call an "Objective world." But the starting point for any objectification of the world or our experience of it began by questioning it.

The gain for poets that accompanied their acceptance and employment of doubt came in the form of tropes that bestowed relation rather than demonstrated it. No longer forced to appeal to higher orders that arranged meaning to be read deductively downward into experience, poets were at once destitute and free. They lacked guarantees for meaningful conclusions, but they could now vacate the maps that often before had indicated orthodox or conventionally sanctioned paths of reasoning. In "Skunk Hour" Lowell could exchange the all-inclusive "white" of "the chalk-dry and spar spire / of the Trinitarian Church" for the "white stripes" that delineate "Main Street" and identify the back of the "mother skunk . . . who swills the garbage" and who, though Lowell comes upon her when she is vulnerable because she is feeding and with her kittens, "does not scare." Solomon summarizes the gain that follows Husserl's initial stance of doubt by saying that "it is the intentional act that *constitutes* the object." We can find what we set out looking for. We choose where we look, and whether or not we "scare." If we proceed with this constitutive principle in mind, then we are free in ways that certainly were not unimagined before Lowell's generation but imagined differently enough that those earlier choices, made with the hierarchies of a prearranged tradition in the background, were often in danger of ending in equations or, turned round, in oppositions. Reasoning by oppositions was a method employed both early and late by Lowell. Both equivalence and opposition are locked much the way discursive reasoning is locked. All offer preexisting paths that can preclude the poetic imagination's ability to make discoveries through similitude.

The examples of Husserl and Lowell suggest that, as a presupposition, doubt can lead independent thinkers to significantly similar methods for arranging experience. As I outlined earlier, Husserl divides the consciousness into three categories, the experiencing, transcendental, and eidetic egos, and these seem to have a lot in common with Lowell's existential threesome of experiencing, recollecting/transcending, and imagining selves. But the similarities between Husserl's proposed structures and those employed by Lowell are more suggestive than conclusive, and, though Lowell also can be read from an existential perspective, the knotty relationship between phenomenology and existentialism is not resolved by comparing Lowell's practice and Husserl's proposed method. It is furthered, but in a way that remains too local for philosophical debate. Still, Lowell's second period does begin by sharing Husserl's first premise, doubt taken from the level of predicament to a means for proceeding. And taking doubt to be a method rather than a weakness or failure is what led to personalism, confessed or in other ways bracketed or parenthesized, in the poetry of many of those writing after World War II. For still other poets writing during the same period, doubt led to the simile-like trope's replacement of symbol and other figures of correspondence.

The most successful modality for poets has not been minimalism or realism. Enjoying greater freedom of movement by neither appealing to nor opposing any one system, similitude has been the most generative mode of thought. Simile-like modes have been able to fill the gap, however locally, created by a loss of authority that came in the wake of the modernists. Likening creates new relations that, at the time and within the terms of equivalence, would not otherwise be recognized. Likening draws a wider net than causality, equivalence, or opposition can draw.

Phenomenology and existentialism share in the tradition that has followed Descartes. Husserl's concern in *Cartesian Meditations* is with how we know things, with intentionality (or expectation), and with the way these work constitutively for the consciousness. The existential project has much more to do with human action. Combined, the two would appear to take us from the precepts of teach and delight to discover and do. Or, regarded another way, they urge us from autobiography to biography, from a subjective basis for knowing to an objective one. For Kierkegaard, anxiety begins with a distinction similar to the one between autobiography and biography, with a finite subject proceeding till it encounters an infinite object. An individual realizes his or her freedom only then to discover the limitations to that freedom. The subjective self is discovered among other selves, an objectifying process that is both liberating and restraining. An everyday example of this is the way children use similitude to move from self-sympathy to empathy.

The idea that the self is dependent on others for its existence is essential to Heidegger, and sets him at a remove from his mentor Husserl. The personal irony attendant to Heidegger's emphasis on the self's relational character, its being in the world, is his political thought. A problematical figure for his woeful affiliations with the Nazis and with nazism, Heidegger posited ideas about poetic thought that are nevertheless useful. Seemingly blind to some of the implications of his own stance, Heidegger contrasts utilitarian thought with poetic thought. The former is goal-oriented, and characterized by its not being on the margin but very much a part of whatever is at stake. It is language put to the purposes of power, in one manifestation or another. It is the orchestration of language in order to prove an idea already held or to gain an object already valued. Poetic thought has no agenda. Rather than the holding-over-against of argument, poetic thought is a giving-over. In *Poetry, Language, Thought* and in numerous other works Heidegger addresses issues of major importance for poetry. In his own meandering and convoluted way, he investigates language and poetic thought, and he explores questions such as what is our relation to the tradition and how does similitude (in the hands of poets, simile-like tropes) work as a cognitive and constitutive instrument.

These are such acute topics in part because, as seen in the cases of Nemerov, Justice, Pack, Van Duyn, the later Lowell, plus others, many contemporary poets share Heidegger's resistance to dualistic systems. Tropes that equate do not work because there is nothing on the far side of the equal-sign. Poets writing today find themselves at large in the world, as Heidegger would have them be. In Heidegger's essay "What Are Poets For?" vulnerability is considered a part of what individuals have to contribute. As Heidegger extracts his understanding from a poem by Rilke, referred to as "improvised verses," he sees people as the objects of something that "ventures" them even as they "go *with* this venture." Poets seem unusually fine examples of this principle. The imaginative, or poetic, use of language increases possibilities. In short, to be ventured is not to be thrown away, especially insofar as you knowingly accept risk. Venture is not beyond caring, and there is "a safety" in the "unshieldedness" of those at risk, a safety in being vulnerable to what, to judge by his title, Heidegger (not being a poet, or much of one) has decided ahead of time that poets are "for." Unfortunately, there seems to have been no irony intended on Heidegger's part in the teleological, possibly even utilitarian, "for" applied to people, but the idea of thinking poetically in order to uncover new possibilities, however subject to the dangers of abstraction that notion might be, remains clear and profitable.

Contemporary poets have stressed individual instead of cultural experience. They have tended to remake more than rediscover their frontiers of experience. Tropes that liken—simile, metonymy, synecdoche, mimicry, metaphor that is fluid, and others—that work constitutively have flourished. Because they also establish the play between sameness and difference, rhetorical devices such as anacoluthon, anaphora, apostrophe, chiasmus, homoeoteleuton, and zeugma have proved capable of operating as additional occasions for simile-like tropes. Various tautological arrangements— title and work, epigraph and text, poet and persona—have operated as similes, as have echoes the language carries forward from earlier texts.

The evaluative question that we should ask about contemporary poetry has to do with the figures poets use more than the forms that surround, display, and sometimes provoke those figures. Insofar as the figures by which poets think meld with the forms they use, forms of course are a part of poetic thought, but figuration is the basic stuff. Of course, form holds its ground. It can serve as both a structure and an obstruction that generates new thought (an idea dear to Winters and Tate), and of course it has the capacity to make language more memorable than it otherwise would be. Form heightens utterance. But it is the figurative modes of thought, couched in form, in the poetry of the poets who are discussed in the following chapters that provide the most conclusive demonstration of mastery over that very formal medium, language. Is there a better way to differentiate between Apollo and the faun, other than by judging the intellectual and aesthetic play that occurs between figurative modes of thought and the forms that surround and feature them, and sometimes may provoke them?

It appears that for now in the perception of many contemporary poets, the New Critical staples of irony, paradox, and ambiguity have shifted from the status of written tropes, which uncover new meaning, to read tropes, which work in a prescriptive way that covers over the play of meaning. With the precision of their use in the academy, these last three have become such reliable tools for reading that often they appear to preclude the fluidity of meaning for which the modernist poets and exegetes of the New Criticism originally prized them. Despite this contemporary perception, irony, paradox, and ambiguity are modes of thought used in the belief that language works, and in this they are much more rewarding than certain techniques recently substituted for them.

Physical substitutes for irony, paradox, and ambiguity have flourished and often done so in ways that are predictable, even formalized, but they have worked by tearing down the structures of language, not by expanding them. The minimalists' removal of punctuation, the use of vague pronoun reference, and the excessive use of enjambed, foreshortened lines, to give three examples, disrupt the reader's syntactical expectations. The effect results from a kind of formalized disarray. The uncertainty created by these disruptions may make things *seem* ironical, paradoxical, or ambiguous, but the reader has been given a mechanical substitution for an intellectual problem. Substituting the mechanical arrangement of foreshortened lines that disrupt the flow of language for the very real problems we have with the intelligibility of experience is not only a retreat from the profound causes for doubt but also, in the act of retreating, a kind of stalling within the condition.

For some, the question of organism may raise its analogical head. Without rehearsing the ways conflicting schools (New Critics and Black Mountain school, for example) have used it to justify their very different positions, the problem with organism is that it is governed by its object. The Brooksian formulation that likens elements of a poem to the "parts of a growing plant" has the advantage of using, for its analogy and by implication having in its intention, a complex object, or an object *seen* in its complexity. The organism found in contemporary poetry (I restrict my examples to anthologized poems by Robert Creeley, A. R. Ammons, and James Wright) that opposes such complicating turns of thought as irony, paradox, and ambiguity, often is based on noncomplex objects, or objects apprehended by modes of thought that in their restrictiveness make the things to which they are applied equally restricted. This is a risk that goes with the less extensional, simile-like tropes, for which I neverthless wish to argue. Likening is no more rewarding than the objects likened are rewarding. Reading an object metonymically is only as useful as the object is able to invoke and sustain its relation to a larger more substantive structure. Here questions of context, and, implicitly, questions about the tradition, are never really absent. Influence is a useful litmus test, *now* tested by *then*. Anxiety, whether Kierkegaardian or Bloomian, is not a negative. Belatedness is itself both a predicament and an opportunity, as the echoes that show we come late also allow us the chance to incorporate their preceding contexts, so the dimensions of our contemporary meaning extend back and enjoy a textual depth of field. But this takes us from a restrictive or object-based idea of organism to a broader mode of achieving meaning.

From Harold Bloom's *Anxiety of Influence* (1973) to James E. B. Breslin's *From Modern to Contemporary: American Poetry, 1945–1965* (1984), explanations of change in American poetry have tended to focus on the oppositions and influences that exist between generations. In the preface to his *Situation of Poetry: Contemporary Poetry and Its Traditions* (1976), Robert Pinsky identifies the concept of "influence" as part of the romantic tradition and states his preference for the term *affinity*. The virtue of Pinsky's preference lies in the freedom it affords us. Although having literary parents does provide or withhold imaginative power,

Pinsky's choice about how he will regard the matter helps to free him from a push-pull understanding of poetry-as-primacy. It is important we see that the distinction between older and younger groups of poets has more to do with the context of the time during which their poems are written, and with their beliefs about what can be said, than it does with dates of birth and questions of rank. Bloom's application of the Oedipal paradigm is a profound description of opposing wills struggling behind texts, but so is Heidegger's prospect for poets stepping into "the will as venture." The self-individuating and oppositional will and the self-ventured will are in dialogue throughout contemporary poetry. They appear in the guise of poems that speak and poems that sing.

Poetic speech is meant to resist situations that threaten the individual, and in doing so it recognizes differences, holding the world at an arm's distance. Poetic song gives over rather than holds over. It is open to the resources of language, including our language's history in the tradition, as the individual's voice is transposed into an ablative melody intended to go beyond the discrete will. The ideal behind poems that sing, whether ever fully realized or not, is the wholeness of the self and the use of language for a nondisjunctive way of seeing the world. But of course the absence of wholeness is an equally viable motive for song; as Hollander tells us at the conclusion of his "Piano Interlude," "Song is not born in rooms emptied by fulfillment, / But only in long, cold halls, hollow with desire." Song can either affirm wholeness or lament loss and fragmentation. The ideal of wholeness informs both actions. Song projects the ideal of duration, not completeness but the sense of wholeness by which a voice extends itself.

When speech and song are pitted against each other in the same poem, they can initiate a simile-like maneuver. Wholeness and continuity suggested by song are matched against the speechlike breakup of these, which opposes them yet in doing so retains them in play. Speech and song are modes by which we can hold opposing ideas simultaneously far and near, playing them variationally in order to see each from as many perspectives as possible. Moving between the extremes of speech and song dramatizes the ideas they suggest. Such movement is the play of likeness and difference, the likeness of continuity between the self and the world it inhabits and the difference of discontinuity between the self and its world. Similitude is in continual play. Ultimately, speech and song invoke the same originating idea. They are the negative and positive of one value, which when played back and forth can create as easily a complex series of responses to wholeness as they can responses to the lack of wholeness.

Contemporary poets appear to have favored, in place of symbol and allegory, simile-like tropes because they are free of the tradition's hierarchical arrangement of theistic and moral assumptions embedded in antecedent texts. Such tropes are valuable for their applicability to personal experience, though in the case of echo, for example, that experience includes something from the tradition. Among the poets I wish to consider, the shift has not been one of rejection or rebellion against the tradition so much as it has been a change in emphasis that led them to seek authority on more local terms. Following the modernists, local surroundings seemed a necessity. As Heidegger says, a tradition that has become "master" covers over what it has to "transmit." Poets writing after World War II confronted a tradition that was very much the "master." Therefore they found that the modes of thought by which they could uncover new meanings had to be ones that were not overly dependent on tradition or hierarchy for their authority.

Another reason that certain tropes have been favored has been because they articulate themselves almost physically; they bend, deflect, swerve, liken, and differentiate. They are almost anatomical in their figuration, and this is of benefit to a poetry inclined toward personalism. Poets who employ a simile to describe a predicament automatically deflect it and put themselves and their readers outside it, however briefly, as the play between similarity and dissimilarity continues. Viewed on the level of the individual trope, emphasis is given to the play of meaning, rather than to one "correct" interpretation. In contrast, insofar as symbol and allegory appeal to the tradition for their significance, they initiate a kind of genetic philology because the original meaning of a thing is an arche.

Nemerov is as skilled with trope as any poet writing in the second half of this century. He employs, in addition to the usual modes of figuration, a kind of synaposematic mimicry. Synaposematism is a defenseless species' mimicry of another species that possesses some means of protection. Seen on a physical level, Nemerov's version of this sort of mimicry allows him to use poetic figures to deflect and displace a nonanthropomorphic world in which single events are random and generalizations about those events are best restricted to terms of probability. (For company, Nemerov often seems to prefer physicists to poets.) Regarded on another level, by articulating the jeopardies of a decentralized metaphysics, Nemerov mirrors back those truths that threaten. Mirroring is a way of becoming indistinguishable from the object mirrored, thus possibly safe from it. Even if we cannot overcome a problem, when we articulate it we put it at a distance from us, as though we mirrored it back. Because the mimic mirrors his object, he holds himself both near and apart. He opens an area in which the play of similitude becomes possible. Nemerov mirrors back what he fears, and by this deflecting, reiterative gesture he shields himself, creating ataraxy before various gorgons. The mastery of Nemerov's ontological mimicry in "The Loon's Cry" compares favorably with a modern landmark such as Wallace Stevens's "Sunday Morning," which explores the viability of a symbolic life. Comparing the two poems provides a good illustration of the differences between the best of modern tropes that operate by equivalence, even as systems of equivalence are seen to fail, and the best of what has followed.

In "Sunday Morning" Stevens is writing at the beginning of the century about the failure of myths, especially Christianity and Neoplatonism. Stevens presides over a set of vacant symbols. Having entertained the contradictions that accompany dualism, here heaven and earth, he concludes with a sort of twilit nostalgia and longing. Once he has used his ample store of figures to display the recollection of hope, which entails the condition of despair characterizing the winged soul that circles ambiguously through "Sunday Morning," Stevens concludes with our symbols echoing not only their past meanings but also their current hollowness. The soul that Stevens describes propositionally has been placed in the despairing position of what Kierkegaard would call "an experimental god," made sick by memory and expectation.

Nemerov takes his measure from the second half of the century, and whereas Stevens is the master of vacant symbols, Nemerov is the master of seeing, the master of the tropes by which he likens experience—as in the "The Blue Swallows," where "intelligible things" owe their existence to "the mind's eye," which lights "the sun." In "The Loon's Cry," instead of seeing a Neoplatonic soul sinking to "darkness on extended wings," Nemerov works finally by hearing, likening a nonanthropomorphic loon's cry to an example of our technology, a train whistle. Stevens's arrangement is a short-circuited deduction. Meaning, or the absence of meaning, is read from heaven downward, or from the memory of once-held hopes for heaven downward. Nemerov's mode of thought works in the reverse direction, likening upward from two disparate sounds into the one sound made human finally by the reflecting thought of a poem.

All is not immediately constructive with similitude, however. There is the figure that turns away and hides or covers over the relations between things. Richard Wilbur finds that the disguise in a lie's "toxic zest" does this, whereas Robert Pack focuses on the incongruities that initiate humor. Some figures give us the differing side of similitude, that moment when something reveals itself to us in the form of what it is not. Heidegger's example is disease, with which he means to represent the gap between the symptoms by which the disease may appear and the actual disorder that remains potent yet hidden. But even disguise leaves traces that can be followed back to the source of what is experienced. Differences are relational; thus *different from* points back to what may be currently out of sight. In the poetry of Justice, this occurs often through a conjunction, by which he either turns our perspective or turns the object he places before us. His "Nostalgia of the Lakefronts" is masterful in its use of rhetorical turns in order to modify perspective spatially, temporally, and psychologically.

A poem is a double hermeneutic. It is written to interpret experience (cultural, personal, or both) and to be interpreted. Modern poets such as Eliot, Ransom, Tate, and Winters were distinguished for their erudition. They were at home in the academy, and for them the interpretation of their culture's literature was a personal matter. After World War II, the skepticism about language and meaning that made poets less inclined to consider philological questions and much more apt to base the authority of their poetry on personal experience meant that certain modes of thought prized by modern poets no longer seemed, as they once did, appropriate or accurate. With modernist assumptions about hierarchies set aside, there was no need for the equivalences generated by symbol and allegory. Because the goal of less extensional, more connotative tropes is to discover relation rather than demonstrate equivalence, poetic language has been free to work constitutively, if locally. There have been few positions to be taken, except those that by similitude could open a meaningful free play.

1

Symbol, Allegory, Causality, and the Phenomenal Flux

> If we have been right in assigning to music the power of again giving birth to myth, we may similarly expect to find the spirit of science on the path where it inimically opposes this mythopoeic power of music.
>
> —FRIEDRICH NIETZSCHE

> I'm fed up with people who say, Boo hoo, somebody stole my myths.
>
> —W. D. SNODGRASS

> (sung to "Somebody Stole My Gal")
>
> Somebody stole my myths,
> Stole all their gists and piths. . . .
> Hear me crying,
> Don't much like forever dying—
> Somebody stole my myths.
>
> —X. J. KENNEDY

I

As a protégé of T. S. Eliot, Allen Tate, and John Crowe Ransom, Robert Lowell enjoyed early recognition in part because his work exemplified the aesthetic standards of the New Criticism. Later, when a major revision in poetics was afoot, Lowell made a dramatic break with New Criticism and modernism. Consensus has it that the changes in his career make Lowell a representative figure for his generation. There has been general agreement both about the worth of his poetry and the barometric gradient of his career. But our understanding, and our evaluation, of the developments in recent American poetry are clarified by a look at the different modes of thought employed during Lowell's two periods. He remained modern, more than anything else, but his relation to modernism was complicated. Discussing *Lord Weary's Castle* (1946), Randall Jarrell summarized Lowell's poetry as "a unique fusion of modernist and traditional poetry" in which there rest "side by side . . . certain effects that one would have thought mutually exclusive." Jarrell says that Lowell's is "a post- or anti-modernist poetry," and he makes a completely accurate prediction of the influence that Lowell's work was to have on contemporary poetry.[1]

The questions of trope and source for a poem's authority, whether they come from tradition, mentor, myth, or experience as, say, represented by the language of realism, reveal the paradox of Lowell's modernist antimodernism. Where should he look for likeness? Early in his writing, Lowell had three kinds of authority at easy reach. When Jarrell wrote his summary, Lowell had the tradition, examples of what could be done with the tradition represented by his mentors Ransom, Tate, and Eliot, and the central myth for his imagination supplied by his Catholicism, a belief he shared with Tate. Lowell's first book, *Land of Unlikeness* (1944), began with an introduction by Tate, and it took its title from Etienne Gilson's *Mystical Theology of Saint Bernard* (1940), which stated that "the essential condition of knowing is [a] 'similitudo,' [a] phantasm, the presence of which in the mind" enables "it to transform itself to the likeness of the object, enables it by that very fact to know it."[2] (C. S. Lewis's *Allegory of Love: A Study in Medieval Tradition,* published in 1936 between the times Gilson lectured on Saint Bernard and published his book, made a similar point about the "similitudo."[3]) Authority came from one's likeness to God, but taken out of context, or in the context of Lowell's later skepticism, this precise formulation could be part of a premise for a phenomenological treatment of experience. A change in context was ultimately what did happen with Lowell, as he grew increasingly distant from his first sources for authority—the tradition, his mentors and their embodiment of the tradition, and the Catholic church. But this did not happen until after Lowell's profoundly formative beginnings, modernism and the church.

Authority remained an issue in Lowell's later phase, and often something very close to Gilson's "similitudo" or "phantasm" had a secular existence in the phenomenological workings of the imagery in Lowell's experientially based poetry.

In his discussion of Saint Bernard, Gilson states: "For there is a primary likeness to God that no man can lose as long as he lives, remaining in him as testimony to the higher likeness he has lost. It consists in this, that the soul is everywhere and at one and the same time present in its body, even as God, whole and entire, is everywhere and at once present in all His creation."[4] This was the first mature world for Lowell's imagination. With "charity" qualifying the experience, Gilson equates "sight of God and likeness to God."[5] The young Saint Bernard was a figure of renewal the young Lowell found attractive. A poet converted to Catholicism, Lowell felt himself to be an agent for renewal who was writing in a secular century, a "land of unlikeness." The figurative language of his poetry was a means for some "sight of God."

What happened to Lowell when God slipped from sight, or imagination? He could no longer assert correspondence between himself or the world and a divine object, but the activity of likening through poetry continued. Even as he played against it, the proposition of likening—which assumes that there are worthwhile, if not normative, objects out in the world waiting for comparison—remained central to Lowell's imagination. To use the previously cited epigraph from Nietzsche, music's formative power to give "birth to myth" must have been replaced by some element of science, which "opposes [the] mythopoeic power of music."[6] In Lowell's later poetry, the influence of science presented itself as a combination of doubt and objectivity. The music did not stop completely, but it became clear to Lowell's readers that the process of likening vertically had been replaced by a process of likening horizontally, through thing and word.

Lowell's career dramatizes the struggle between systems of realism and idealism, what during Lowell's formative years Lewis termed "sensibles and insensibles." To borrow from Lewis again, Lowell began writing with an idea of the "fundamental equivalence between the immaterial and the material" worlds. Allegory may have been secondary to the romantic and sacramental symbol, which initially was a primary mode of thought for Lowell, but both modes took their authority from a hierarchy that began in an immaterial world.[7] The change in Lowell's poetry was a movement from idealism to factualism. As a "study in the concrete polarity of actuality and potentiality," the symbol appeared to overreach its authority.[8] What replaced it was a reliance on the world of "facts."[9] Lowell, therefore, dramatizes the options that exist between several ontological arrangements—the symbol projecting upward and forward, the fact refusing to project, the resourceful simile moving between these two extremes.

The idea that "Lowell is essentially a post-Symbolist poet" who wrote a "realistic or documentary or metonymic lyric" is an accepted explanation of his career as it is understood to have progressed from *Life Studies* on.[10] But the first steps toward the "realistic or documentary" in Lowell's poetry were taken well before *Life Studies,* when Lowell was writing and revising "The Mills of the Kavanaughs." Whenever you date it, however, Lowell's poetic shift was more dialectical than an act of abandonment. By this I mean that the significance of his later poetics was in reference to what had preceded it. The meaning of the new poetic principle of personalism resided partly in its opposition to the partly fictional and finally impossible notion of impersonalism. The authority for a confessional poem came in part from its being, at least in appearance, so much more opened than the self-testing and self-sealing ironies of modernist poetry. The realism of a younger group of poets was convincing because it played off of a generation's disillusionment with aesthetic principles that seemed to have promised more meaning than recent history could come close to validating. Lowell's change in poetics remained relational, whatever terms we use to describe his poetry. Replace "sensibles," "factualism," the "realistic," "documentary," or "metonymic" with the qualities of doubt and objectivity commonly associated with the scientific mind, and you have a compatible perspective. What both sets of terms overlook is the ongoing exchange that occurs between oppositions such as symbolism and realism. Focusing on the realism of Lowell's later poetry can cause us to miss the positive role that doubt plays . . . the way that through figures it ventures but does not abandon what has been questioned. Symbols may be passé, but the possibilities they represent still remain. As with

lament, doubt reminds us of the potential for stubborn reclama-
tion. Thus, whatever terms are used to describe it, Lowell's poetic
shift should be read as a thrust that over time entailed a counterthrust. His exchange of symbolism for realism was relational. It
existed in the context of what had preceded it. Insofar as Lowell
and others of his generation are understood to have repudiated
the modernist preference for symbol yet failed to disengage themselves from modernism, symbolism and realism remain linked.

"Waking Early Sunday Morning," from *Near the Ocean* (1976),
begins, "O to break loose, like the chinook / salmon jumping and
falling back, / nosing up to the impossible / stone and bone-
crushing waterfall—." A religion's symbolic fish is here understood in a biological sense that applies to generations. Throughout
this poem Lowell maintains a balance between his early concentrated, multilayered poetry and the agility of his writing from *Life
Studies* on. "Waking Early Sunday Morning" cannot avoid being
in dialogue with Stevens's "Sunday Morning," which in turn is in
dialogue with Christianity, Platonism, as well as some of Stevens's
literary ancestors. At the same time, off-rhyme, a four-beat line,
and the absence of capitals (which reinforces the poem's flexible
enjambment) provide the agility we associate with Lowell's late
poetry. A similar balance is struck by the poem's diction—"O to
break loose" opens the first stanza. The realist's "Stop, back off"
opens the second. Throughout the poem, Lowell moves back and
forth between what a symbol such as a fish *might* project and
what realism reduces it to—"our monotonous sublime."

Because it operates by equivalence, symbol fails to satisfy the
requirements of realism or science, which deny the metaphysical
side of the symbol's equation. Once one half of the equation is
negated, the other half is also lost. But simile moves well within
either understanding. Through the play of sameness and difference
it ventures what is lost as much as it likens what is retained. Simile
carries less baggage; thus it is better able to relocate. Lowell's
fierce desire in "Waking Early Sunday Morning" "to break loose"
exists in terms of a simile, "like the chinook." God's "vanishing /
emblems," or symbols, his Congregational "white spire and flag- /
pole sticking out above the fog," are "like old white china door-
knobs, sad, / slight, useless things to calm the mad." The knob of

the flagpole no longer points upward but through simile is made horizontal. It is likened to the way a doorknob presents itself to us, the aspiring flagpole now oddly set on its side.

The significance of Lowell's shift is not just that he exchanged religion or some form of metaphysics for realism or for the systematized realism of phenomenology. Lowell's poetics kept either understanding possible. Symbolism may oppose the skepticism of scientific or phenomenological thought, but simile precludes neither, as indeed neither does the history of our intellectual development. The real issue raised by a shift such as Lowell's is the way it reveals the change in our understanding of likeness and possibility—from Gilson's emphasis on our "likeness to God" to the phenomenologist's sense that one likeness exists only in relation to other likenesses, the latter being a primo for the play that contemporary poets have made out of simile, simile-like figures, and rhetorical patterns that occasion simile-like structures.

When Lowell abandoned the church, the authority required for his poetry came to be generated from experience, with experience as something both internal and external. As Lowell once said of William Carlos Williams, who from *Life Studies* on served as a literary father, "man is what he experiences."[11] This shift in Lowell's understanding and practice of poetry removed God as the object to which he might liken himself and introduced many smaller objects as replacements, and it was a decision in which the observer was added to the data.

Categorized as a turn to confessionalism at the time it occurred, Lowell's addition of the observer to his experience was like the change made by Husserl, placing the self within the material to be observed. At the same time, the goal of objectivity in Lowell's effort, which entailed a considerable amount of irony about himself, gave his work the detachment of phenomenological discipline and restrained it from becoming excessively expressionistic. Lowell had mythology and the symbolism of the Catholic church as early paradigms for instruction. What he reached after his disillusionment over World War II and various events in his personal life was a point at which he retained a capacity for symbolic systems but no longer gave them an external grounding, the grounding of religious belief, for example. Lowell was like the stubborn "mother skunk" in "Skunk Hour," surrounded by structures she passed by in favor of her own singular purpose, which includes not only "sour cream" but also the kittens she leads. He came to the plateau he describes in "Fall 1961":

> A father's no shield
> for his child.
> We are like a lot of wild
> spiders crying together,
> but without tears.
> Nature holds up a mirror.
> One swallow makes a summer.[12]

Recalling the spiders that fascinated Jonathan Edwards, Lowell realized that any one mode of reflection he might use would be perspectival, and as singular as a spider's signature left in the way it weaves its web. The Euclidean parallel between heaven and earth, which made sense of Christian symbolism and allegory, no longer held. It was impossible to describe things in absolute spatial or temporal terms. Lines might as well cross and diverge as never touch. The strained figure of "one swallow" making "a summer" announced its own acute limitation.

Experiencing this sort of randomness, we approach the nihilist's world that Vereen Bell sees in Lowell, the "world as is."[13] Yet Lowell's *method* of observation never abolishes its basis in the monkish hope for wholeness that lingers not only behind modernism but also behind the scientific method. And there is a matching characteristic to take into consideration with Lowell. His figurative language posits the world in terms of *as if,* as well as in terms of *as is.* Poetry remains the artifice of possibility as much as it uncovers factual truth. The Lowell who moves between *if* and *is* means the most to us. The figurative and the factual are in constant play. Pursuing such play in "Dolphin," the title poem of *The Dolphin* (1973), his poetry is the "eelnet made by man for eel fighting," something that the man himself necessitates. Each part of a net is like the others and is attached to them. The net of likening, of simile-like tropes, catches and particularizes each eel. The divided self, whose words end "Dolphin," says "my eyes have seen what my hand did." This Cartesian speaker makes a net. He divides and then likens his experience in order to make sense of a world in which, as Lowell says in "The Flaw" (*For the Union Dead* [1964]), "all's possible, all's unpredictable." The poem ends:

> Hope of the hopeless launched and cast adrift
> on the great flaw that gives the final gift.
>
> Dear Figure curving like a questionmark,
> how will you hear my answer in the dark?

Somewhere between fact and figure Lowell wavers, exemplifying the competing powers of realism and poetry's capacity for making new relations.

Because poetry was for him a mode of thought used to gauge experience, poetic style did not merely reflect Lowell's thinking, it was the primary means for thinking. Thus, with his rejection of Catholicism, Lowell had no choice but to alter his style. His poetry exchanged its condensed, highly charged lyricism for a relaxed, often prosaic line. In the epigraph from Nietzsche, myth and science are antagonistic. Whereas the former is associated with music, the latter "opposes" music's "mythopoeic power." Nietzsche contends that "the tremendous historical need of our unsatisfied modern culture" and our "consuming desire for knowledge . . . point to . . . the loss of myth."[14] Lowell's poetic shift was mainly a change in the modes of thought which he believed he could use to make sense of experience.

At first Lowell used his religious understanding to explain events. Highly formal, his poems characteristically came to a dramatic close whose finality bespoke the world-ordering Christian cosmos that he believed fit the world he experienced. But with the church no longer a source for authority, Lowell's mode of thought took a different form. Instead of ending a poem by saying, "Stand and live / The dove has brought an olive branch to eat," as he did at the conclusion of "Where the Rainbow Ends" (*Lord Weary's Castle*), in his last phase Lowell chose to end "Waking Early Sunday Morning" more casually: "No weekends for the gods now" and no "advance" . . . despite the promises of science. Here the prediction for the future was the opposite of earlier prognostications, which typically were quite final. Lowell's later vision indicated a modern version of the Hundred Years' War, an inconclusive conflict grown too familiar for hope or heroism, and one with no transcendent order to distinguish between right and wrong:

> Only man thinning out his kind
> sounds through the Sabbath noon, the blind
> swipe of the pruner and his knife
> busy about the tree of life . . .
> Pity the planet, all joy gone
> from this sweet volcanic cone;
> peace to our children when they fall
> in small war on the heels of small
> war—until the end of time
> to police the earth, a ghost
> orbiting forever lost
> in our monotonous sublime.

The change in sources for authority took Lowell from a faith in which he was once described as being "more Catholic than the church"[15] to a sense of acedia that he found in himself and the world around him. Early in his career, he ended "The Quaker Graveyard in Nantucket" (*Lord Weary's Castle*) with "The Lord survives the rainbow of His will." Eighteen years later, the title poem of *For the Union Dead* ironically describes the technological benefits science has made possible for the republic: "Everywhere, / giant finned cars nose forward like fish; / a savage servility / slides by on grease." The fish in the Boston Aquarium are gone just as surely as *fish* no longer carries value as a symbol for Lowell's previous religious beliefs. The progress Lowell describes, in which "Parking spaces luxuriate like civic / sandpiles in the heart of Boston," has not brought freedom but "servility." A poem in *For the Union Dead* entitled "The Drinker" begins: "The man is killing time—there's nothing else." When the man sleeps he "hears the voice of Eve, / beseeching freedom from the Garden's / perfect and ponderous bubble." Outside the garden and seeking freedom through political and technological means, we miss what we intended. The poem concludes:

> Is he killing time? Out on the street,
> two cops on horseback clop through the April rain

to check the parking meter violations—
their oilskins yellow as forsythia.

Lowell ends with a quotidian example of the way we gauge our
lives, our "killing time" by limiting it to the regulations of parking
meters. The auditory pun created by "cops . . . clop" and tick-
tock reminds us of the way relation persists, but in skewed and
eccentric ways. In such a world "oilskins" are just as bright as
"forsythia." Yellow is yellow, a color we experience without
assigning value to it.

The coda for Lowell's later attitude toward religious beliefs he
once held is provided by "Jonathan Edwards in Western Massachusetts." This is one of several poems Lowell wrote about Edwards, each of which explores the predicament of a New England
divine who embodied the contradiction between religious belief and
rational thought. Lowell made a study of Edwards, who early on
became an important model for the central discrepancy Lowell
found in his own thinking:

> Edwards' great millstone and rock
> of hope has crumpled, but the square
> white houses of his flock
> stand in the open air,
>
> out in the cold,
> like sheep outside the fold.
> Hope lives in doubt.
> Faith is trying to do without
>
> faith.

This is the central predicament of mind that Lowell and, in various ways, others of his generation faced. Those who would "hope"
to find more than traditional "square / white houses," which by
themselves preclude the individuation of shape and color that
would give them identities, must, for personal identity, proceed by
"doubt." The enjambed statement "Faith is trying to do without /
faith" suggests we avoid anything as pronounced as theology,
which would be too predictable in its interpretations to be an adequate mode of discovery. By the use of a kind of hopeful form of

"doubt," a language that likens replaces inherited "square / white houses," whose traditional plans falsely prearrange meaning. Tropes that likened were the answer to the ontological problems suggested as early as 1944, by the title of Lowell's first volume, *Land of Unlikeness*. With the destruction of Edwards's and others' "great millstone and rock / of hope," there was no permanent image of God left by which the soul could be understood. Self-location was carried out by the mind's synthetic likening through language. But Lowell's process of writing-as-thinking reached a new level with the dramatic turn that occurred around the time he was writing *The Mills of the Kavanaughs*.

Discussions of Lowell's shift in style usually focus on *Life Studies*, where the changes are most obvious. What has been generally overlooked, however, is that the basis for much of his later development is a poem written long before *Life Studies*, the title poem of *The Mills of the Kavanaughs*. As much as the success of *Life Studies*, the failure of "The Mills of the Kavanaughs," his most ambitious poem, dates the major shift in Lowell's poetic thinking. Based on a Christian cosmology, "The Mills" originally lent itself to the traditional four levels of interpretation (literal, allegorical, moral, and anagogical) invoked by exegetes from Aquinas to Northrop Frye and Tate. Many of the poem's key stanzas were written in 1937 while Lowell was staying in Monteagle, Tennessee, with his mentor Tate.[16] As it originally appeared in the *Kenyon Review* 12 (1951), "The Mills" represented the then current objectivist modes of irony, paradox, ambiguity, and mythical allusion. Between the poem's first version in the *Kenyon Review* and its second, as the title poem of Lowell's third volume, many of its Catholic references were removed.

The most obvious deletions are references to the Virgin Mary and Saint Patrick. One passing reference to the Kavanaugh family church is also missing. In place of these deletions, Lowell adds elements that, regarded as a whole, state his new skeptical position. In the second version of "The Mills," the inclusion of epigraphs from Matthew Arnold's "Dover Beach" and Williams's *In the American Grain* amounts to the removal of a Catholic framework. This is the case with Arnold because his poem confronts the minimal possibilities of a life for lovers such as Anne and Harry Kavanaugh when the "Sea of Faith" has been lost. The epigraph from Williams, that "Morals are the memory of success that no longer succeeds," suggests the ethical wash that Harry Kavanaugh is in with his dismissal from the navy during wartime. The Kavanaughs' failed Catholicism and dwindling family fortune are particular instances of what Williams calls "success that no longer succeeds."

There is also the addition of Daphne to the poem's second version. Replacing the Virgin Mary, Daphne complements the Persephone motif, but she does so by suggesting actions opposite to those represented by the Virgin. As opposed to the acceptance of God and of love's triumph, Daphne represents the rejection of a god and love's failure. The metamorphosis she requests while fleeing Apollo erases the condition in which his love can reach her. Another result of the removal of a Catholic framework for the poem's action is that Harry's suicide becomes much less significant. It becomes a morally ambiguous event open to varying interpretations.

In the first version of "The Mills," the central Catholic motif was the symbolism of the Virgin Mary. After the revision, Persephone's role as the wife of Hades was no longer balanced by references to the Virgin, and though other allusions, particularly to classical mythology, were still employed, the poem's meaning came to be based less on myth than on a secular world view. Instead of using symbol and allegory to refer to the fixed order of a Christian cosmos, the poem's narrative created its particular sense of realism by placing events in sequential and causal relation to one another. Setting, characterization, and prior events, instead of a fixed cosmos, became the sufficient causes for the poem's action.

By 1949, when existentialism was beginning to exercise a strong influence in America, Lowell found his own horizons, if not absurd, at least increasingly cloudy. He was divorced from Jean Stafford (who was Catholic) and no longer in any way associated with the church itself. In a letter to Marcella Winslow dated 20 April 1949, Tate summarized Lowell's condition as precarious, citing the church, marriage, and poetry as what "held" Lowell "together."[17] In retrospect, Tate's description appears a little formulaic. Lowell's problem was first of all physiological. But Tate identified the central issue with Lowell: certain forms of relation provided the basis for identity. They had been the church, marriage, and poetry. By Lowell's new understanding, the self existed, to a considerable degree, in isolation. Lowell continued his strong friendship with others. Throughout the mental difficulties he experienced at this time, and later, there was his marriage with Elizabeth Hardwick. But in many ways his understanding of relation had taken a large step away from the ideals of extensive and eternal ties taught by the church. A brief look at two stories by Stafford, "A Country Love Story" and "An Influx of Poets," the latter published after Lowell's death, not only demonstrates the autobiographical basis for "The Mills of the Kavanaughs" but also gives added scope to the turmoil Lowell lived through around the time he was writing his most ambitious poem.[18] Several years later Flannery O'Connor, who had been with Lowell at Yaddo during 1949 when his first real bout with mania was beginning, wrote to Sally and Robert Fitzgerald in April 1954 and made the following wry assessment of what continued to be a transitional Lowell:

> Cal Lowell [writes that he is not] "rejoining the flock." He thought he "could do more good outside, at least for myself." And some other claptrap about Henry Adams being a Catholic anarchist and he was the same, only agnostic too. I wrote him that his not being in the Church was a grief to me and I knew no more to say about it. I said I severely doubted he would do any good to anybody else outside but that it was probably true he would do good to himself inasmuch as he would be the only one in a position to.[19]

O'Connor might have made the same assessment of anyone who entrusted himself or herself to ways of thinking at odds with her fiercely held beliefs. In any event, anarchy was the political manifestation of Lowell's doubt; agnosticism, the religious.

Lowell's personal crises were made more difficult by their occurrence at a time when traditional bases for meaning were under attack. As the reference to Henry Adams suggests, Lowell increasingly understood the world as the embodiment not of transcendent order but continuous process. At most, all that could be recognized was a general law of history, specifically, for Lowell (as for Adams) a vision of American decline. (It is no coincidence that both men wrote books entitled *History*.) And at the very least Lowell's new vision allowed for an approach to a personal law of history, as indicated even in the titles of *Life*

Studies, Notebook 1967–68 (1969), *The Dolphin,* and *For Lizzie and Harriet* (1973). Relation had been scaled down from the metaphysical heights of Catholicism to the local reaches of family and a regional and personal past. At the same time there remained an absolutism in Lowell which surfaced from time to time, a desire for apodictic truth. And in this Lowell was finally less like the Adams of naturalistic historiography than the Adams of *Mont-Saint-Michel and Chartres.*

What Lowell experienced around the time he was rewriting "The Mills," however, was not only that his Christian mythmaking was out of place but also that the prophesied apocalypse of his earlier poetry was illusory. The Boston-as-Babylon depicted in "As a Plane Tree by the Water" deserved what a Last Judgment would bring; its moral degeneration amidst a world at war made it the basis for Lowell's revelation of God's righteous and seemingly imminent vengeance. But by the time Lowell was writing and rewriting "The Mills," neither divine nor human vengeance had touched Boston. Indeed, the closest thing to a rain of fire and brimstone had been the allied bombing of Axis cities (something to which Lowell was completely opposed), a vengeance wielded not against but by America. The events of the war seemed to invalidate Lowell's earlier artistic mode of thought.

Dissatisfied with his poetic practices, and reacting to new pressures outside poetry, Lowell embraced the opposite of his previous attitudes and methods. Thus, while objectivity remained his final goal, Lowell added the observer to the field of observation. What was on one level the modernist ideal of objectivism was in part relinquished for a brand of subjectivism, for autobiography. Similarly, the fixed cosmology of Lowell's Christianity, arranged from heaven downward, was rejected in favor of an existential process in which meaning was created by human initiative. Deduction from a traditional myth such as Christianity was no longer valid or authentic; induction, however, provided a poem with the dramatic persuasiveness of a participant or eyewitness.

What lies beneath this change is that for Lowell poetry is more than anything else a mode of thought, but the unique character of artistic knowledge is that the real life of a poem starts as the poem itself breaks off and the interpretive process begins. In and of itself the poem is incomplete. It needs a reader, an interpretation.

There are problems of text and context, work and audience. Thus, at the beginning of the fifties Lowell was under pressure to change his poetic mode of thought for two reasons: his own doubts plus what appeared to be an increasingly secular audience. The early, religiously informed version of "The Mills" did not fit the context that was evolving in the wake of World War II.

Finding himself dislocated by a secular understanding that saw the world not as revelation but as mere process, Lowell made his poetry a means for locating the self within that process. In order to do this he developed a Januslike imaginative consciousness. By writing a series of lyrics in *Life Studies* which looked backward and forward, he created a continuum of retentional modification. Particular experiences were no longer discrete events but parts of a continuous whole that he fabricated. By such a method he was able to bracket the present, to parenthesize it, and to locate himself in relation to it, but only after it had passed.

Realizing while he was revising "The Mills" that he needed to abandon symbol and allegory, Lowell turned to another kind of mediation. As the protagonist of the poem, Anne Kavanaugh served as a persona for him. Her reverie was an early bit of phenomenological-like bracketing. She was the first means by which Lowell managed to telescope images of his past and probable images of his future. Aspects of the various scenes from his first marriage (many of which appear in Stafford's two stories) surface obliquely in Anne's reverie. At times the poem is a dramatic unfolding of marital frustrations and suicidal tendencies. Viewed another way, "The Mills" is a collage of tidbits taken from Lowell's family history, as well as from his personal experience. In order to establish a pattern with sufficient authority, Lowell turns to imagining the process of Anne's reverie, continuously shuffling and reshuffling details. An example of this method is the fusion that takes place between Lowell's harsh personal experience with the military as a conscientious objector and his father's interrupted naval career; the two are combined to shape Harry Kavanaugh's disgraceful return from the navy in the middle of World War II.

In Lowell's poetic shift, however, there are changes other than personal departures from the tenets of objectivism. Lowell's source for authority in his poem after he removed it from its grounding in Catholic faith was sequence and a sort of common-sense employment of causal reasoning. For Immanuel Kant, causality is part of the mind's capacity to synthesize red now/blue now/green now into experience. It is the mind's ordering of appearances through time, which thus appear connective and become experience. But causality gives us experience only on a phenomenal level. It offers none of the anagogical or apodictic truth claims that Tate, the sometime impresario, would have urged on a young Lowell visiting him in Monteagle, Tennessee, in the thirties. What can an imaginative piece of writing give us as haut meaning when it appeals to sequence and causality as they appear in practical garb? As part of the effort to work out his original intentions, the events Lowell described in "The Mills" were a substitute for what allusion to the tradition previously handled. They appealed to a reader's notions of realism but lacked the truth claims that Lowell's Catholic faith had assumed. Similar to the way readers accept it as operating through Lowell's use of setting, characterization, and previous events within narrative, Kant's notion of causality represents connection between otherwise discrete events, but it exists "only in appearance," not in the world of pure reason.[20] The sense that one event is caused by a preceding event remains on the empirical level; thus this understanding lacks Lowell's original goal—the absolute truth claims that a Christian cosmology and the four levels of interpretation had promised. Lowell's drive for certainty drifted through a good deal of silt, eventually resting on the shifting bed of phenomena commonly presented as personal experience, as well as regional and family history, delivered with varying versions of his relaxed causal reasoning to support things.

In the second version of "The Mills," the reverie by Anne Kavanaugh which largely constitutes the poem is less the New Critics' static, synchronic artifact of irony and wit and more a diachronic movement of the mind of the persona through a series of re-presentations of her past. The poem's opening stanza begins with an objectivist description of Anne and her setting. Fourteen lines later, however, Anne addresses Harry and begins a meditative monologue, which runs the entire length of the poem. Objective description by an omniscient voice is interspersed regularly, but the predominant consciousness in the poem is Anne's. What enables "The Mills" to overcome much of the narrowness that can result from using one character's point of view is Anne's reverie.

By it she telescopes a series of events, selecting those most significant for closer inspection.

If the poem's main action centers around what Dudley Fitts has
called "one ancient bedroom joke," the joke is seen through the
wife's eyes, not the husband's.[21] Harry is quoted but not heard,
his disintegration recollected rather than dramatized, because the
poem's real action is Anne's unraveling of the meaning of events,
and this takes place within her isolated, subjective consciousness.
Such a re-presenting of self, established through the connection of
time, is what Lowell matures as his method in *Life Studies*.

Revised, Lowell's narrative in "The Mills" is no longer symbolically and allegorically prismatic but time-locked as he begins
to wrestle with a restricted understanding of being. No longer
skyward-looking, his poetic consciousness becomes that of a
Janus, capable of seeing the future and the past simultaneously
but blind to the present immediately beneath this consciousness.
It is a mind balanced between the past, which it makes part of the
present tense, and the future, which is informed by expectations
built out of former experience. The future is given structure by
the shape of past experiences. Because he is *in* process, Lowell
can never grasp the present. But he can frame the present by continuously looking forward and backward.

"Beyond the Alps" is one of the clearest examples of such a
consciousness. The train's movement from Rome to Paris represents Lowell's own mental movement from the city of Christianity
to that of art.[22] The individual's practice of art has replaced the
corporate practice of religion. For Lowell, knowledge now is
achieved by personal gathering, rather than from an institutional-
ized faith. Its motion is analogous to Lowell's consciousness
making constant revisions between a known past and an expected
and unfolding future. If myth can no longer be used to make
modern experience intelligible (as Eliot, another early influence
on Lowell, maintained it could be) and if, in particular, Christianity is now seen as just another myth, then poetry is left with only
empirical means by which to establish its truthfulness.[23] That is, a
work's realism, its ability to convince the reader, now accrues
through a series of causes and effects, whose net result establishes
a sufficient basis for the believability of events in the narrative.
But each effect leads back to a cause that was the effect of a pre-

ceding cause, carrying us through an endless regress—a chain of
events that is too long for us to fetch some absolute reason for
what happens, like a first cause. Even the detailed reasons for the
central action in "The Mills," Harry's suicide, are too many to be
explained. For example, Anne's personality plays a major role in
Harry's disintegration, but tracing its machinations would require
a labyrinthine poem.

The most important point, however, is that Lowell fell into a
poetry subject to questions of causality in the first place. Without
an enveloping myth within which his narrative could operate on
several levels of signification, Lowell's poetic process was reduced
to a local activity. Beginning with the revision of "The Mills," it
lacked the umbrella-like system of reference it needed for bridg-
ing that gap between permanence and process, the transcendent
and the immanent. From a practical standpoint, the deletion of
the Virgin Mary apparatus reduced the significance of Persephone
as an opposing figure. Similarly, the deletion of Catholic references lessened the significance, both dramatic and purely analytical, of Harry's suicide. Piling up causes for suicide, Lowell stacked
the deck for dramatic effect, but by doing this he invalidated the
poem's perception, which is finally not realistic but melodramatic.

When we add Anne's supposed infidelity to the guilt that went
with Harry's failed career and his inability to restore the Kavanaugh fortunes and create heirs for the family, Harry's actions
appear almost dictated. Lowell satisfies our tendency to explain
things causally, and, due to a set of deterministic reasons, Harry's
suicide achieves its moment. We tend to feel there was no other
choice. Yet, amidst such weight, the significance of Harry's suicide
still depends upon his freedom to choose otherwise, a freedom
that Lowell's new poetic mode lessens. Removal of the promise of
life is certainly realistic enough in the minds of most readers,
skeptical or not. It is a weighty development, but its final result
is to reduce the significance of the loss of life.

Rather than achieve dramatic meaning through either myth or
realism and causality, Lowell's later poetry often sought to perceive contingencies just under the surface of meaning. But even
contingencies were causal. Meaning had undergone a leveling
process. No longer able to aspire to something as ambitious as
ontology, as Jacques Maritain would have poetry, Lowell's poetry

narrowed to something more like a personal phenomenology by which he bracketed experience.[24] This change took place near the time when Maritain was sponsoring Tate's entry into the Catholic church. Maritain's example as a Catholic intellectual was highly important to several of Lowell's circle, especially Tate and Caroline Gordon, but, from the "The Mills" onward, Lowell understood the world to be not deterministic but increasingly indeterminate. In reaction to this, he created a poetry that, paradoxically, was increasingly determined by modes of thought operating in the governing position that myth once occupied. Gilson and Lewis represented positions of faith, whereas Husserl and Sartre represented positions of doubt. Lowell moved between these contraries, and his method for traveling was realism sometimes, other times a simile-like mode of thought. The reasons for the movement away from myth and symbol in Lowell, which contributed to a major change in contemporary poetry, should be kept in mind. They reveal an implicit reduction in the horizon of a known past and an expected future, a narrowing of experience from the possibilities of a transcendent world to the probabilities of a historical world of fact and realism. But possibility was not completely ruled out. Likening had been tipped sideways, the way in "Waking Early Sunday Morning" the Congregational flagpole was leveled so its top presented itself as a doorknob. But doors still opened on new rooms. In his later poetry Lowell was mainly guided by a sense of realism and a tendency toward "relentless trivializing of life," but trope enabled him to think variationally about the scaled-down world he saw before him, and it did so in ways that matched the constraints and variations of phenomenological method.[25]

II

Poets of Lowell's generation and after tend to emphasize personal experience as the basis for meaning in their poetry. Usually their stylistic choices are intended to fit an individual rather than a cultural consciousness, as meaning is achieved inductively rather than deductively from a culture's cumulative learning. In its second phase, Lowell's poetry coincides in certain important ways with some of the proposals made by the phenomenologist Husserl in his *Cartesian Meditations*. This does not mean that Lowell and others of his generation consciously embraced phenomenology but that their beginning with doubt as first a predicament and then a method led to certain telling similarities. The parallels between Lowell's internalization of experience and his turn to realism and Husserl's proposed methods for dealing with experience illuminate some reasons for the limited truth claims behind some of the most celebrated contemporary American poetry.

Husserl's way of using doubt to overcome doubt matches the use contemporary poets make of personal experience in their poetry to overcome the isolation of personalism. The characteristic moves made by contemporary poets have been to turn away from the hierarchies of tradition, as our language hands it down, in order to focus on an individual's isolated experience, then turn back to language in order to apply tropes to that experience. Matching what they see with figurative language, poets apply new torsions to their surroundings. The ideal is to uncover new relations, but within objective constraints intended to generate reliable results in the manner of scientific procedure. The similarities between Husserl's model, in *Cartesian Meditations,* which narrows its field of observation the way a scientist would limit data, and Lowell's practice in *Life Studies,* where information is gained from a focused area of experience, provide us with a new approach to the poetic modes of thought that work on a personal level and help to explain why they have seemed appropriate, while the impersonal modalities championed by the modernists were rejected. Along the way of thinking about doubt as both predicament and method, certain evaluative questions suggest themselves, the main one being why poets writing after World War II felt their work required less extensional modes of thought.

Both Husserl and Lowell begin in a state of doubt, and each radicalizes his predicament by making it his method. Husserl proposes a series of models meant to arrange experience. Lowell uses a series of poems, and his opting for doubt, rather than the Catholic faith of his early period, causes him to write a poetry that assumes nothing beyond an isolated self operating within memory. There is a parallel between Husserl's phenomenological triad of experiencing, transcendental, and eidetic egos and Lowell's existential triad of experiencing, recollecting/transcending, and imagining selves. In *Cartesian Meditations* Husserl chooses to "begin in absolute poverty, with an absolute lack of knowledge," which parallels Lowell's rejection of what before had been his central wealth of understanding, a Catholic balance between belief and knowledge.[26] Were Husserl and Lowell operating within a theistic framework, then doubt would be the opposite of what was required. But they are not. They have accepted what Husserl calls the "poverty," the "lack of knowledge" of the subjective consciousness understood in "absolute" terms, the alternative to basing apodictic truth in the mind of God being to place it in a self made wholly responsible for truth. However, Husserl and Lowell only begin with this Cartesian brand of doubt. René Descartes's model is intended first to prove God's existence, then that of the world, but Husserl and Lowell only put doubt to the task of gaining *knowledge* about experience. In this sense, *Cartesian Meditations* might have a different title.

For Husserl the stuff of observation is the eidos; for Lowell it is the image. They are similar. Initially Husserl divides consciousness into two elements, an experiencing ego and a transcendental ego. This division makes a third consciousness possible, the eidetic ego, capable of imagining eidetic variations upon the material gained by an experiencing ego as it is filtered through the transcendental ego. Here, in his own way, Lowell also parallels Husserl. His division of consciousness into two entities (an experiencing self and a recollecting/transcending self) makes a third entity possible, the imagination that likens in order to uncover new relations.[27] Husserl's five meditations are models for gauging experience. Although his purpose is different from Descartes's, Husserl nevertheless begins with two Cartesian assumptions. The first is that doubt is a positive capacity of the mind by which it asserts its independence from external objects. The second is the mind's ability to apply doubt to itself.[28]

From *Life Studies* on, Lowell's writing is also a tool used to gauge experience. In his later poetry he divides himself into the experiencing, existential Lowell who has a personal past, a distinguished family, and New England history behind him and the poet Lowell who by the distancing advantage of memory transcends the past in order to imagine variations on it. For Husserl past phases of an eidetic ego are collected like a column of slides fed into a slide projector; for Lowell, a similar function is performed, but with past images of his life (rather than the phases of an eidetic ego) gathered like a stack of snapshots. In both systems a third locus is created. A triangle for consciousness is established, somewhat the way a pilot takes sightings on two known objects for a running fix that will tell him where he is or, rather, where he has just been.

A series of triangulations constructs a world of possible experience for the eidetic ego, or poetic imagination. Lowell is able to use his past, experiencing self as a second locus, and when that past self is seen to have encountered another self with its implicit locus and experiential world (what Husserl calls an horizon structure), a whole world structure becomes possible for an otherwise time-locked and isolated consciousness. This process works in multiples; the experiencing consciousness encounters a whole series of other consciousnesses, other selves, carrying their implicit horizon structures. Operating systematically, Husserl can work himself back to the "one identical world" he originally found it necessary to doubt;[29] operating imaginatively, Lowell can do much the same thing. He can orchestrate the points of view of several people present at one place during one afternoon—for example, the setting of his grandfather's farm described in "My Last Afternoon with Uncle Devereux Winslow"—in order to rediscover a "one identical" truth about that event.

Triangulation can occur only after a "Pairing," such as that between ego and alter ego, has taken place. "Pairing" is an "Appresentation" of an "Other," an "organism" that proves it is other by its "continuous change in behavior from phase to phase." Lowell's example of this kind of thinking psychologizes it, something Husserl wished to avoid. But the modes of thought are much the same. In Lowell pairing is done by splitting the self into an experiencing ego and a transcendental ego, which, in an act of doubling, watches its other, the experiencing ego's variational progress. In "To Delmore Schwartz," for example, Lowell as transcendental ego regards his former self, or experiencing ego, living with Schwartz in Cambridge during 1946. Details are represented—the "furnace" that went out, "the antiquated / refrigerator," efforts to meet "T. S. Eliot's brother," a "stuffed duck" that belonged to Schwartz. The entire setting recalls incongruity, the "Rabelaisian, lubricious, drugged" duck, which finally wound up with its "web- / foot, like a candle" stuck "in a quart of gin" that Lowell and Schwartz had killed, and the woefully telling, borrowed and half-joking lines by Schwartz, *We poets in our youth begin in sadness; / thereof in the end come despondency and madness.* Speaking for both young poets, Schwartz replaced Wordsworth's "gladness" with "sadness," as if early on he wished to predict the emotional tenor of a poetry forced to give its attention to the eccentricities and absurdities that accompany too isolated a perspective.

Standing alone, without consolations such as nature or church, Lowell has his former self to regard, and he has his life with Schwartz, who in some ways serves as a variant other for what Lowell was in 1946 in Cambridge. The later "despondency and madness" that both Lowell and Schwartz experienced are bracketed here by Lowell's backward gaze and the reiterative gesture of his poem. One is reminded of other Lowell poems, which are often a snapshotlike series of past phases within his consciousness— "Dunbarton," "Grandparents," "For Sale," "Buenos Aires." Yet as an eidetic ego that transcends his time-locked flowing of experience or as a poetically imagining consciousness capable of imaginative free play and projection, Lowell can not only trace his past development but by eidetic variation he can explore possibilities, including possibilities held somewhere out ahead—the poems in *For Lizzie and Harriet,* which are dedicated to Elizabeth Hardwick and to Lowell and Hardwick's daughter, Harriet, for example. Here is the first of numerous poems to Harriet, entitled "Harriet":

> Half a year, then a year and a half, then
> ten and a half—the pathos of a child's fractions, turn-
> ing up each summer. Her God a seaslug, God a queen
> with forty servants, God—you gave up . . . things whirl
> in the chainsaw bite of whatever squares
> the universe by name and number. For
> the hundredth time, we slice the fog, and round
> the village with our headlights on the ground,
> like the first philosopher Thales who thought all things water,

and fell in a well . . . trying to find a car
key. . . . It can't be here, and so it must be there
behind the next crook in the road or growth
of fog—there blinded by our feeble beams,
a face, clock-white, still friendly to the earth.

This vision of progress through an obscured landscape is analogous to the variations Lowell builds with poetic imagery. If
what he is looking for is not "here" then through eidetic variations
it can be found over "there," beyond "the next crook . . . or
growth."

"End of Camp Alamoosook" is addressed to Harriet and describes a day in late summer when "the unexpected, the exotic, the
early / morning sunlight is more like premature twilight." In "The
Hard Way" Lowell tells his daughter: "Don't hate your parents,
or your children will hire / unknown men to bury you at your
own cost." And it is perhaps best seen in this sort of fey play with
the psychological verities that Lowell's project is not at all systematic, the way Husserl's is. Husserl argues that he has moved
from the realm "of the 'as if,' " a realm of "phantasies," to "Objective experience" dealt with by "scientific activity."[30] But Lowell's imagining is never intended to carry the heft of scientific
rigor. He remains in the "as if" of poetic tropes—though in terms
of its guardedness about assumptions, his later poetry stands much
closer to the spirit of "scientific activity" than it does to that of
myth.

At times it is impossible to distinguish between Lowell's manic
yet valuable ruminations and ideas that are simply the product of
his illness. Lowell himself tended to think that individual illness
was related to cultural disorder, and the personal character of his
poetry further obscured any distinctions one might make between
Lowell the thinker and Lowell the mental patient. His habit of
questioning, what Stephen Yenser calls his employment of "contraries," parallels his behavior during manic episodes—the canon-
ization of Flannery O'Connor and Robert Fitzgerald as new saints
who would purify the church, when he was still a Catholic, or
later his episodic abandonment of family and home in order to
take up one new residence or another.[31] This habit of imposed
doubt is related to Lowell's decision to reject Christian dualism

and the modernist style of Eliot and Tate in order to adopt the more direct method of Williams, a physician trained in the scientific method. Despite the gray areas associated with his illness, Lowell's rejection of some of the central tenets of modernism provides us with the key to his methodical employment of doubt as a mode of thought comparable to that of a phenomenologist.

O'Connor had the acumen and the opportunity to observe Lowell frequently during the early fifties. In addition, she had an affinity with him that gave her special insight into his changed thinking. Friendship and the sense of community that combined with her strongly held Catholicism generated her keen interest in Lowell's vacillations with the church. In another letter describing Lowell's vicissitudes, O'Connor summarizes what few others saw in him until the publication of *Life Studies:*

> You ask about Cal Lowell. I feel almost too much about him to be able to get to the heart of it. He is a kind of grief to me. I first knew him at Yaddo. We were both there one fall and winter. At that time he had left his first wife, Jean Stafford, and the Church. To make a long story short, I watched him that winter come back into the Church. I had nothing to do with it but of course it was a great joy to me. I was only 23 and didn't have much sense. He was terribly excited about it and got more and more excited and in about two weeks had a complete mental breakdown. That second conversion went with it, of course. He had shock treatments and all that, and when he came out, he was well for a time, married again a very nice girl named Elizabeth Hardwick, and since then has been off and on, in and out, of institutions. Now he is doing very well on one of these drugs—but the Church is out of it, though I don't believe he has been able to convince himself that he doesn't believe. . . . The last thing he wrote was called *The Mills of the Kavanaughs.* Right now he is writing an autobiography. This is part of some kind of analytical therapy.[32]

Occurring as he completed "The Mills," Lowell's departure from the church accompanied a familiar transition. No longer able to say "I believe, therefore I know," he took the cogito's predictable route of "I doubt, therefore I am." And, as Husserl had done earlier, Lowell not only accepted doubt but also radicalized it. Predicament became method.

Because of its imagery, Lowell's poetry appears to represent a spatially dislocated self. But because, as Husserl says, "two possible variants of" the self cannot occur simultaneously, the dislocation is temporal. Lowell's "dull and alien room," his "cell of learning," in "Myopia: A Night" is an image brought forward—a past self seen through his surroundings by the present self writing the poem. (The triangle that gives a fix tells where one was a moment ago. Its exact meaning is past tense.) This is apparent first in "The Mills." Anne Kavanaugh's reverie becomes a means by which she (as Lowell's persona and transcendental ego) represents past phases of her experiencing ego and thus locates her present, reflective self. In the poem's opening lines there are three horizon structures of possible experience. Inside the poem, Anne's present, reflective self represents a transcendental ego, and her past self is an experiencing ego. Harry provides another horizon encountered by Anne's experiencing ego. As children, Harry and Anne provide still others, as do Harry's mother, Red Kavanaugh, and, distantly, Anne's father. Ultimately, each of these characters provides a different perspective (Husserl's horizon structure) for Lowell's imagination.

In "The Mills" Anne Kavanaugh uses memory to pose and counterpose past instances of her life. The same method is used eight years later in *Life Studies,* but it takes place in a series of lyrics rather than in the consciousness of one character in one long poem. In both cases, however, images from Lowell's past operate as what Husserl would call past phases of an eidetic ego—made possible by an *ego cogito,* which transcends the groundless present of a world seen as continuously fleeting. Husserl's elevated ego functions with a Januslike consciousness that looks simultaneously to the past and to the future but that cannot see immediately beneath itself. For the Janus, the present tense is groundless and in that sense does not exist. For Lowell the skeptic, the present is also groundless. It is continuously fleeting because, without the historical fact of Christ, time is mere process, "the querulous hush-hush of the wheels" of Lowell's train in "Beyond the Alps" as it moves from Christian Rome, where history is circular, to Paris, the city of art, where time does not round back. Put as a hyperbolic pun, "The lights of science" cannot "hold a candle / to Mary risen—at one miraculous stroke." The loss of circularity is seen in an oblique and comical way—especially the pope's purring "electric razor" matched by his "pet canary," which chirps "on his left hand" after "the Vatican [has] made Mary's Assumption dogma."

Following "Beyond the Alps" in *Life Studies,* there are three variations upon the present: "The Banker's Daughter," "Inauguration Day: January 1953," and "A Mad Negro Soldier Confined at Munich." Scrutiny proceeds at a rapid pace. Each of these poems provides a frame for Lowell's postwar life, the first treating the abuses of power within a historical context (Marie de Medici), the second dealing with power in a contemporary framework (Ike the victorious general and national leader), and the third confronting the way power is often experienced on a personal level, as entrapment. In a Husserlian sense, Lowell is bracketing his experience. The information he needs serves a reflexive purpose; the range at which his object stands is read in reverse, telling him where *he* stands relative to what he sees. The middle poem, "Inauguration Day: January 1953," which is short, begins at a highly concentrated pitch, "Manhattan's truss of adamant," and grinds down to a quotidian note, "the Republic summons Ike." Here Lowell writes in conflated terms that match the modernists', especially Tate's and Ransom's gnarled ironies, while he ends on a note that is ironical but also factual and somehow seems as small as the state of the nation and the state of mind he wishes to suggest: a diminutive name such as "Ike" played against "the mausoleum in" the "Republic" that "summons" him. Broad strokes over a small canvas, perhaps, but in Lowell's later poetry a sort of shorthand that seems to have worked for most readers.

"The Banker's Daughter" and "A Mad Negro Soldier Confined at Munich" are experiencing consciousnesses that Lowell explores variationally so that he may pilot a coast shaped by the worlds these other consciousnesses re-present. The former begins with an objective voice then moves into Marie de Medici's consciousness, whereas the latter is an overlay of Lowell and a soldier's consciousness and is taken from the time Lowell spent in an American mental hospital run by the military in Munich, where he was exposed to a group of violent patients. The earlier poem equates power with "the easy virtues of the earth," death finally. The later poem is kaleidoscopic in its twisting and twisted references— "American," "Kraut," "boys," and at the end, an "ant-egg dole."

Transposed into another voice, that of Marie de Medici, "The Banker's Daughter" offers a variation on Lowell's world, and the shift in perspective provides another consciousness, essentially focused on the problems with power. At the same time, of course, the use of an objectifying persona, such as Marie de Medici, is a traditional device used by Lowell's modernist elders. All four poems—"Beyond the Alps," "The Banker's Daughter," "Inauguration Day: January 1953," and "A Mad Negro Soldier Confined at Munich"—provide what Husserl would call an "other," the appresentation of another consciousness that regards the experience of still other consciousnesses and allows Lowell to perceive the world with multiple reflexivity.[33]

In the second section of *Life Studies,* "91 Revere Street," Lowell relates his present self to the past by gathering former images of himself and allowing them to qualify one another, creating a collective self for the present. The poem reflects Lowell's acceptance of the sane world of prose and his abandonment of the manic concentration of his early poetry. The flat, factual narration of events is in marked contrast to the intense narrative of "The Mills." The assertive, compounding allusions that were characteristic of the first phase of his poetry are absent partly because Lowell is writing prose, but also because of a general lessening of concentration. More relaxed now, he regards past phases of himself as an experiencing ego. No longer craning his neck toward heaven for a celestial fix, Lowell can still locate himself, but in "91 Revere Street" he does so as a Janus would, by looking backward and forward on a horizontal plane rather than upward for the vertical meaning obtained through Christian belief.

The book's third section, consisting of four portraits of other modern literary figures (Ford Madox Ford, George Santayana, Delmore Schwartz, and Hart Crane), represents eidetic variations on Lowell's own character. He regards his experience plus that of the other four as five sides of the modern man of letters. Each individual represents an experiencing ego whose horizons are identified so that he may round out an objective world for Lowell as poet. Lowell represents the four figures as isolated consciousnesses not only because each is alienated in some way but also because each functions as another consciousness aware of its surroundings and thus serving as a variant for a transcendental ego.

As the observer, Lowell is also alienated, and his eidetic variation of four others, who are like him in that respect, is the way he exploits such a predicament in order to overcome it. As Husserl uses subjectivity to get past it and to enter an objective world, Lowell articulates alienation, a condition of subjectivity, to get beyond it. Writing at a time when existentialists were describing a world of alienation, absurdity, and inauthenticity, Lowell used the portraits of four literary figures, who in their eccentricities represented these characteristics, as overlays for himself.

The final section of *Life Studies* is divided into two parts, both autobiographical. Its poems are directly concerned with Lowell's past. One poem in the last section of *Life Studies* will illustrate the building process that informs much of Lowell's poetry from "The Mills" on. That poem is "My Last Afternoon with Uncle Devereux Winslow." Here a transcending, present self regards a past, experiencing self, and by doing so locates its present situation and, by implication, develops expectations for the future.

The reader is presented in this poem with the world of Lowell's childhood. Lowell, as an experiencing ego, is present, and there are several other characters who serve as experiencing egos within the poem, each carrying his or her own set of memories and expectations. Taken collectively, these help to round out Lowell's horizon. There are four consciousnesses in the poem which are substantial enough to contribute to what takes place. Foremost, there is Lowell; in addition, there are his Great Aunt Sarah, his Uncle Devereux Winslow, who is dying, and his Grandfather Winslow. The poem recollects the initiation of Lowell at "five and a half" into his first understanding of death. The "earth and lime" with which he plays carry a retrospective significance. Uncle Devereux will soon be dead. Other physical details work similarly, all within the experiencing ego of Lowell as a child. Additional pockets of experience are implicit in the presence of other characters.

Great Aunt Sarah represents an isolated, eccentric, and defeated life. She supposedly "jilted an Astor." Then, as a pianist, she "failed to appear" for a recital that was to launch her career. She now practices on a dummy piano to avoid disturbing Lowell's Grandmother, who is tone-deaf. Uncle Devereux, who knows that he will be dead soon, nevertheless wants to go abroad. And

Grandfather Winslow is responsible for the world these characters inhabit. He has made it possible with "his *Liberty Bell* silver mine," though he also owns "fools'-gold nuggets." The point is one an existentialist of the fifties would appreciate. There is no wealth or freedom here, in any human sense, but poverty of spirit and entrapment.

Uncle Devereux will sail "for Europe on a last honeymoon" when he is dying; Great Aunt Sarah practices furiously on a dummy piano and will never actually make music; Grandfather Winslow inhabits the world that he has built but that has turned out to be "overbearing, disproportioned"; and young Robert is at his most formative stage, soon to confront mortality yet stereotyped like a mannequin in "Rogers Peet's boy's store." Each character is in some way short-circuited, and each prefigures the truncated world of "the tranquillized *Fifties*" mentioned in "Memories of West Street and Lepke," a world Lowell knew all too well. But Lowell recovers and uncovers this world in a way that takes advantage of, even insists on, the isolation of experience and the incongruities that arise among different perspectives. Viewed with the eye of an existentialist, the world he describes is absurd. Considered through the kind of poetic figuration that Lowell used in his later phase, it is a place where understanding does not work and where doubt is not only a reasonable conclusion but also a reasonable method by which to continue.

"My Last Afternoon with Uncle Devereux Winslow" gives parenthesis to a past phase in Lowell's life, and by adding the implicit consciousnesses of his great-aunt, his uncle, and his grandfather it rounds the experience. The poem gives Lowell a related but different location by which he can measure his present situation. Lowell's Anne Kavanaugh is an early instance of this process. Her reverie creates a Januslike continuum by which she clarifies an important part of Lowell's marriage to Stafford. As a series, the poems in *Life Studies* work similarly for different periods in Lowell's life.

III

In order to locate themselves in process, skeptics must create strategies to grasp their fleeting world. The similarities between Husserl's and Lowell's division of the self approximate one method for doing this. In its divided subjectivity, the self is just as poor as Husserl suggested it was—nothing more than the accumulation of horizons, the past phases of an isolated but expectant consciousness moving through a space-time continuum. One's past is gathered in a series of images which informs one's expectations for the future. Yet despite all this activity the best that can be said of such a method is that it is a strategy. As such it is incomplete.

Husserl says that a phenomenological method will give adequate but not apodictic knowledge. Judging from the critical acclaim Lowell has received, such an approach has satisfied many of his readers. Yet we should not forget that Lowell's late-modern poetics is in many ways a response to what Heidegger calls "the default of God."[34] O'Connor's summary of Lowell's troubles from 1949 through the early fifties indicates that certainly for Lowell God appeared to have defaulted in some terrible way. However, it is only fair to add that for O'Connor and many others there was no such default. For some, Lowell's late poetry is closer to the truth than his early poetry because it excludes the metaphysical assumptions embedded in a hierarchical tradition. Such assumptions are implicit in the symbolic, allegorical, moral, and anagogical levels of meaning. But for others, such as Lowell's friends the Fitzgeralds, the Tates, and O'Connor, the revised poetics of Lowell's second period merely lacked the larger dimension of meaning that a metaphysical understanding provides.

For those who hold to some idea of a transcendent, Lowell's second phase, influential as it has been, represents our fall from "The symboled world." It marks the inauguration of a minimal poetry whose language signifies but cannot symbolize. Finding horizons to have become local, such a poetry's expectations are equally local. In Husserlian terms, a restricted expectation will produce an equally restricted experience. Translated into what happened to Lowell, rejecting the possibility of a transcendent world precludes experiencing it. To those who are skeptical about higher order, however, Lowell's poetry represents a realist's going forth without illusions, a reduced but nevertheless honest mode of reconnaissance. Husserl's decision to proceed in a roughly similar manner suggests that Lowell's shift in understanding had significant corroboration.

Lowell's generation made a revision on its revisionist forebears. The modernists, who sought to avoid the subjectivity associated with the writers of the fin de siècle, found that many of the younger poets whom they had nurtured set about rejecting their tenets by returning, in varying degrees, to subjective positions. Antimodernist, Lowell's generation actually shares characteristics with antemodernist grandfathers. If the 1890s produced the dandy with top hat, cape, and cane, the 1960s produced the dressed-down dandy with long hair, jeans, and sandals. The self-consciousness is the same. Although Lowell's dress was carelessly conventional, and thus between either extreme, the subjective turn he made with his poetry took him much closer to the antemodernists of the 1890s than one might think. Ernest Dowson's "Non sum qualis eram bonae sub regno Cynarae" is not that far from the condition Lowell describes in "Man and Wife." In both poems the speakers are, as Dowson says, "desolate and sick of an old passion." And in both cases subjectivity manifests itself through recollection, alienation, then confession.

"The querulous hush-hush of the wheels" of Lowell's train in "Beyond the Alps" occurs as he travels from faith to the same doubt that Husserl employs. Both Lowell and Husserl are close to the condition Nietzsche spoke of as a "Socratism which is bent on the destruction of myth" and in which "mythless man stands eternally hungry, surrounded by all past ages, and digs and grubs for roots, even if he has to dig for them among the remotest antiquities."[35] Within the limits of poem-query as poem-answer, Lowell evolved a useful strategy for framing experience. Categorized as confessional by many, from *Life Studies* on his later poetry satisfies that category at times but at other times does not. As the echo of John Milton's Satan in "Skunk Hour" suggests, Lowell's strong sense of personal dislocation precludes some of the communal implications of confession. In his later phase, what issued from Lowell's treatment of the past was not the sequence of events as they happened but the way things coalesced for him afterward, when he reconsidered them, not in tranquillity but isolation.

In order to make events coalesce, Lowell's thinking operated causally. He no longer wrote to number the possibilities of a transcendent order but narrowed possibility, most often to the historical probabilities of a personal past. Thus, in "91 Revere Street" the lineage, technical bent, and military training of Lowell's father were set beside a boyhood with no father, diffidence as an adult, and marriage to the domineering Charlotte Winslow Lowell. What were his father's chances? What are anyone's chances within the sort of understanding Lowell employed in this description of his parents, which is restricted to the probabilities of a push-pull world of psychological forces operating causally—Charlotte Lowell's taste for the sort of domination she had found in her father, versus her husband's passivity.

In "91 Revere Street" past instances of Lowell's life with his parents are arranged. Its narrative reveals the polarity that existed in Lowell's mind between mother and father. If his imposed doubt meant that Lowell thought by contraries, surely he did so in part because of the positive and negative exchanges between his parents, both over him and through him. Lowell made doubt a positive method in his poetry much the way "91 Revere Street" reveals that as a boy he understood matters by being on both sides of each question that was raised between his parents. The potential for tearing down was implicit in Lowell's bipolar relation to his parents. But this bipolarity is most important because it parallels Lowell's later poetic method.

The bipolar tendency Lowell displayed as a child in his parents' home matured into his vision of the contrast between the heaven of Catholic orthodoxy and the Boston-as-Babylon of his New England heritage. But, during the first phase of his writing, the objects of his bipolar process tended to be external. Later, Lowell moved inward, and his bipolar tendency led him to counterpose a personal past to a personal present in a series of poems which bracketed subjective experience. His poetic process became an internal one in which the mind posited itself as its own boundary.

Poetry cannot do philosophy's job. Recent poetry is not applied phenomenology. Lowell did not copy Husserl's method. He simply arrived at a point in his life which presented him with many of the same problems Husserl had encountered in a less personal way earlier in this century; and in large part Lowell developed modes of thought in response to those problems that were similar to the modes that Husserl had already described. The pressures of a given period are felt by all of us, and a comparison between the similar solutions developed by two different disciplines tells us something about the context within which those pressures are experienced, a context within which we all must function. Husserl's cautious procedure in *Cartesian Meditations* is useful to us in part because his proposed method parallels many of the steps an absolutist by temperament such as Lowell took to establish certainty amidst the reduced surroundings that he inhabited from the time he was revising "The Mills" on. That these two very different thinkers turned to similar modes of thought argues not so much for the value of those modes, though certainly they are important, as for a common predicament confronted by the mind that has submitted itself and everything else to doubt.

2

Emaciated Poetry and the Imaginative Diet

I

Symbol, allegory, irony, paradox, and ambiguity were handled by the New Critics in a complex way that made a matrix of the text, with the tradition standing behind as the ultimate context. One of the first problems for poets schooled by the New Critics was not to sound like the property of a thorough New Critical reading. To many of those writing during the fifties and early sixties, symbol, allegory, irony, paradox, and ambiguity seemed to exist as much by their presence in the readings made by followers of the New Criticism as they did for their appearance in contemporary poems. The use of these devices seemed to repeat old patterns, rather than to create new and independent work. In this light, a "traditional" poet was someone standing belatedly inadequate before the present. Under the banner of experimentation, numerous alternatives were tried. And many of these alternatives, which seemed vital at the time, now appear tired and derivative. But their effects upon the modes of thought employed by contemporary poets have nevertheless been real, partly because they have helped to identify which streets are dead-end ones.

I would like to concentrate upon one type of poetry in particular that has been created as a substitute for the aesthetics presented to us through the New Critical reading of modernism and the poetic tradition. That alternative is what I call the emaciated poem. The trades in modes of thought made by those who adopted this kind of poetry give us an important outline to our contemporary literary economy, in which serious gains and losses have resulted from aesthetic shifts. There are numerous practitioners of this poetry. Two of the most interesting and useful examples are Robert Creeley and A. R. Ammons.

The first characteristic you notice about the change to which Creeley and Ammons have contributed is a shrinkage in margins that has produced a stylish, highly marketable thinness. For two decades one of the most publishable forms of poetry seems to have been the lyric broken into lines that would fit in a newspaper column. Editors are always cramped for room to include everything they would like to publish, but more than a question of space is involved here. At the same time its margins have narrowed, this poetry has been restricted in other ways. It is thin in more senses than one. And its thinness is part of a seriously considered change in the modes of thought used by poets such as Creeley and Ammons.

The publication of *Life Studies* in 1959 made it clear that a major change in American poetry had taken place. At a time when the influence of existentialism placed a premium on authenticity, Lowell deserted the traditionalism of Eliot for the immediacy of Williams. A general shift in poetry was under way. Haut bourgeois was out, déclassé was in. The rigors of poetic form amounted, it was now thought, to an inauthentic treatment of experience that, understood existentially, had to stand outside conventions as a unique moment. The isolated poet now set traditional categories of thought aside; the scales were removed from the shaman's eyes as poems about one's return to origins (which, like victims, are assumed to be innocent and good) proliferated. Moments from one's formative childhood and from dreams were accompanied by primitive objects, stones, bones, caves, and other items that seemed irreducible and thus appeared as the indices of the unconscious, essential humanity. What could be less ordered and therefore more existentially authentic than the unconscious? Like a caveman's experience, it was free of the clutterings of intellect and culture which stood between the eye and its object. The primitive, representing the unconscious, became a means for projection downward to dramatize human meaning, much as religious belief and the traditional use of symbol and allegory had been upward projections for transcendent meaning.[1]

A change in poetic style is always connected to a change in thinking, as the example of Lowell makes clear. Just as existentialism reached full stride, Lowell's personal experience seemed to have achieved a matching gait. From the forties until the end of his life, Lowell was a highly celebrated figure, and the scaled-down poetry of *Life Studies,* which he began writing in the early fifties, significantly affected other poets. His example urged that poets should cease using classical and Christian allusions to constitute meaning, especially through the use of symbol and allegory and, to a lesser extent, through the use of irony, paradox, and ambiguity. In place of these extended tropes, which to some poets made the poems that used them seem like marginal additions to the tradition, poets should turn to personal experience in the guise of a confessional aesthetics. Having left the church and faced his own dark world of the unconscious, Lowell began writing out of his own experience, his family's experience, and the history of New England. The Christian myth, a basis for timeless meaning, had been replaced by history and personal dislocation. However one judges his later poetry, Lowell did what he had to do in order to remain faithful to the truth of what he saw in our process-ridden era.

The urgency for poetry to make experience intelligible in a time-ridden era (whether one should use myth, as Eliot suggested, or reason, as Winters urged, or Jungian depth imagery) did not change with the experimentation in style which Lowell and others undertook. Because of the theistic assumptions embedded in their traditional uses, symbol and allegory had become problematical in the face of a postwar skepticism, and on the surface the classroom virtues of irony, paradox, and ambiguity taught by Cleanth Brooks and other influential critics half a generation earlier also appeared to have been set aside. Beneath that surface, however, the temporal problems that the Brooksian categories addressed did not disappear; poetry continued to respond to them. Whether one was concerned with religious experience (as Eliot was), with "preternatural" experience (as Winters at times said he was), or with the unconscious mind, poetry's task continued to be that of ferreting order out of the doubt and disorder of modern existence. What actually happened was that a poor man's version of irony, paradox, and ambiguity sprouted as part of an excessive reliance upon enjambment. An abbreviated version of the Brooksian virtues appeared as the result of the use of excessively short lines, and it did so in the poetry of those who had rejected the New Criticism and who clearly stood in opposition to what the New Critics represented. We are familiar with the Brooks version; here is a variation on it, Creeley's "I Know a Man":

> As I sd to my
> friend, because I am
> always talking,—John, I
>
> sd, which was not his
> name, the darkness sur-
> rounds us, what
>
> can we do against
> it, or else, shall we &
> why not, buy a goddamn big car,
>
> drive, he sd, for
> christ's sake, look
> out where yr going.

This poem presents a wry speaker worrying about one's movement through the dark, the unintelligible. For Brooks and the New Critics, words are linked with their particular bits of cultural baggage, and, out of the various torsions that these words generate as a group, a greater, more complex meaning is constructed. Irony, paradox, and ambiguity are the results of a building up, of putting words in tension with one another. In contrast, Creeley's method in "I Know a Man" is to break down. Ambiguity is created because the poem's foreshortened lines frustrate the reader's syntactical expectations. A mechanical substitution is offered for an intellectual problem. The lines are so short that they cannot function as run-on lines, only as syntactical interruptions. Readers teeter between the end of one line and the beginning of another with the vague feeling that things are ambiguous, ironical, or paradoxical because the units of language to which they are accustomed have been interrupted. Rather than irony, paradox, and ambiguity existing as a nexus of meaning, one is given the *impression* of these elements. Being a physical disruption rather than an intellectual complication, the trick is similar to the surprise generated by the home movie that is reversed just after a child dives into a swimming pool.

Creeley's excessive line breaks leave the reader struggling to get through the poem. Line breaks separate subjects from their verbs, interrupt phrases, and split individual words into lesser parts. The reader's pace is slowed to such an extent that what would be recognized as a commonplace when confronted at ordinary mental speed sounds oracular at this halting pace. Readers casually familiar with poetry who discover a poem written this way may think they have heard something substantial, but there is not enough here to sustain wit or argument. What they have heard may sound like a poem because it sounds different, and this is for no greater reason than the mechanical imposition of foreshortened lines.

Here is Creeley's poem "Quick-Step":

> More gaily, dance
> with such ladies make
> a circumstance of dancing.
>
> Let them lead
> around and around, all
> awkwardness apart.
>
> There is
> an easy grace gained
> from falling forward
>
> in time, in
> simple time to
> all their graces.

This poem might well never have been written had Williams not already written "The Dance," particularly the phrase "they go round and / around." There are some nice moments in "Quick-Step," though it is at best a wistful lyric. It creates the clear impression, however, of being much more than wistful. As an individual's exaggeration in dress and movement will hold our attention and suspend our ordinary going-about-our-business, the truncated lines in this poem work against the forward pressure of what the poem says as it moves at an exaggeratedly halting pace. We are briefly arrested, slowed, and charmed more by the slowing than by what we are told. A major element in Creeley's method is to call greater attention to what is visual in the poem than we would normally grant it. Stumbling over line break after line break, we tend only to picture things that have been named because so little is being said about them. In "Quick-Step" the act of dancing seems more vivid because so little else is there to compete with it, not even the momentum of the poem's own language.

This is the same poem put into conventional lines:

More gaily, dance with such ladies
make a circumstance of dancing.
Let them lead around and around,
all awkwardness apart.
There is an easy grace gained
from falling forward in time,
in simple time to all their graces.

Given breadth, the language in "Quick-Step" demonstrates the same accented-unaccented alternation that has been with us since *Beowulf*. Yet Creeley's use of foreshortened lines indicates that he was not seeking this sort of rhythm when he wrote the poem. The lines Creeley settled upon are too disrupted for rhythm to work. But it exists in the language, whether the poet hears it or not.[2]

Although greater momentum is generated by the use of conventional line lengths in "Quick-Step," the poem still produces a rather ordinary event. Little happens in the poem. Nothing can be done about what Creeley's practice of disassembly did to its content, particularly its overreliance upon enjambment and that which is visual. There is a question as to how one should read the poem at the end of the first line, because punctuation is needed there. (Creeley would probably say the point is that punctuation should not be there. He is interrupting our syntactical expectations with the absence of punctuation as well as with line breaks.) Generally, however, the reader can move through the regularized version of the poem at a speed close to that at which we usually think. Doing so demonstrates the poem's essential slightness, in content as well as form.

Written with the oracular effect that excessive enjambment creates as an organizing principle, "Quick-Step" presents us with a trick in the first line; "such ladies" pretends to a specificity that does not exist. The final word in the poem, "graces," is made to carry more significance than it can bear. The preceding words "awkwardness," "grace," and "falling" do not create a context for the ladies' "graces" to close the poem with anything definite enough to be meaningful. One is reminded of a vague, unrealistic, and high-handed male attitude that recent feminists have been quick to identify. Creeley's poem is an unfocused wish directed toward an indefinite object. It is sentimental.

Creeley's use of enjambment disguises much that is disappointing in the poem because his line breaks present a serious problem that disturbs the reader: the unreliability of language to provide a truthful approximation of what is real. The reader may not initially feel that Creeley's poem is simplistic, because he has skewed his writing so that the *way* he says things becomes the object of contention rather than *what* he says. Often the way a poem says what it means is nearly as important as what it does say, but in such situations the manner of statement, or suggestion, does not take the place of meaning. Creeley's willingness to expose himself to linguistic chance in his poetry is not a source of strength.

II

Amidst many variations there are two particularly striking characteristics that appear often in poetry written since the late fifties: assumed primitivism in style and content, and an overreliance on the image which results in neglecting poetry as an auditory art. Much of the attraction these characteristics hold for poets stems from their desire to ferret meanings from what they consider to be the unconscious. The influence of psychology has led us to a new sort of allegory (though there are other instances of the allegorical impulse; for example, science fiction and children's literature). Poems are now more apt to try to bridge the gap between the conscious and unconscious mind than that between a physical and metaphysical world. The world of dreams is generally a silent one—thus the deemphasizing of auditory concerns in poetry; it is primitive, and it is usually experienced visually—thus the excessive reliance upon imagery.

W. H. Auden's lines from "In Praise of Limestone" provide an appropriate comment here: "The poet, / Admired for his earnest habit of calling / The sun the sun, his mind Puzzle." Auden is acknowledging the openness and capacity for wonder that are essential if one is to write poetry, whether the poet be open to reason, belief, the unconscious, or all of these. He is not urging ignorance as the basis for authenticity, however. The worst result of the poetic shift considered here has been the shamanism of poets such as Allen Ginsberg, Robert Bly, and (too often) Creeley. The best result of this shift has been the adjustments made by poets such as Auden, who have stood ready on the one hand to exploit structures of the language, many of which exist in traditional poetic modes, and ready on the other hand to accept the mind as "Puzzle" and to regard experience from a position outside accepted categories of thought.

Winters once faulted Tate for an excessive use of enjambment.[3] Although Winters had accurately identified a departure from end-stopped lines, which was soon to be taken to an extreme, he was too scrupulous where Tate was concerned. As with Lowell's early work, Tate's poetry grew out of a sustained rhetoric that overran the boundaries of end-stopped lines as a natural result of its own momentum. The headlong pace of such rhetoric compounded meaning almost as quickly as a cluster of images might, though with one important difference. Whereas an image conveys a nexus of meaning immediately, as with Pound's "black bough" or Williams's "red wheel / barrow," the use of rhetoric in a poem requires time, as meaning is built synthetically from moment to moment.

Rather than seeing the truth as though it were projected on a screen, the way Milton's angels were supposed to have done, Tate and others generated meaning out of the ongoingness of their own language. In part we have a distinction between poetry that generates meaning synchronically, with imagery, and poetry that operates diachronically, with rhetoric. The latter also uses images, but they are only part of the recipe. The rest of the formula includes statements, questions, a wide variety of syntactical units, all sorts of tropes. It also exploits the rhythms inherent in our language in a way that is discussed most successfully with the aid of phonetics.

Another element in the synthetic poetry of Tate and others who still make use of the rhythmical line should be mentioned. The emotional thrust of the headlong pace of such poetry contributes greatly to the way the poem affects the reader. As Winters knew, the rhythm in a poem reinforces meaning on an emotional level. What Winters saw toward the end of his life, however, was the growth of a poetry devoid of rhythm. Thin, usually very brief poems populating the pages of various periodicals ignored the rhythmical possibilities in language, relying instead upon imagery. Their lines were too short for effective movement to be established, the voice having no chance to gain momentum. What these lines did establish was the dominance of enjambment. As they had been for centuries, end-stopped lines were the norm that gave significance to the reservation Winters made about Tate's (and, indirectly, early Lowell's) use of enjambment. But with the general turn made by poets to foreshortened lines, enjambment was taken to such an extreme that its use was no longer significant. The rhythm to which it contributed could no longer be heard.

The momentum of language enables a poem's ending to stand on the ground of immediate conviction. The systematic disruption of that momentum by line breaks, however, can leave a poem standing on the ground of immediate doubt. For us, doubt is a familiar condition. But is the disruption of language that occurs in the poems discussed here a significant expression of doubt, or is it simply the incongruent exertion of an individual will? Showing that there are gaps in language is meaningful only if one's overall purpose is to close them in some way. Language is self-sealing, and to a remarkable degree naming gaps seems to close them. In contrast, the excessive use of enjambment makes one feel there are empty spaces in language, but that feeling names nothing, discloses nothing. It is the result of contrivance rather than an honest attempt to articulate a linguistic shortfall and correct it. The use of foreshortened lines has led poets to employ certain narrow modes of thought in place of other more inclusive modalities.

Irony, paradox, and ambiguity are intellectual answers to various linguistic shortfalls. They do not provide a complete solution to the problem of meaning, but they contribute to one. And they do so, finally, in an additive manner. As modes of thought, they rely on the extensiveness of meaning contained in language. The overuse of enjambed foreshortened lines for syntactical disruption is a physical response not grounded in the extensiveness of meaning but dependent on the reader's expectations and the writer's will, the momentary surprise created by that will. Both methods are skeptical responses to experience. But the Brooksian formula proceeds additively on the assumption that language works, that it grasps what is really before us. The second formula proceeds subalternately on the assumption that reasoned language is arbitrary and inauthentic.

Here is A. R. Ammons's poem "Loss":

When the sun
falls behind the sumac
thicket the
wild
yellow daisies
in diffuse evening shade
lose their
rigorous attention
and
half-wild with loss
turn
any way the wind does
and lift their
petals up
to float
off their stems
and go

Although this poem is quite different from the poetry of Eliot, Tate, and early Lowell, its method is not new. On the one hand, we are provided an example of the pathetic fallacy, a phrase invented by John Ruskin; on the other hand, "Loss" is reminiscent of what the Imagists were doing at the beginning of the century, and in some ways the Decadents before that. In a Paterian mood,

Lionel Johnson would say what he said when defining English decadence in *The Century Guild Hobby Horse,* namely, that Ammons is trying "to catch the precise aspect of a thing, as you see or feel it."[4] One of the most striking characteristics in Ammons's poetry is that often he restricts himself to literal imagery almost all the way through a poem, reserving only one or two moments when he breaks out into figurative imagery. His previous restraint makes this shift all the more effective, though his reliance upon this method is one reason his poems frequently are not successful when read aloud. The shift from literal to figurative imagery is a mode of thought that seems suited to painting, and Ammons has turned to painting in recent years. Poetry's affinity with painting is a longstanding matter. If we look no further than the Pre-Raphaelites, "Loss" reminds us of Dante Gabriel Rossetti's "The Woodspurge." In other ways, however, "Loss" is much closer to an Imagist poem, particularly in its use of foreshortened enjambed lines.

As in Creeley's two poems, "Loss" works by a fragmentation of normal syntactical units that gives priority to the poem's imagery. Greater amounts of time are created for smaller units of language as the reader is encouraged to meet experience visually, with hierarchies, categories, or presuppositions set aside. "Loss" is primarily an artistic exercise in nominalism. Forcing us to focus on the particulars of nature more than on its patterns, the approach Ammons uses is skeptical, especially because of its minimal expectations. As part of this skepticism, sentimentality creeps in, "daisies" that we are told are "half-wild with loss." But not much is being lost here. Although in part we are provided a play on the daisies' wildness mentioned earlier in the poem, the emotion of this statement outstrips its meaning.

Rather than finding a matrix for meaning in an image, the way a successful Imagist poem did, "Loss" dramatizes the incoherence that will always result when we fix upon a thing subject to process. In this circumstance Ammons has dramatized a few moments in an isolated consciousness that happens to be looking at daisies. The poem generates a self-fulfilling prophecy for that consciousness: it uses imagery to give permanence within its own boundaries to daisies that, we are told, are nevertheless subject to time. A sense of loss is inevitable if not trustworthy.

Eliot's contention that the use of myth can make modern experience intelligible is based on assumptions about permanence similar to those made by Ammons and others where imagery is concerned.[5] In both cases, a spatial priority is established for what is being said, but with an important difference. We should not confuse the synchronic impulse to freeze predicaments spatially by using an image with a nevertheless similar tendency that occurs in the use of myth. Freezing a temporal predicament through the use of myth is a different matter, because myths are stories and thus have duration: they carry histories. Images are often extensive, parts in networks of meaning, but characteristically their significance is not born of the past or of a supposed past. When an allusion is made to a myth, the reader familiar with that myth suddenly recalls a chain of events: time is gathered. When an image is used, relations are invoked, but the projection of a temporal predicament into an atemporal image, which is the method Ammons and many others use, avoids the problem of time. The reader is offered only part of a solution for an intellectual problem that is basic to our process-minded era. In "Loss" the disruption of our syntactical expectations through enjambment and the overreliance upon imagery operates on the basis of the same trick in timing that one finds in Creeley's "I Know a Man" and "Quick-Step." These poems are written to be read much the way Burma Shave signs were placed to greet travelers along the highway.

A wide range of excellent poetry has been written over the last forty years, some of the best of it in free verse. In the restrictiveness of its short lines, however, the emaciated poem is not free but rigid. The lines are not long enough or balanced enough for rhythm to be established. I suspect that Creeley and Ammons would say that their thin poems are honest and authentic and that Eliot, Tate, and company wrote poetry that was self-consciously learned and bulky, thus posed and inauthentic. The question of authenticity, however, is predicated upon doubt, the same uncertainty about oneself and the world one inhabits which caused Lowell's poetic shift. Although the most influential recent episode has been the existentialist's alertness to the absurd, there is nothing new about doubt in our thought. Using the *cogito,* we have turned our predicament into our method: uncertainty has become our most reliable means for certainty as we have learned to rely upon the self-sealing character of language, which by allowing us to name a problem allows us in some way to move beyond it. Husserl's five meditations are intended to do this. Because we begin with uncertainty rather than belief, we must emphasize existence rather than essence. Because of the self's precarious position, as an entity standing in a world of process which dissolves entities, misshapen exertions of the will are inevitable, the most common of these being a very old and familiar exertion—sentimentality.

III

Writing an emaciated poem is not the only way to slow a reader and to emphasize images. Reversing the rhythm in a line or placing a caesura in a line are common ways to achieve the same effect and to do so without creating an interrupted surface that distracts the reader from what is being said. This is the first stanza of "Painting a Mountain Stream" by Howard Nemerov:

> Running and standing still at once
> is the whole truth. Raveled or combed,
> wrinkled or clear, it gets its force
> from losing force. Going it stays.

Opening with the bold statement of a paradox, rather than a vague feeling of contradiction created by truncated lines, this is an ambitious poem. The first stanza employs a series of metrical reversals, suggesting the mutual dependence of apparent opposites. We think of a stream as nominal. It is a thing whose properties remain the same; thus we try to paint it. The real nature of that stream, however, is that it streams. Rather than nominal, it is verbal in its ongoingness, which defies being fixed in a painting within a frame. Nemerov's answer to the intellectual problem of forcing something that is diachronic into synchronic terms in order to understand it is to say "paint this rhythm, not this thing." In other words, the narrow thingness of Williams's red wheelbarrow is quickly exhausted, and we must move up to a level of abstraction—namely to the process within which wheelbarrows, boughs, daisies, and streams exist, in order to understand what we see. Having made such a move, we are capable of making more satisfactory statements. Having made a statement, Nemerov succeeds where Ammons fails. As a quiet part of what he is telling us, Nemerov sets up metrical reversals; they appear throughout line two, in the first half of line three, and in the second half of line four. The poem's concluding stanza resumes the metrical and syntactical balancing act:

> The water that seemed to stand is gone.
> The water that seemed to run is here.
> Steady the wrist, steady the eye;
> Paint this rhythm, not this thing.

Anyone who wishes to can break this poem into truncated lines, but doing so is unnecessary and would be cumbersome. Nemerov has already satisfied his poem's need for reversals, and he has done so in a way that directs you to the meaning he intends rather than distracting you with syntactical interruptions.

For those intent on other ways of creating pauses, here is an even quieter use of the caesura, taken from Nemerov's "The Blue Swallows":

> Across the millstream below the bridge
> Seven blue Swallows divide the air
> In shapes invisible and evanescent,
> Kaleidoscopic beyond the mind's
> Or memory's power to keep them there.

Lines one, two, and four have an extra unstressed syllable each, placed after the second foot as a kind of vestigial caesura. An interruption or slowing occurs, but its force does not exceed the surprise created by what is being said. Line breaks substituted for Nemerov's caesuras not only would sacrifice the convincingness created by the poem's rhythm: being heavy-handed, they would be the first step toward sentimentality, the emotional force given the statement exceeding the significance of that statement. Rather than making experience the object of his poetry, as Creeley and Ammons do in a way resembling Pater and the Decadents, Nemerov has relation as his object. He is concerned with appropriateness—the appropriate relation between mind and thing, or things. Consistent with this concern, his poem demonstrates an appropriate balance between perception and articulation.

An impressive number of highly distinguished poets writing since World War II have continued to produce poetry that, while it does not restrict itself to traditional modes, takes advantage of them—a poetry that is successful auditorially as well as visually. Rather than using one poetic technique to the exclusion of others, and restricting the modes of thought they can use in their poetry, these poets have been quick to exploit a wide range of tools traditionally available to poetry—most importantly, various forms of trope. They have relied upon rhyme, assonance, consonance, lines regular enough to allow rhythm to be heard, literal and figurative imagery, simile, synecdoche, metonymy, metaphor, a form of mimicry, plus various rhetorical devices that often occasion tropes, including anacoluthon, anaphora, apostrophe, chiasmus, homoeoteleuton, and zeugma. In addition, these poets have tended to be interested more in ideas about relations than in the "precise aspect" or nominalistic detail of an isolated experience.

Here is a masterpiece among miniatures, Donald Justice's "Thinking about the Past":

> Certain moments will never change, nor stop being—
> My mother's face all smiles, all wrinkles soon;
> The rock wall building, built, collapsed then, fallen;
> Our upright loosening downward slowly out of tune—
> All fixed into place now, all rhyming with each other.
> That red-haired girl with wide mouth—Eleanor—
> Forgotten thirty years—her freckled shoulders, hands.
> The breast of Mary Something, freed from a white swimsuit,
> Damp, sandy, warm; or Margery's, a small, caught bird—
> Darkness they rise from, darkness they sink back toward.
> O marvellous early cigarettes! O bitter smoke, Benton . . .
> And Kenny in wartime whites, crisp, cocky,
> Time a bow bent with his certain failure.
> Dusks, dawns; waves; the ends of songs . . .

Justice opens his poem with a statement about our paradoxical relation to the past and reinforces what he says with a metrical re-

versal. The first two feet are trochaic; after that the line settles into
iambs with an extra syllable at the end. The rest of the poem is a
working out of what the opening line states. By marshaling particulars into a relation that gives them significance, Justice demonstrates that the past is both fixed and continuous, at least in our
"Thinking." At the same time, because we *are* "thinking" we are
not fixed but strangely discontinuous with the object of our thought.
The past is permanent somehow, and we were part of it yet are
impermanent now. The prospect where we find ourselves viewing
what has gone before requires that we recollect the past, which
Justice does through his poem, and that argues our estrangement
from an earlier time. Our "Thinking" is the prime evidence of our
removal from an earlier time. We are engaged in a synthetic, ongoing process, but the past is neither of these. Because we are removed, the best we can do is catalog what we nevertheless know
to have been, and still to be, a continuum. Compared to this, the
catalog's discrete particulars seem inadequate, but they are the
best our "Thinking" can do, even when it is our past lives we are
considering, which we had to think in order to live. Justice is after
a paradox of mind and a predicament of being that has the pathos
we experience, for example, when we hear a once-favorite song
and it brings back a matrix for our former selves.

Line two of "Thinking about the Past" is completely regular,
iambic pentameter with a caesura after the third foot. In the following lines metrical substitutions, extra syllables, caesuras, and catalogs (especially in lines three, nine, and fourteen) are used to vary
the rhythm as the reader moves down through what is a subtle
modulation of tone achieved by naming key particulars—the "mother's face," "rock wall," and "upright" all in their own ways "loosening downward." Line four, which contains "Our upright loosening
downward," is hexameter with an extra syllable in "loosening."
The added length of the line plus the way "loosening" slows things
with the hint of a caesura in its extra syllable create the sense of
extensiveness that Justice is after. Line five begins, "All fixed into
place now," three trochees, then, after a caesura, shifts into iambs.
It consumes as much time as line four, is slowed by the voiced
stop /d/, a caesura, and metrical reversals—all to the purpose of
ending the poem's opening movement.

The individuals and objects recollected—the mother, the piano

(Justice maintains an active interest in music), Eleanor, Mary, Margery, Benton, Kenny—operate reflexively as small bits of the speaker's former self, which existed both in isolation and in conjunction with others. Breasts, tobacco, "wartime whites," "Dusks, dawns; waves; the ends of songs"—all of these hold individually an implied whole that Justice cannot bring back in any literal way. What he can bring back is the tone as he felt it then and somewhat differently must feel it now, "moments [that] will never change, nor stop being." And that tone is created by the way the poem itself moves through time—rhythmically, phonetically, and logically. The poem's movement is Justice's own torsion on "Time a bow bent." He bends it around another way through the unique timing of his own utterance. Although this poem's movement *is* unique, we agree that its movement is integral to what it says and we can agree generally on the way it moves. The last line has seven syllables yet is iambic pentameter. "Dusks, dawns; waves;" represents three stresses, and the punctuation between each word (especially the semicolons) emphasizes their discreteness. We can take the comma and two semicolons as unstressed syllables; thus again we have a metrical reversal. "Dusks, dawns; waves; the ends of songs. . . ." That is, three things that are part of our diurnal process metrically counterposed to that moment when process stops, here, "the ends of songs." More generally, things such as age, death, good-bye—all that "the Past" at once withholds and evokes. For Justice, time makes a chiasmus.

Or, to use Justice's own words, "Time a bow bent." Time curving back through "Dusks, dawns; waves;" and music. But, more importantly, the doubleness of bow and bend. Each is the other. And this relates to what the activity of "Thinking about the Past" means. The past was thought as we lived it; thinking about it now amounts to thought about thought, the meaning now of the meaning then, a curving back into another curving back. One crosses the other. To *bow* is "to bend," and the noun *bow* used here goes back to the Old English *bugan,* "to bend." Initially we may think of a bow as something used with an arrow, but its first definition is simply something that is bent into a curve. It also is a warping, a knot, a wooden rod with horsehair used in playing instruments in the viol or violin family, and a stroke of that rod used in playing such instruments. The noun *bend* is the act of bending, the state of being bent, and something that is bent or curved. It is also a knot, and it is a musical term, varying the pitch of a constant note. But the word used by Justice, the verb "to bend," means to constrain to tension (as a bow) or to turn, press, or force something that then is curved. So Justice is telling us, "Time a curve curved." Very much the way melody works in a song. Thus "the ends of songs" curve back upon their beginnings the way a bow bends, or the way "Thinking about the Past" curves back—this time in multiples because of what Justice does by using poetic modes of thought *to think* about his subject.

One can also read "bow" as the bow of a ship, with "Kenny in wartime whites"; that is, navy whites. That would allow a fusion of "Time" and the ocean, where the poem is generally set. But Justice's intention was not to use water as a symbol of life, with a "crisp, cocky" friend bending it to his will, the direction of his ship. His friend was "bent" to "failure," apparently by dying in a war that seemed inevitable. The tonic chord Justice strikes is the complex way thinking thinks itself, this time poetically. I have spent some time with this poem in part to demonstrate, not exhaust, its complexity. It is visual enough but does not restrict itself to the bare, staccato description of an emaciated poem. Justice makes use of many of the stops and starts, squeals, blares, and tweedles our language provides. Making such aesthetic decisions for a poem not much longer than those by Creeley and Ammons discussed earlier, he makes more sense by using richer modes of thought.

This poem is highly formal, but it takes many liberties with the conventions of form. Someone opposed to the distinction I wish to make between emaciated poems and healthy ones might begin his or her objections with an overly strict interpretation of what form entails. The tactic to use if you oppose form is to hold a formal poem to too narrow an interpretation of its own aesthetic principles. Then you can argue that it never was formal in the first place. Or, agreeing it is formal, you can make it appear to fail by its own standards. But of course form exists as much by variation, the other half of its license, as it does by rule or pattern.

In going back over the numerous metrical variations in "Thinking about the Past," imagine someone who expresses reservations as to whether the poem actually is written in pentameter. Is it possible that the poem is in free verse? For many contemporary readers, I would suggest, the degree of tolerance for metrical variation within iambic pentameter and other metrical patterns is considerably narrower than should be the case. Maybe that is the basis for sensitivity about free verse. Given a strict approach to formal verse, free verse looks like the only haven for variations. (But variation is meaningful only when the sort of repetition created by iambic patterning and other meters definite enough to be experienced is maintained.) Here are a few reasons for saying that "Thinking about the Past" is not written in free verse but is a formal poem. It is fourteen lines long (reminiscent of the sonnet, with which iambic pentameter is associated), and the majority of its lines have five stresses and are more iambic than anything else. In determining what the meters are, a plurality carries the vote.

Let us examine lines one and eleven as examples of the way variation works in Justice's poem and contributes to its overall formal qualities. I read these lines as having feminine endings. Do the lines, as someone might ask, instead have reversed accents (not feminine endings, but trochees preceded by regular iambs) in the last position, a highly unorthodox place for this kind of substitution? If so, does this mean that either the poem is not written in traditional meters or that the poem is not successful in its traditional meters? Let me quote the lines here (line one, "Certain moments will never change, nor stop being—" and, line eleven, "O marvellous early cigarettes! O bitter smoke, Benton . . ."). What some readers may overlook is the way Justice forces us to read punctuation with the emphasis usually given actual syllables. The commas in these two lines have the value of an unstressed syllable; thus in line one "nor" rather than "stop" gets the stress, and in line eleven the pause after "smoke" resulting from the comma, as well as the deliberateness caused by the voiceless stop /k/ of "smoke," makes the line end this way: -'-. In further support that the poem is not written in free verse but makes dynamic use of traditional meters, the dash following "being" and the ellipsis following "Benton" suggest an outriding effect or continuation at the lines' ends, which complements the effect that their feminine endings generate.

"Dusks, dawns; waves; the ends of songs . . ." is the poem's final line, and here the comma and the two semicolons operate as unstressed syllables to produce a line with the timing of three trochees and two iambs. If you measured the way the line's punctuation tells you to read it with a stopwatch, you would find you were giving the same amount of time, and attention, to the pauses caused by punctuation as you would give to unstressed syllables. This is by no means a universal practice in Justice's work, but a familiar one. Justice is a highly skilled musician. He knows how effective a rest can be.

So let us return to the question of reservations for a moment. We can see that punctuation causes the same effect that a musical rest causes; but acknowledging that punctuation creates various effects that modify the movement of a poem the way syllables do may bother some readers. The problem with the way we associate convention and formal poetry stems from our tendency to appeal to the authority of consensus rather than the freedom a poet writing a poem may exercise at any time. When we appeal to consensus, convention is turned another one hundred and eighty degrees. We move from what in the practice of writing formal poetry is an opportunity for variation to what in criticizing that poetry becomes the basis for constraint. This is a line of thinking by which formal verse has all of the orthodoxies stressed; there are numerous taboos, so many in fact that one might despair over the future of formal verse. In contrast, free verse is understood to be liberated from all repression. But all verse survives under the mutually constitutive opposites of repetition and variation. Because for free verse appropriate restraints and liberties must be established over and over, poem by poem, it seems likely that the principle of repetition is more troubling for free verse than it is for formal verse.

There are other ways for short poems that are not emaciated to ken our contemporary ranges of experience and meaning. An example of poems that are very short but often carry considerable intellectual heft are J. V. Cunningham's epigrams. They are short, not thin. But a clearer comparison can be made with "To the Reader," a poem by Cunningham that *is* thin, though not emaciated:

Time will assuage.
Time's verses bury

Margin and page
In commentary,

For gloss demands
A gloss annexed
Till busy hands
Blot out the text,

And all's coherent.
Search in this gloss
No text inherent:
The text was loss.

The gain is gloss.

Here, unlike the examples from Creeley and Ammons, the lines are short, but rhythm works in them. They are iambic dimeter, with trochaic substitutions beginning several lines and with outriding, unstressed, extra syllables concluding lines two, four, nine, and eleven as part of feminine rhymes. Along with rhythms that reinforce what the poem says (consider the trochees beginning lines one and ten, as well as the four lines ending with feminine rhymes), in Cunningham's poem the reader's syntactical expectations are not continuously disrupted as we read down through the stanzas. Despite the shortness of the lines, the line breaks occur at logical (that is, aesthetically intelligible) points. By its argument, in this case by taking up the sedimenting effects of the critic's "gloss," the poem resists any attempt on the critic's part to engulf it with "commentary." It possesses an intellectual core that engages us and does not let go or let us reduce it to something less. There is a vigor in this that never loses touch with the context in which the poem should be read. The poem presents itself in finished auditory form and, by its reliance upon poetic statement, obstinately calls up the appropriate cultural concerns for understanding what is being said. This may not be most readers' favorite poem by Cunningham. For the purposes of my argument here, it is better that it not be. This is because even as a middling performance on Cunningham's part, "To the Reader" has a resilience that keeps it intact, which insures that this relatively obscure poem stands in marked contrast to the particulars of two familiar anthology pieces—the malleable daisies of "Loss" and the vaguely

imagined ladies of "Quick-Step." The thinness of "To the Reader"
is athletic rather than starved.

In "The Aged Lover Discourses in the Flat Style," Cunningham
relies upon wit. The poem has a serious point to make about the
isolation of individuals even when they are in the most intimate
circumstances. This incongruity is the basis for the reader's laughter, but such incongruity itself is, here, a serious problem. That is,
it is the basis for the poem's humor and our initial laughter, but
given additional thought the poem actually resolves in wit, as the
reader recognizes the similarity between the two estranged lovers.
They are together, but each is mentally somewhere else. Thanks
to its wit, the poem retains an intelligible and memorable problem
in a playful presence that is always ready to reengage the reader:

> There are, perhaps, whom passion gives a grace,
> Who fuse and part as dancers on the stage,
> But that is not for me, not at my age,
> Not with my bony shoulders and fat face.
> Yet in my clumsiness I found a place
> And use for passion: with it I ignore
> My gaucheries and yours, and feel no more
> The awkwardness of the absurd embrace.
>
> It is a pact men make, and seal in flesh,
> To be so busy with their own desires
> Their loves may be as busy with their own,
> And not in union. Though the two enmesh
> Like gears in motion, each with each conspires
> To be at once together and alone.

The "flat style" creates a place where humor and wit intersect. In
the latest edition of Holman and Harmon's *Handbook to Literature,* wit is characterized as "primarily intellectual, the perception
of similarities in seemingly dissimilar things," while humor "deals
with the foibles and incongruities of human nature, good-naturedly
exhibited."[6] In addition to the obvious pun intended, Cunningham's reference to "the flat style" is in part his way of achieving
the comedian's deadpan expression. At the same time, it is an
adaptation of the plain style, championed by Cunningham's mentor, Winters. The epigrammatic tendency in almost all of Cun-

ningham's poetry reveals a neoclassical temperament that makes him comfortable with the classical simplicity of the plain style. As handled here, it amounts to an unobtrusive means for presentation of the poem's oscillation between humor and wit, which are the central modes of thought by which the poem works. And in its apparent passivity, it parodies the lovers, who find themselves flattened in various ways. The quietness of Cunningham's style reveals a modesty for which emaciated poems aim. The difference between the two aesthetics is that Cunningham's organization is built out of syntax and rhythm native to the language, a patterning that works without drawing attention to itself as patterning. The disruption of syntactical expectations, in contrast, is a highly self-conscious attempt at patterning by dispatterning.

"Montana Fifty Years Ago" is another Cunningham poem that gives us an alternative to the problems with the emaciated poem. The plain style supports a metonymic gathering of particulars which travels in the direction of one powerful yet muted strophe.

> Gaunt kept house with her child for the old man,
> Met at the train, dust-driven as the sink
> She came to, the child white as the alkali.
> To the West distant mountains, the Big Lake
> To the Northeast. Dead trees and almost dead
> In the front yard, the front door locked and nailed,
> A handpump in the sink. Outside, a land
> Of gophers, cottontails, and rattlesnakes,
> In good years of alfalfa, oats, and wheat.
> Root cellar, blacksmith shop, milk house, and barn,
> Granary, corral. An old *World Almanac*
> To thumb at night, the child coughing, the lamp smoked,
> The chores done. So he came to her one night,
> To the front room, now bedroom, and moved in.
> Nothing was said, nothing was ever said.
> And then the child died and she disappeared.
> This was Montana fifty years ago.

Here the plainness and simplicity of utterance that Creeley, Ammons, and others are after, for reasons that by themselves are admirable, is achieved without throwing away the auditory advantages given us by accentual-syllabic patterning. The alternation between stressed and unstressed syllables, which is natural to our language (try scanning the speech of those who angrily deny this), and the modulations that result from the greater and lesser duration of certain phonemes within an accentual pattern give the poem a quiet intensity from line to line that argues honesty of feeling, which is the virtue sought by the unadorned appearance of the emaciated poem. But unadornedness turns out to be an empty category if there is laxness of thought and utterance underneath. The poem's muted speech dramatizes the power of silence. There is the silence between the man and woman in how they met and how they live afterward, the isolation that goes with the kind of work they do and where they happen to live, and the silence that follows the boy's death and the woman's disappearance. Out of a list of harsh, realistic facts, Cunningham creates an otherworldly effect. We are haunted by what the abandoned house represents now in terms of its vacancy, and the plain style employed here supports that experience. The poem establishes a dwelling for what it describes as missing; at the same time, the shaping Cunningham provides turns into hollowness, one that he says and, because of the *way* he says it, one that we feel is an intense experience.

As these examples from Nemerov, Justice, and Cunningham demonstrate, the issue here is not the poem's general shape or brevity but its intellectual substance, whatever the length, and this is the result of the modes of thought the poet employs. Some modalities build meaning on the belief that language works, however imperfectly. Other modalities are built subalternately on the belief that reasoned language and the forms it traditionally inhabits are hollow shells left over from an earlier time. The problem with this oppositional stance is that its significance as a position is made possible and defined, finally, by the tradition it seeks to overthrow. The emaciated poem is not a postmodern development free of the tradition. It is dependent on the tradition for its identity. In order to be significant, it requires the tradition, so that the reader can understand from where it makes its departure. The arbitrariness of its lining, for example, requires standard syntax and the tradition of end-stopped lines as normative patterns off which to play.

Edgar Bowers's "The Mountain Cemetery" is a slightly longer alternative to the emaciated poem:

With their harsh leaves old rhododendrons fill
The crevices in grave plots' broken stones.
The bees renew the blossoms they destroy,
While in the burning air the pines rise still,
Commemorating long forgotten biers,
Whose roots replace the semblance of these bones.

The weight of cool, of imperceptible dust
That came from nothing and to nothing came
Is light within the earth and on the air.
The change that so renews itself is just.
The enormous, sundry platitude of death
Is for these bones, bees, trees, and leaves the same.

And splayed upon the ground and through the trees
The mountains' shadow fills and cools the air,
Smoothing the shape of headstones to the earth.
The rhododendrons suffer with the bees
Whose struggles loose ripe petals to the earth,
The heaviest burden it shall ever bear.

Our hard earned knowledge fits us for such sleep.
Although the spring must come, it passes too
To form the burden suffered for what comes.
Whatever we would give our souls to keep
Is only part of what we call the soul;
What we of time would threaten to undo

All time in its slow scrutiny has done.
For on the grass that starts about the feet
The body's shadow turns, to shape in time,
Soon grown preponderant with creeping shade,
The final shadow that is turn of earth;
And what seems won paid for as in defeat.

As with Ammons's "Loss," Justice's "Thinking about the Past," and Cunningham's "Montana Fifty Years Ago," Bowers's poem has given us, in part, a memento mori. But though in theme this poem is much the same as "Loss," otherwise it is quite different. If the poems by Creeley and Ammons occupy the experimental end of the poetic spectrum (or what used to look like the experimental end), Justice's poem enjoys a middle ground that benefits from various sources—a jazz musician's taste for variation, which Justice plays against rhythms and phonemes that have characterized our language for hundreds of years—while Cunningham's unadorned voice sings a muted solo. In contrast to these, Bowers is highly traditional in the voice he generates. For his dynamic elements, he relies upon a varied, even at times archaic diction, and he does so out of a belief in the extensiveness of meaning held in a sort of etymological present tense by the language he has inherited and inhabits.

For Bowers, meaning has a more temporal than spatial character; thus imagery plays only a partial role in a poem. "The Mountain Cemetery" is primarily descriptive and in that regard visual and spatial, but everything we are given is put to the task of unraveling the riddle of time. Riddles are abstract realizations about concrete things that conflict. As Nemerov does in "Painting a Mountain Stream," Bowers moves in the opposite direction from Williams's mandate for things over ideas. Ideas come first, and they bring a great number of things together for our consideration. For Bowers there is a fundamental paradox in the fact that the process that brings us into this life is the same one that inevitably carries us out again. We live in light but note the contrast of "shadow." The final shadow is "turn of earth," the grave, a time when "what seems won" over the course of a lifetime of work is "paid for as in defeat." Bowers's stoicism is a complex understanding with a history of considerations which originates from a cultural base that is too complicated for an emaciated poem to handle. But ideas, conveyed by abstract diction and statements, can handle such material.

The use of "biers" introduces an archaic bit of diction, which Bowers employs to dramatize the extensiveness of death and by implication the extensiveness of life, which always faces death. Words such as "biers," "semblance," "imperceptible," "just," and "preponderant" change the poem's prospect toward its subject. The diction of the poem moves its meaning from the anatomical to the abstract, where greater connection can be demonstrated, without violating the poem's literal meaning—we remain in the cemetery. While on one level Bowers is giving us a descriptive poem, the language in his description operates reflexively. It gives us the object, and it reflects back through our familiarity with certain words into a whole body of human thought existing prior to the speaker, who takes up the subject of one cemetery. The above words are not simply abstractions; they exist within the poem's context. But they are cognitively qualified in a way that forces us to view the cemetery described in a context much larger than what description alone would give us. There is death, which we get with the daisies in "Loss." But much more important for human beings, who are able to anticipate death, there is the riddle implicit in the absolute process by which we understand ourselves. And mostly that understanding abides abstractly. Of course, Bowers could draw from a much different pool for his diction. He could use slang, the language of plain conversation, or the concision of wit and achieve other effective ends.

Matching Bowers's abstract diction, which gives his poem a scope that goes beyond the ken of most contemporary descriptive poems, is his use of statement—a practice championed by Winters and expanded in its usefulness by Robert Pinsky.[7] The ideal behind this practice is that successful poetic statement achieves a compression of human experience and understanding which because of its concentration hits the knowing reader more powerfully than anything else a poet writing a lyric might use. And the ideal example is Ben Jonson's "On My First Son," in which he says, "O could I lose all father now!" His son is dead, yet he remains a father. Like Justice's "Time a bow bent," he remains shaped without the thing that gave him shape, thus terribly hollow. Yet he is still capable of reason; thus the poem's concluding statement, which identifies our frequent confusion between what we merely "like" and what we love.

A statement such as "The enormous, sundry platitude of death / Is for these bones, bees, trees, and leaves the same" enables Bowers to yoke the particularity of the cemetery with our mortality, the general condition that cemeteries represent. (Cunningham's "Nothing was said, nothing was ever said" concentrates the argument of "Montana Fifty Years Ago" with the same intensifying results.) We all must die, yet for each of us death is different. In the older sense of another mildly archaic word, death is "sundry," different for each of us. It also is a "platitude," and in another sense of "sundry" it is miscellaneous. Death is an enormity that is separate from everything else every time it happens, yet so common we must call it a "platitude" as well. Bowers's yoking the role of death as a commonplace on the public level with its stark uniqueness on the private level (the particulars of the cemetery that he lists) is consistent with his yoking the two lines just quoted. The first line names the general; the second catalogs the particular.

The disparity between the general and the particular both offers us a distinction and works additively for greater meaning. That is a strength of poetic statement. Rather than breaking down an already existing meaning and offering nothing in its place the way a truncated line often does, poetic statement is able to span the fragmenting effect of details and gather them into a collective meaning. But additive distinctions are made in Bowers's work not only by statement but also by abstract language. A term with abstract overtones, such as "semblance" or "imperceptible," is also able to gather the particulars of a poem into a collective meaning, although this time the collecting is done more suggestively than is the case with statement. In both cases, however, details in a poem can be marshaled, either by diction or by statement, and raised to a central role in the poem's argument.

Here is another little masterpiece, "On a Child Who Lived One Minute," the opening poem in X. J. Kennedy's selected poems, *Cross Ties* (1985).

> Into a world where children shriek like suns
> Sundered from other suns on their arrival,
> She stared, and saw the waiting shape of evil,
> But couldn't take its meaning in at once,
> So fresh her understanding, and so fragile.
>
> Her first breath drew a fragrance from the air
> And put it back. However hard her agile
> Heart danced, however full the surgeon's satchel
> Of healing stuff, a blackness tiptoed in her
> And snuffed the only candle of her castle.
>
> Oh, let us do away with elegiac
> Drivel! Who can restore a thing so brittle,

So new in any jingle? Still I marvel
That, making light of mountainloads of logic,
So much could stay a moment in so little.

Perhaps this poem's most striking feature is the way Kennedy uses feminine rhyme to effect our movement through what he has to tell us. Where Nemerov uses metrical reversals and the caesura or an extra unstressed syllable to give the effect of a caesura and jostle the reader's movement through the poem, Kennedy uses an extra unstressed syllable at the end of lines two, three, five, seven, eight, and ten to fifteen. In each case, the line's eleventh syllable is part of a feminine rhyme. One can either describe what Kennedy is doing as adding an extra, outriding syllable or, because of the absolute regularity here, say that he is substituting an amphibrach for the last foot in those lines that contain feminine rhyme. The effect is the same. Kennedy disrupts our movement through the poem with an eleventh syllable, which leaves us unsettled and therefore catches our attention. He complicates this unsettled feeling with the agreement of rhyme, but the rhyming sound comes on the less emphatic eleventh syllable of the line, which is unstressed. Disruption goes hand in hand with agreement, balancing these two opposites into a poised assertion and qualification that match Kennedy's attitude toward the infant girl's death. This balancing act is also carried out by the poem's shifts in diction and by its last line.

In attitude, the poem shifts between the delicate language of "fresh," "fragile," "fragrance," "tiptoed" and the tough, realistic tones of "shriek," "satchel," "stuff," "Drivel," "brittle." In the second stanza, Kennedy counterposes "fragrance" to "satchel" and "stuff," as well as "blackness" to "tiptoed." These choric movements by means of diction finally exchange their strophe and antistrophe for the epode of the stanza's last line. Here Kennedy brings a brief pause to his balancing act between gentle words that alone might slip into sentimentality and the harsh words that offset any softness. The stanza's little epode occurs through figurative language. The poem speaks figuratively all the way through, but here there is a purposeful distancing carried out by the localized irony of "castle" and the almost overly familiar use of "candle." The infant has her *candle snuffed,* and the commonness of this expression tells us the speaker knows how common death is, even for children. The complexity and dearness of life, suggested by "castle," do not make life safe from the blunt limit of death.

Kennedy continues the debate between gentleness and harshness in the third stanza through his diction and by the balanced conclusion of the last line. He is going to "do away with elegiac / Drivel," even as he is writing an elegy. And he calls his elegy a "jingle," and doing so divides a metrical foot with a question mark. The *gle* of "jingle" is the unstressed half of a foot that "Still" completes. There is to be no "Drivel," and, just to show you he means it, he hits his own line with a hammer and splits the self-deprecatory word "jingle." Having counterposed gentle and harsh attitudes all the way through the poem by alternating the tone of his diction, Kennedy has acted out a very real response to death, especially when it happens to someone so small, innocent, and vulnerable. We are tugged in two directions at once. We feel protective toward the child and unnerved by her death. The dying of someone so "fragile" is almost too much to look at directly or for very long. However, we experience a kind of fist-shaking rage directed toward the circumstances that let such a thing happen, and with this we welcome the harsh diction Kennedy gives us.

The resting place for the poem, given in the last sentence, is worthy of Frost's "Design," though it carries more emotional heft because of its subject. Just as Frost concludes with an inscrutable design behind the moth and the spider—one that either appalls us with its carnivorous terms for exchange or that further appalls us with the absence of even such a grim principle as carnivority—Kennedy concludes with our having to accept the contraries of "so much" and "so little." There appears to be a nice logical balance to such a conclusion, but Kennedy's contraries operate as a trope. Nothing could be farther from balance or stasis. What we are given is the fusion of an abiding absurdity with which we all live. We experience our lives in their unique intensities, but we understand them in normative terms that are cold and distant compared to the way we feel. We are self-alienated by the contradiction between the way we feel about being human and what, in this century especially, we have learned to think about being human. Kennedy literally means "making light of mountainloads of logic"—the logic that tells us about the cheapness of life, the logic that tells us about its dearness, but more than anything else the logic that operates by size, quantification, number. The modes of thought by which we measure things are meaningless here. They do not begin to approximate the range of possibility that life brings. Rather than striking a nice rational balance like a tonic chord at the poem's conclusion, Kennedy tells us in the most winning and controlled terms, even rational ones, that we inhabit an irrational world and that understanding alone is not enough to put things right. Here apparent closure ends as a troubling disclosure.

Nemerov, Justice, Cunningham, Bowers, and Kennedy combine many of the most sensible elements of modern and late-modern technique. Although they recognize that reason comes to us as form, they realize that experience often arrives wide of any one categorization, but not wide of figuration. For these poets, and others like them, the mind's ability to discover order is just as real as the world's disinclination to stay ordered. Thus, poetry's task is always in need of being performed again. The work of each poet is built on the oppositional relationship existing between an old and new poetics and the continuing tensions between order and disorder. The answer to both oppositions is a poetry of mediation, in which poetry's most fluid elements are allowed to operate freely.

IV

There are variations on the aesthetic choices in poetry I have described. Along with the emaciated, there are the obese. Some poets write lines elongated to the point that one seems to be reading prose. The existence of "poetic prose" is one truism among many that have been used to break down the altogether real distinction between poetry and prose. The prose poem, the one-word poem (which is four words), the concrete poem, and the emaciated poem have all resulted from half-truths. Although the image has been the most common device for those interested in forming a new poetics, throughout the twentieth century first one then another characteristic of poetry has been taken, to the exclusion of the rest of what constitutes poetry, and expanded to make a poetics. Because the method is easy to use, its results are easy to find.

Linked with the role the image plays in these variations is a question of talent that partly originates in the influence painting has had on the poetry of this century. In its silence and spatial fixity, painting remains quite different from poetry, which is auditory and, like music, exists first in time. It is hard not to think that poets writing emaciated poems are geared to the visual in poetry because the image is such an accessible mode of thought. At the same time, poets writing overly thin poems have failed to employ some of the most effective poetic tools the language provides. And their poetry has suffered accordingly. Because poetic technique with language cannot be separated from poetic thought, writers who narrow their aesthetic narrow their range of meaning. Everyone recognizes the limitations of a painter who is colorblind. What about a poet who is tone-deaf or who lacks a sense of rhythm? Creating the kind of poetry that Bowers, Cunningham, Justice, Kennedy, Nemerov, and many others have written is not a realistic possibility for many poets writing today. These poets would argue that what they are doing is the authentic thing to do. For those who have no choice, of course it is.

3

Poems That Speak, Poems That Sing

I

Two types of contemporary poetry stand as opposites—plain-spoken poems that are reticent about their intensity and lyrical poems that are both compulsive and musical. There are many other ways to distinguish contemporary poems, which must compete during what is a pluralistic period; but in thinking about different poems, especially the presuppositions behind the different modes of thought they employ, I wish to posit the extremes of speech and song in order to uncover what they suggest about the resources available to poets. There is more to such a distinction than our usual ideas about speaking and singing take into account. If we focus our attention on poems that speak and those that sing, we will see fundamental differences in the assumptions made by poets about the truth claims available to them.

While poets who speak present themselves as realists who are skeptical about unity and wholeness, those who sing seem to act on the assumption that they and what they sing about are unitary subjects. Even when the self or its subject appears fragmented, the fragmentation derives its significance from a concept of unity that precedes it. The significance of a disintegrated view, songsters might say, depends upon a preexisting concept of unity that makes disintegration meaningful. Heidegger would say that by naming disintegration we hold unity near.[1] The dynamics of near and far affect two other categories—formal poems that sing out of a disintegrated view and free-verse poems with a highly ordered view. Another arrangement occurs in the guise of poems that speak at one point and sing at another. But to begin with—because degree rather than category controls the distinctions I wish to consider here—the extremes of singing and speaking are, in their polarity, sufficient.

There is a kind of entelechy in poems that sing, an association of sounds which develops the way melody, rhythm, and harmony lead composers and listeners ahead through music. The opening notes of a melody may be chosen from a huge range of alternatives, but the music that completes such openings is, by comparison, highly determined. There is also something teleological at work in melody and in poems that sing. Neither entelechy nor teleology is meant to describe a philosophical principle. Here they are meant to approximate a poetic activity in which a tone, an image, a first line, or even a word directs the opening of a lyrical poem.

Poems that speak create a *sense* of realism. They tend to move from one fact to the next in a rational sequence. They also have the convincingness of an eyewitness news account provided by a prudent and reasonable person. Our sense of realism in contemporary poetry is influenced by popular notions about scientific objectivity. While it often is based on a rhetorical device as much as anything, a poem that speaks, such as William Stafford's "Traveling through the Dark," appears to proceed empirically and rationally as an objective mode of thought, in a quasi-scientific manner. In fact, insofar as poets restrict themselves to a here and now they draw from a perspective that spatially and temporally is quite subjective. Even a scientist experiences this sort of problem. A scientist who studies tree frogs begins by having to decide what location he or she will use for purposes of observation, what an appropriate sampling of the population will be, what characteristics are significant for observation. The methods used will be as objective as possible, and the goal is to obtain repeatable results, but the subjective beginning persists.

Perhaps because the poem that speaks is not required to achieve repeatable results, the way a scientific experiment is required to do, the poet who speaks tends to have it both ways. Part of the artistic convincingness of a poem is its ability to feign modes of thought that it does not employ, nor should it. Certainly we do not expect a poem to generate precisely the same reading time after time. For one thing, the contexts within which the poem is read must change continuously. But there remains a source of authority for poems that speak resting in our popular ideas about the objectivity of science and in the poet's mimetic powers to create the aura of the unadorned *real*.

A poem that grounds its truth claims in the language it uses, as well as in cultural experience and the poet's experience, has access to a kind of variational play that extends thinking—that does not stop with one *here* and *now* . . . or achieve its convincingness from the appearance of doing so. Instead it uses tropes, plays figures to join thought and thing. In contrast, a plainspoken poem that gains its authority from the attitudes of empiricism and realism reduces its access to other sources. In a poem that aspires to songlike wholeness, the extending qualities of figurative language, or trope, as it is used in new ways and as it exists in a literary tradition, can go beyond the isolation of personal experience. So the songster, who initially appears to be the more subjective artist, the expressive one, can vary things to tap a larger range of experience than can the realistic, empirically grounded poet who relies on description.

What we encounter are mixtures of approaches, though there are significant differences in those mixtures. There also are reversals. Poems that speak may only appear to be realistic and to have gathered their evidence by empirical means. That is a variation on the poem that speaks, which becomes available to poets as soon as they identify the poet-as-realist's technique of plain speaking. Seen in primary outline, however, poems that speak are grounded in modes of thought, such as description, cause and effect, literal imagery, limited figurative imagery, a persona. They tend to be products of discrete experience recounted additively by means of a realist's vocabulary. In their unadorned directness, they generate a sense of realism, factualism, and honesty, but their literalness precludes some important levels of imaginative projection; for example, the symbol in its role as "a study in the concrete polarity of actuality and potentiality."[2] Or, less ambitious but for now more successful, there is the simile-like trope's capacity to bestow order with great variety simply by likening.

Tending to rely less on experience and more on connotation

and figurative thought, as well as baggage from past cultural experience, poems that sing are not limited to a *here* and *now* and are able to span a larger, and in that sense potentially a more objective, range of experience. Because language is at once our most comprehensive and revolutionary grounding, poems whose modes of thought emphasize language's resources have obvious advantages over those that base their truth claims primarily on the localizations of an individual's experience. Language is our radical, both origin and extreme. Our most radical poets are those most skilled with language.

As they are used in poetry, speech and song cross over constantly in many different and interesting ways. Although my purpose is not to trace the history of such crossovers but to establish the two opposing positions from which crossing over becomes possible, a look at the way crossing over works in several poems will show how speech and song are joined, separated, and played against each other. Robert Frost was a master of the play between speech and song. He would say his poems, but the effect was often that of song.

In Frost's late poem "Directive" (1947), the voice is modulated between saying and singing. Frost presents his poem as if it were spoken, even as he demonstrates all over again that he is one of our most gifted lyrical poets. In "Directive" there is a strong emotional drive for unity behind the voice that "only has at heart your getting lost." This discrepancy is the source for the poem's and its speaker's acute angularity, which is finally our angularity. The match between giving directions (a speechlike thing to do) and the rhythmically compulsive and highly associative account of traces of the past found in the landscape by the poem's speaker (what turns into a songlike thing to do) results in a poem that speaks with lyrical intensity. It speaks song, or sings speech. This positing by negating is a basic trope in Frost's poem, and it takes place in various ways.

Frost tells us "There is a house that is no more a house / Upon a farm that is no more a farm," both of which are located in "a town that is no more a town." Out of the "loss" he enumerates, we are to "Drink and be whole again beyond confusion." On our way we are to make ourselves "up a cheering song of how / Someone's road home from work this once was." We are to become "lost enough to find" ourselves. The descriptive "road" down which he has led us is a "ladder road." Out of the lostness of the *here* and *now/there* and *then* that we are given, we are to grasp a "goblet like the Grail" and rediscover wholeness. "The goblet [is] from the children's playhouse," which is not a place for realism but a "house of make believe." Belief is a game; the goblet is only *like* the "Grail." The simile leaves it both alike and unlike. Two things brought into proximity because of their likenesses are then seen to be different. Because of the play of similitude, they also remain likened.

The entire poem moves by means of pairings, and Frost's voice, which both speaks and sings, is the primary means by which he balances them. That voice proceeds by the things it enumerates— the realistic detail of the "cellar hole" likened downward so we see it "closing like a dent in dough," plus the other signs that prove that once there was "a house in earnest," that is, a house *in fact*—these, versus the suggestiveness of a "spring as yet so near its source, / Too lofty and original to rage." The spring is a poor man's "Mont Blanc." Both of Shelley's poems entitled "Mont Blanc" pertain here—the longer poem concerned with source and the brief, five-line poem concerned with oblivion. Source and oblivion are Frost's subjects in "Directive." His voice holds both before us by means of pairing: "A broken drinking goblet like the Grail" and "I stole the goblet from the children's playhouse." The grail is a symbol for source that once introduced is not allowed to remain symbolic. It is "broken." It is further demystified by the erosion of the speaker's grasp on reality. He has stolen what he now calls a "goblet" from a "playhouse," a house devoted to imagination and here to likening, rather than to the correspondence that the "goblet" suggests.

"Directive" is a late poem for Frost and an early one for a contemporary poetry that was finding simile-like tropes increasingly valuable. The poem remains dynamic for us because Frost never resolves the oppositions he introduces. He means they are both true and not true at once, like the poem's quietly mad persona, who tells the truth about his wish to get us "lost," the truth about untruth. There are no "wrong ones," and there are plenty of "wrong ones," including the speaker, whose voice is tensely modulated enough to rise to song. Unity is held in dramatic proximity by the compulsive enumeration of fragmentation, and the heart of this economy is the way the poem crosses back and forth between visions of realism and myth, oblivion and source, and modulations of voice between speech and song.

In his earlier poem "Design" (1936), Frost gives us a sequence of events that constitutes his experience. He tells us he has found the "spider," "heal-all," and "moth" and then recounts how they came together. The poem's discursiveness gives it a speechlike character, yet "Design" possesses the concentration we associate with song, especially its rhythm, rhyme, and rhetorical patterns. The repetition of the "spider," "flower," and "moth" (later as "dead wings") in lines seven and eight works like a refrain. The further repetition of the same objects in lines nine, eleven, and twelve sustains the effect of refrain and also works somewhat like a riddle. The total effect of Frost's repetition resembles that of a song such as "Captain Woodstock's Courtship." Yet Frost enumerates a sequence of events; he speaks what happened. By the end of the poem any idea of unity or "design" should "appall," unless the more appalling truth is that there is no "design" at all in what has happened. In both "Directive" and "Design," Frost balances between the opposing propositions of unity and fragmentation by means of balancing between speech and song. As the titles of these two poems suggest, a large part of Frost's project here is his questioning of loosely held versions of entelechy and teleology. His alternation between speech and song is the appropriate aesthetic device.

Many poems are not balanced the way "Directive" and "Design" are and tilt in favor of either speech or song. Their success in either direction is most accurately understood in terms of degree. Nevertheless, we can polarize these two tendencies and say that poems that sing operate to a considerable extent by the ear (consonance, assonance, alliteration, rhythm, even rhyme) and by associative reason (synecdoche, metonymy, simile, metaphor, mimicry). And, for the purposes of both sound and meaning, these modes of thought tend to arrange a musical structure for a poem's particulars. But while poems that speak also use these devices, they more commonly abjure much that an auditory imagination might offer as *songlike*. They tend toward aggregation, with their latitude influenced by a concept of realism. Compared to this, poems that sing seem projective. Because they derive their convincingness more from figurative language than from a realistic grounding in experience, they urge more than the empirical eye gives them. Poems that sing appear to be written on the assumption that being exceeds the senses and that our power to name things is part of the extensiveness of being. Poems that speak are more guarded in their assumptions.

If a poem that sings does project beyond one place and if a poem that speaks tends to burrow into and exploit the entirety of one place, why should we place one aesthetic practice above the other? Perhaps the greatest achievement occurs when a poem does both, yet what is important here is not hierarchy but the nature of the modes of thought used in these two types of poetry, or tendencies in poetry. These modes reveal certain presuppositions about the world, and they control what can be uncovered by the poems in which they are used. Lyrical projection operates like a Janus that looks through language back on our history and forward through figuration to change and possibility. A poem that speaks tends toward empiricism and realism as it looks backward and forward out of one setting. It also can address change and possibility, of course, but the concept of realism, which gives credit to what it says, also tends to base its authority on some *here* and *now*. This is one way for distinguishing between song and speech. And it is only partly satisfactory.

I wish to give to song, or to the tropes that often accompany poems that sing, some of the province Heidegger gives to "Saying," as a "lighting-concealing-releasing" activity carried out in a relation of "nearness" that surfaces otherness.[3] The simile-like structure that creates the play of similitude is a means by which we hold likened things near and far at once, as we see them as simultaneously both alike and different—near to being the same yet far from complete correspondence. When they are paired, they light and release things about each other; however, their pairing conceals characteristics that are separate, unique, and outside what makes the two a pair. Here is one more qualifier.

Heidegger considers language a doing, an activity, rather than an artifact. As we shall see in chapter four, Howard Nemerov takes a similar position—opting in "The Loon's Cry" not for "the nouns of stone / And adjectives of glass" or "the seawall of the solid world" but for "the verb / Which surge[s] in power properly eternal." A poem is its doing. It is its writing or reading. The Heideggerian maxim that language is "the house of Being" is better understood here if we think of such a house as a mobile subject to continuous winds. The mobile appropriates the space around it by annexation, but the annexes it creates are constantly appearing and disappearing as the mobile moves. Our concepts of realism give us an intellectual stasis that stands over against constant winds, which never let the mobile rest. Such concepts miss what language is, and we are language before we are anything. These ideas can work, in their way; our "metaphysical-technological explanation" gets us many things. But when language really works *as* language, its speaking or saying amounts to a "lighting-concealing-releasing" emerging from the sense of wholeness, if one's interest is poetry, then emerging from what songlike qualities suggest. As Heidegger explains, "Saying is the mode in which Appropriation speaks: mode not so much in the sense of *modus* or fashion, but as the melodic mode, the song which says something in its singing. For appropriating Saying brings to light all present beings in terms of their properties—it lauds, that is, allows them into their own, their nature."

In the same passage Heidegger remarks that "language . . . is the keeper of being present." It comes "to light" by "the appropriating show of Saying."[4] So far as poetry is concerned, the way around "the metaphysical-technological explanation" that Heidegger cautions against is for us to focus not only on melody but also on the "appropriating" and annexing uses made of trope in the "show of saying." Some implications of this idea shall be explored in chapters four and five.

II

Theodore Roethke's "In a Dark Time" and "The Waking" are far from pure and uncomplicated examples of poems that sing. They have their speechlike qualities. But they are lyrical enough for our purposes here. Their songlike intensity derives from Roethke's sense of personal vulnerability set against a concept of unity that he is unwilling to relinquish. When he asks "Which I is I?"

Roethke asserts his own fiercely Cartesian answer, doubting in order to assert. Having drawn himself into question, he writes his own powerful answer. "The Waking" performs the same unifying function that "In a Dark Time" performs, and it demonstrates even more clearly the central aspect of song in Roethke's poetry, which presupposes a unified self and subject—or, lacking the complete thing, the *value* of such unity set against what, to borrow from Nemerov again, is the "undermining" process of the "verb" that is Roethke's own being. On the one hand, Roethke gives us the stasis of the villanelle, whose repeated lines create an almost spatial fixity. On the other hand, the lyricism of the poem means it progresses the way a song does, and by doing. Roethke says he learns "by going where" he has "to go"; that is, by activity. The poem is about "The lowly worm," what time does "To you and me," the way identity is eroded; yet stylistically, the repetitiveness of "The Waking" denies forward movement. In English, the villanelle means something different from what it means in French. Because in English there are few rhymes while in French there are many, the repetitiveness of the villanelle is a much more distinct experience for an English ear. The strictness of this form, especially its repeated lines and rhymes, denies change and centers the speaker, insisting upon repetition similar to the refrains in a song, even as Roethke is telling us just the opposite—that there are no repeats in this life.

Both of Roethke's poems work on the basis of mutually dependent opposites; we are told our identities are continuously dissolving, but we are given this grim news through a formal poetry that at least appears to have originated from an opposing belief in order. All art operates by the opposing principles of repetition and variation, but here there is a new emphasis given to this principle. In poems that sing, form and lyricism are aesthetic devices that create a feeling opposite to fragmentation, even when these elements are used to articulate fragmentation. "The Waking" is as skilled and controlled a formal poem as Pound, Eliot, Tate, Ransom, or Winters could ask for, yet Roethke, having said he "wakes to sleep" and thinks "by feeling," questions "What is there to know?"—a response that characterizes Roethke in terms somewhat different from Ransom's and Winters's frequent appeals to the rational mind or Pound's, Eliot's, and Tate's confidence in the tradition. Here Roethke speaks the part of a younger, more skeptical generation.

What we gather from "The Waking" and "In a Dark Time" is not so much something Roethke might claim to know as the way these poems articulate a unitary self. Caught in what Heidegger calls "a destitute time," it is a self that *thrives* by singing, even as it questions unity. *Thrive* originally meant "to clutch," "to grasp." In a Heideggerian sense, Roethke concludes "In a Dark Time" by grasping himself. Ending with the line "And one is One, free in the tearing wind," he understands himself by what Heidegger might call "singing, to the trace of the fugitive gods"; that is, singing to an obscured metaphysics.[5] Our dark time is what in part we might generalize as our post-Cartesian understanding of ourselves and our world. Unity in this sense is not just the singleness of an integer, "one," or even the totality of related parts or the unification of those parts, "One," but is the self's freedom to doubt itself, which is its only means for concord within time seen as an eroding process, "the tearing wind." Unity can be concord in a musical sense, as a chord that is temporal and has harmonic effect, but only in the sense that it does not resolve, has no appropriate end. Unity is verbal instead of nominative.

Another way to describe the effect of Roethke's two poems is to think of them in terms of wholeness. In *The Quest for Wholeness,* Carl G. Vaught says that "wholeness is not to be equated with completeness" but that process continues. In order to understand what Roethke's poems do we must see each of them as a mode of thought, "a way of thinking that acknowledges the integrity of the quest for wholeness with direct experience; that understands the need for a description of it within the context of reflective discourse; and that attempts to connect the two levels without subordinating experience to reflection, and without holding these two dimensions apart in absolute opposition." Vaught would add that we should not subordinate reflection to experience and that we should avoid modes of thinking that carry the "exclusive reliance upon either experience or reflection."[6] Similar to the way Frost manages to balance his questioning between song and speech, Roethke's two poems achieve the balance Vaught encourages.

Written in free verse, Philip Levine's "They Feed They Lion" sings wholeness in what appears to be a completely informal manner. However, with the possible exception of Roethke's villanelle, Levine's poem is more restrained than the poems discussed earlier. This is the first stanza:

> Out of burlap sacks, out of bearing butter,
> Out of black bean and wet slate bread,
> Out of the acids of rage, the candor of tar,
> Out of creosote, gasoline, drive shafts, wooden dollies,
> They Lion grow.

The use of anaphora, the repetition of "Out of" and later "From," serves as Levine's main means for achieving a compulsive, song-like catalog. The catalog he recites gives what Vaught calls the "direct experience" necessary for "reflective discourse." At the same time, Levine uses anaphora to chant against the fragmenting particulars of the landscape he itemizes—an industrial scene that evokes blunt speech. Levine chants a long list of details which one normally considers only within the rules of speaking. (How many people sing about "creosote, gasoline," "drive shafts," or "pig balls"?) The play back and forth between a very traditional arrangement for elevated utterance and debasing detail forms the dramatic basis for the contrast Levine wishes to make between the integrity of the individual and the assaults on that integrity made by various forms of abstraction—technology, industrial assembly lines where people are asked to perform the same witless and dehumanizing task over and over all day long day after day, corporate structure, capitalism, and so forth. Each of these arrangements represents an assault on human values because of a kind of generalization of thought. Ironically, the agents of these abstract forces, the corporate bastards, are never brought beyond the barriers they would create for themselves, though of course somewhere they are a real part of the factory world that Levine describes. To the extent that they are not brought forward with the same complexly sympathetic eye that focuses on the work force, Levine makes these individuals the objects of a whole new round of abstraction and dehumanizing generalization and runs the risk of sentimentalizing his subject.

Levine patterns his poem lexically more than he does by accentual-syllabic rhythm. Anaphora creates cadences. One might ask which method offers more freedom of choice: stressed and unstressed syllables that are neutral in meaning and therefore not very restrictive about what a poem says next or lexical patterning that depends on the repetition of the same word or words and that by denotation and even connotation restricts which words can follow meaningfully. But this line of questioning leads to the way meaning is achieved in "They Feed They Lion." The restraint, the repetition, within the free verse employed by Levine when writing the poem is not an arbitrary set of hurdles he has raised for himself but a central device for articulation, for pivoting or turning things so that sameness and difference are played over and over. "Out of" and "From" point back to parts of origins, our culture finally, that remain relatively static. But the products of these origins that Levine catalogs are constantly different. The repeated use of "Out of" and "From" reminds us of the socioeconomic source behind the human blight Levine wishes to decry. Just as Roethke joined two apparent opposites (a forestructuring form such as the villanelle versus the individual's formless future promised by the process of "The lowly worm" and the fact that we "learn by going where [we] have to go"), Levine joins a catalog of sprawling industrialized America with an artistic commitment to the integrity of the individual, embodied by the assertiveness of the phrases he repeats so insistently—writ large, capitalism versus democracy. Each set of values tends to define its opposite.

Levine's limiting and delimiting presence makes itself evident by the details he selects, and by his distribution of them. Intensity results from formal restraint and lexical patterning, as well as the author's intentions, evidenced by what he selects for his catalog. The repetition in "They Feed They Lion" is tightly controlled. It has drive, and this appears to be the result of Levine's desire for his own understanding of a chordlike unity, his will to have a verbal wholeness retained by individuals who in the world of strikes, layoffs, and debts have very little they can hold on to or that stays in one place.

The specificity with which "They Feed They Lion" is written is a large part of its success. The details in this poem—the "creosote, gasoline, drive shafts, wooden dollies," "Mothers hardening like

pounded stumps," "the furred ear and the full jowl . . . the re-
pose of the hung belly"—contribute greatly to factual heft and
convincingness for the reader, who clearly senses that these things
come from one man's realistic yet passionate reckoning. Levine's
catalog ranges from "West Virginia to Kiss My Ass," to "the
sweet glues of the trotters"—all "on the oil-stained earth," things
too visceral to be understood as signs for something said indirectly. Metaphors and similes alone can lead us down a hall of
mirrors following the names for names, a process at once reflexive
and extensive. In contrast, catalogs enumerate what we must accept, on one level or another, as really existing.

By cataloging things, Levine plays our sense of realism against
the compulsiveness of his headlong speech. He achieves a cross-
over between speech and song. Rather than A equals B, A does
not equal B but is a discrete entity, along with C, D, E, and all the
rest. There is an urgency about the items listed that derives from
what we believe were Levine's intentions when he wrote the poem.
A great deal of the poem's effectiveness, therefore, goes back to the
reader's sense of the wholeness of the angular individual who felt
he had to choose such words. The poem's success results from
that individual's moral anger. It also results from the teleological
sense Levine had to feel had been violated in order for him to
muster enough adrenaline to write with such intensity, to chant
another teleology in place of the violated first one, or to chant
wholeness in the presence of discrete objects that in their separateness are complete but unsatisfactory. Although he is as drawn into
question by our technological quest for power over the physical
world, and ourselves finally, as anybody else who might consider
the subject, Levine writes with a concentration that derives from
what appears to be an undivided stance. Often this is a self-
consciously political stance. The politics are not only present but
also sometimes categorical enough in their inclusions and exclu-
sions to run counter to the realism of the rest of the poem.

Politics are part of Levine's expressiveness. He plays political
generalities against the details he catalogs as a way of addressing
what he sees as the abstract arrangement of political power dis-
tributed by a written document and then greatly revised for the
average individual by capitalism. Political ideals are played against
economic realities as a kind of trope of sameness and difference;

we are all given the same rights, but we have very different degrees of freedom and these degrees are mostly determined economically. The danger in this method for others who might use it is that when a political stance seems too easily assumed, too convenient for the poem, or too quickly assimilated, the authority derived from a sense of realism in the poem is threatened. Despite the sincere political interests many poets hold, poetry works by artifice. Convincingness may equal our *sense* of realism, but it does not necessarily equal reality. With "They Feed They Lion," however, readers believe that the speaker has a strong sense of what human wholeness is and what tears against it. The poem's lyrical intensity derives from the idea of a unitary self, from someone convinced of the integrity of the individual and thus the wrongheadedness of putting technological expedience before human values. We can categorize "They Feed They Lion" as a poem that sings fragmentation out of a sense of wholeness. As with Roethke's two poems, the poem's ethical position derives from the same general theological understanding that Eliot and Tate shared, though Levine never accepts the theological convictions of an Eliot. In fact, Levine's moral position is consistent with a number of his modernist forebears—Eliot, Auden, and Tate. Levine's opposition to the dehumanizing effects of industrialism continues arguments made in *I'll Take My Stand* (1930) by the southern modernist Agrarians Ransom, Tate, Donald Davidson, and Robert Penn Warren. Levine's use of free verse and his opposition to the dehumanizing effects of industrialization are two important family traits that identify him as a descendent of the modernists.

Following in a line that includes Whitman, Hopkins, Williams, and Berryman, Paul Mariani continues the speech-song exchange. Here is "Goodnight Irene":

I am ten and a half and my father
has let me come to work with him again
at Scotty's Esso in Mineola, the wood
and plaster tudor building three blocks
east of the pseudo-bauhaus boy's
Catholic highschool, from which one day
I will venture out to try the priesthood on

(and fail) knowing it is not
for me when I start keeping (against
Brother Clyde's injunction) a marker
in my physics textbook beside the picture
of the lovely in the armlength cashmere sweater
with those swelling upturned breasts.
And from beneath the row of fanbelts
hanging spiderlike I can see the neon
Rheingold sign pulse dully in the doorway
of the Colonial Bar & Grill
where thirteen years from now Wilbur
will split my upper lip with an ice cube
flung across the smoky underwater room
before my brother Walter can hit him
easy with that cross-body block of his
while I reel off my drunky speech to these
my friends a week before my marriage.
But for now I am inside the station
listening to my father singing chorus
after chorus of "Irene, goodnight, Irene,
I'll see you in my dreams," seeing only
part of his face down in the grease pit,
the wrench in his clenched right fist,
his hooded lamp throwing fitful shadows
all across the wall, as he performs
whatever mysteries it is he does to cars.
Useless even to my father, I watch
the yellow sunlight blocked in squares
drift east across the blackened bench
where two halfmoon brakedrums cup
the ballpeen hammer as in a Juan Gris
still-life, the calendar (gift of *Kelly's
Tires*) still turned to August, above which
the cellophane with the nightie
painted on it conceals the underlying
mystery of the lady kneeling there
who smiles frankly at me.
And now the warm smell of leaking

kerosene from the thumbsmeared
darkgreen fifty-gallon tin as I wipe
the opaque bluegreen bottles
of reconstituted oil for the old
"baraccas" as my father calls them.
On the box radio above the wheezy Coke machine
word drones Marines are fighting in a place
called Seoul but there is trouble even
closer home and soon someone is singing
once again the song my father
also loves to sing, "Irene, Goodnight."
And I think of mother back in Levittown
teaching Walter how to read
as my sisters go on playing dolly,
the younger one putting her wedding dress
on backwards while I help my father
put all the bolts into one coffee can
and all the nuts into the other.
And now my Uncle Vic (the one
the strokes choked off three years ago)
grabs his grease-clogged rag
and mutters as he strides out
into the sun to gas up some revved-up Ford,
the static gurgling high above the engine's
macho rumble while my father goes on working
on the underbelly of the car
where the light is coming from,
singing still again "Goodnight, Irene."
But my mother's name is not Irene
her name is Harriet and I wonder why
my father wants to see this other lady
in his dreams but I cannot ask
and will not even know what it is
I want to ask until I am older
than he is this September afternoon in 1950
and now the tears well up for him
and for my mother and myself as I turn
to look back down into the empty pit
to tell him now I understand.

In the opening, this poem is mostly a plainly spoken recollection, not without irony, but grounded in specificity. Thing and place dominate. There are iambic lines that start to climb toward song (lines two to five, part of six, and all of seven). But as "Brother Clyde's injunction" collides with "the lovely in the arm-length cashmere sweater" the language holds to a factual, detailed accounting of what was experienced, and this matches the haunting *"again"* in "my father / has let me come to work with him again," which suggests the father might *not* have done so or might not in the future, entailing a question felt but not understood by the boy as to whether he will be accepted into the male world that by rights should be his to inherit. Because the boy is "Useless even to [his] father," there is even greater reason to wonder whether the father will let him tag along the next time. Viewed on any scale but a child's especially, this phrasing holds the threat of a powerful negation.

There are two perspectives—the person who is "ten and a half," young enough that the extra "half" year is important, and the adult speaker who ranges over his past experiences and eventually steps forward to make sense of them. The two perspectives play back and forth throughout the poem. The lines "Marines are fighting in a place / called Seoul but there is trouble even / closer home" and "But my mother's name is not Irene / her name is Harriet and I wonder why / my father wants to see this other lady" push several realizations together without proper punctuation in order to dramatize the child's inability to analyze, to separate and see, what he is absorbing. Similarly, at the poem's conclusion the speaker—now "older / than" his father was the "September afternoon in 1950" that he has been describing—glides along without any pause of punctuation, rising to the intensity of song as he regards his father and concludes with "and now the tears well up for him. . . ."

The poem describes a *Nachträglichkeit*. Years later, the son is able to look back and understand what he once experienced but could not comprehend as a child. The later recollection generates an intense realization, causing a sense of wholeness that overcomes what before remained separative. The completeness of the past is replaced by wholeness generated out of the poem's repetition of events at a remove that insures the speaker's safety. The realization here is not a matter of what the father did or did not do but a matter of what the people in the poem managed to be for one another. The ordinary use of punctuation throughout the poem makes occasional departures from the norm a powerful tool, one that has the effect of conflating events and what they mean. The pace of delivery is speeded up in order to give the reader all the information as quickly as possible. The result is that the reader takes in what has happened before having the time to really understand it. One has a sense of things but no explanation for them, which increases the attention given them. In addition to dramatizing the speaker's increased pace of recognition and acceptance, which suggests an increase in intensity, this kind of speed-up in timing turns the reader into something like the fish that first takes the hook then sets it home by recognition, by tugging back—the only means for discovering what it has received.

There are "Marines . . . in a place / called Seoul," and over the radio "word drones" on about them. To the little boy, "Seoul" can be *soul* or *sole*—all three finally. He does not understand. For him "word," logos, only "drones." It is dull, monotonous, and indifferent—though it will not remain indifferent. Years later he will imagine the "pit" where his father labored and sang under a "hooded lamp throwing fitful shadows." At this point in the boy's life, however, language, it is suggested, is like a drone bee, without a sting and incapable of gathering honey. It does not work the way it is believed to work. Language itself serves as a metaphor for the father's spiritual and moral condition, which is "hooded" and impotent in its imprecision. The slippage that often characterizes metaphor as it is used in contemporary poetry serves as a pattern for the poem's understanding. A and B are supposedly meant to be equated, but they are only similar. The old cars that get the "reconstituted oil" are called "baraccas," but the word is skewed, and skews. In addition, every place where "is" occurs in the poem the things joined either literally or figuratively clash and cannot be held together. The boy will "fail" when he tries "the priesthood on," realizing that "it is not / for" him. We are told "there is trouble" not only in Seoul but also "closer home" as the radio plays "once again" the song the "father / also loves to sing, 'Irene, Goodnight.'" The boy sees "the light coming from" the wrong place, "the underbelly of the car." His "mother's name is not Irene / her name is Harriet." And the reflective speaker who gives an account of this day "in 1950" summarizes the incongruity of the relationship between him and his father in terms of age reversal: "older / than he is this September afternoon in 1950."

In every case, *is* joins things yet they fly apart anyway, much as *being,* in the guise of the speaker and his parents, is something that fails. *Is* simply does not work, until the end of the poem, when the son accepts incongruity, finding himself older than his father, and then can "understand." Both here and elsewhere, the literal and metaphorical structure of A is B is meaningful for its imprecision as much as it is for accurately matching things, and this is a function of skepticism—about language and meaning, institutions, the tradition. When readers are told that figuratively one thing is another (for example, the mind is God), their response is apt to be a simultaneous *yes* and *no*. Acceptance and doubt turn into the play of sameness and difference, as, due to the way it has come to be read, metaphor creates a simile-like arrangement. So does the hermeneutical process of naming generally.

The father's name for the old cars he services, " 'baraccas,' " is skewed and serves as another example of both the suggestiveness of language and its perils. The "reconstituted oil" is "for the old" cars owned by those too poor to buy new oil. The name the father has for these cars is the confused result of the Spanish words for "donkey," *burro* or *borrico,* as well as *baraca,* "divine gift," and the Italian *baracca*—a hut, booth, shed, army barracks, something poorly managed, or, most importantly, an ill-managed affair. The father thinks he is calling the cars old donkeys. There are auxiliary engines and switching locomotives that are called donkeys, and of course people can be called donkeys. But the main intention here is that the cars are plain and exist for hard lives. The word has intention on the part of the father but ends nowhere, because the confusion of language amounts to a confusion of identity. At the same time *baraccas* carries a set of harmonics that, in retrospect, are highly significant.

As it exists in the poem, the word suggests something like donkey–ill-managed-affair–divine-gift. That is a conflation of much of what the poem has to say about the male world described here. The father and others in the poem do not have the right names

for things, or for one another. Because their identities are relational—mother, son, father, brother, sister—they cannot know
themselves until they know one another. Through the discrepancy
created by the songful Irene and the real Harriet, language will
change and the variations on the conditions of the soul—death
(Seoul), life (soul), and the isolation of "the empty [grease] pit"
(sole)—will become clarified. This change in language is dramatized by the shifts made back and forth in the poem between a
speechlike gathering of experience through the boy's limited perspective and passages of genuine lyrical intensity when the rhythm
steadies into a mnemonic hammering out of what that experience
meant. First an example of the speechlike, accumulative mode:

> And from beneath the row of fanbelts
> hanging spiderlike I can see the neon
> Rheingold sign pulse dully in the doorway
> of the Colonial Bar & Grill. . . .

The first two lines are roughly iambic, especially if one carries
"belts" over into the next line as the unstressed syllable that goes
with "hang." The rhythm breaks up in the middle of line two,
after "spiderlike," reverses itself in line three, which is trochaic,
then fizzles out into the particularity of the name of the bar given
in line four. We are given an aggregation of realistic details that
are presented to us in the matter-of-fact voice of someone who
takes things in but cannot yet modify them, someone who speaks
rather than sings. Then the poem ends with a clear example of the
other end of the register, the figure of "the empty pit" and someone whose voice rises as he pivots on his experience, who turns
on what he has seen and likens it to something else, modifying
realism rather than just recounting it:

> and now the tears well up for him
> and for my mother and myself as I turn
> to look back down into the empty pit
> to tell him now I understand.

The alternation between a more lyrical movement carried forward by iambs and a chopped-up, step-by-step reckoning con-

tinues throughout the poem, and this exchange matches the exchanges that take place between the father's singing a song by a man named Leadbelly, Huddie Ledbetter, and the work he must perform "on the underbelly of the car / where the light is coming from." The light shines as if from the car's lower abdomen. There are two bellies here, two sources—one possibly ideal or transcendent, the other clearly physical. There are other kinds of doubling, several people with two names—Leadbelly who is Huddie Ledbetter, Juan Gris who was Jose Victoriano Gonzalez, Uncle Vic whose name may be an abbreviation of Victoriano, and for the boy a father who is himself and someone different because he is singing about Irene when his wife's name, and more importantly the boy's mother's name, is Harriet. Indirectly, the boy becomes both himself and someone different. Along with surnames and given names, there are other forms of identity that come from our parents; for example, fatherland and motherland. Who the boy is depends on the union of his parents, but here he is confronting a fissure in that union, which he now knows, as he speaks and sings the poem, is a fissure in himself. This does not require soap-opera antics to be true. The father could go home faithfully every night and be withdrawn, be a tyrant, or simply be mildly dissatisfied—and the essential truth of the situation would remain the same. His singing Leadbelly's song reveals he both is and is not the person he appears to be.

The images in the garage are seen as bluntly, even crudely, sexual. The "calendar . . . lady . . . smiles frankly" at the little boy as he notices the "two halfmoon brakedrums cup / the ballpeen hammer as in a Juan Gris / still-life." (On an adult level of understanding, Gris suggests the power to work synthetically, to improvise and invent along the lines of the artist's own sensibility. This is a poem that synthesizes the truth out of a myriad of details left over from one day's real memories. The result of this process comes as a tonic chord reached during the poem's conclusion. The poem moves from the completeness of the realistic scene it depicts to the wholeness of the response of the poet to what is real, a reality that he changes by his adult understanding and acceptance of it.) The "revved-up Ford" is a very limited but quite overt expression of masculinity. The whole little world created by "Scotty's Esso in Mineola" shouts male sexuality, but it is a pitiable scene. Any male bravado, or bravura, is comical and small because of the limitations imposed on each life. "Uncle Vic," who "mutters as he strides out," will work, probably pumping gas, until he is "choked off" by a series of "strokes." The boy's father sings about what he lacks and also promises to dream about it; that is, desire causes pain because it exists as much on a subconscious level as it does in the conscious mind. The father is teaching the little boy to "put all the bolts into one coffee can / and all the nuts into the other." He is teaching a kind of categorization of things that is no more discerning than the black-and-white fallacy that children are warned against in grammar school. The boy's knowledge of his father, at this point, is limited to a bleakly restricted and threatening perspective, "seeing only / part of his face down in the grease pit, / the wrench in his clenched right fist, / his hooded lamp throwing fitful shadows." Once you live with the details of this precluded little world awhile you begin to associate "Esso" with S.O.S. and S.O.B.

Leadbelly was a womanizer, and he was often in jail. His times in prison are a kind of paradigm for the time the father spends stuck in the grease pit, stuck in a life he cannot adequately control, as he sings Leadbelly's song. "Irene" became a hit shortly after Leadbelly's death. As with the father working at Scotty's Esso, Leadbelly never had real economic stability. For both men "Goodnight Irene" is an expression of desire, the wish to hold what you do not possess—another woman supposedly, though probably not another woman but a life that feels whole. The song first suggests infidelity, skewed desire, which could be literal but just as well might be psychological in the sense that the father does not know what the good thing to do with himself is. Put another way, the song is an expression of despair. Singing it articulates knowledge of something one senses but cannot have. The contradiction between knowing about a desirable thing, or knowing about it in terms of some projection for it, some mental pinup, and not possessing it amounts to a psychological tear. Thus, the wish for the wholeness of the world suggested by seeing Irene in a singer's "dreams" leaves us with a real night—desires half realized, half articulated, and unobtainable.

The poem performs another function. Leadbelly was reprieved from one conviction in 1925, sentenced again for intent to murder in 1930, and later pardoned. He had a stormy life, but it ended with a certain measure of recognition. Mariani's poem ends, similarly, with the notion of wholeness, in the sense that the speaker now can "understand" and accept what his surname tells him—who he is. A division is made whole, then, by articulation and trope, by turning the realist's objects so that things are pronounced distinctly, separately, yet at the same time joined by the action of turning them round. The isolation of a "September afternoon in 1950" is rounded into the adult understanding made possible by relation, with all its imperfections and its persistence. As a child, the speaker had no choice but to be divided by the tensions between his parents; as an adult, he exercises the freedom to acknowledge and partly resolve those tensions. He identifies himself and his parents through relation, both biological and figurative.

At the poem's conclusion, the rhythms rise to a songlike suspension as the speaker turns from the things that separated people to a vision of what joins them. He "look[s] back down." The "empty pit," always nearby, now becomes the occasion for a way out of oneself through the re-cognition of others, seeing oneself in others. Of course, no poem literally sings. And making distinctions between poems that are songlike and those that speak is, in a literal (or in a physical or technical) sense, very problematical. However, when two poems are matched or when two or more parts of one poem are matched, we can see a difference in lyrical intensity, and this difference often has to do with the realist's conviction of completeness being pushed suddenly to a vision of wholeness. Certainly that transition is evident in the conclusion of "Goodnight Irene."

In the examples of Frost, Roethke, Levine, and Mariani, limits have been overcome variously. But why the need for restriction in the first place? The wholeness of the self that sings is part of the answer. Meaning is another part. The need for limits derives from the way meaning is built within any mode of thought. In *Truth and Method,* Hans-Georg Gadamer provides an answer to the way closure derives from the need to establish meaning. Gadamer argues that "definiteness" in art "is by no means a fetter for our mind, but in fact opens up the area in which freedom operates in the play of our mental faculties." Art must "please,"

must work for us as viewers, listeners, or readers, "without be-
traying the constraint of rules."[7] And Gadamer points out the
way limit works to give us a center. But the freedom in the way it
works argues there is never any one center; thus *center* can mean
its opposite. (Heidegger would argue we are closer to a center
when we recognize we are decentered.) But why any rules that
restrict us, especially when we are the ones who make them up—
and when we know that being is verbal, that unity and wholeness
are the properties of a process rather than a fixed identity? Aesthetic limits exist for the same reasons rules are used in sport,
indeed make sport possible. The play of identity is a process of
articulation; thus it is verbal in two ways (a saying that is a
doing), both of which require the mutual dependence of apparent
opposites that we associate with music or games—variation and
refrain, or time and boundary, or freedom and restraint.

The arbitrary number of players, the area in which play occurs,
and the time allowed for play are among the many restraints that
are the bases for meaning in sport. A player thus limited can
employ imaginative free play, which becomes meaningful free
play. A *player* can become a *hero*. The fans applaud. Restriction
occasions meaningful free play. Lyrical control, a restriction itself
in poems that sing, works similarly. Thought of this way, lyricism
is a mode of restraint that generates imaginative free play.

Gadamer argues that art's imaginative free play "opens up the
area" of the subject. In poetry, a facsimile of that area is repro-
duced each time the poem is read. On one level, the assumption
of a unified self writing the poem, which is implicit in poems that
sing, constitutes another facsimile. Yet poems *are* written. The
self may be a linguistic appropriation and in that sense drawn
into question, but selfhood is not therefore reduced to a semiotic
process. Someone writes, and someone reads, or listens. I know
of no theoretical accounts that explain why an individual chooses
to write a poem, or has the talent to do it with permanent distinction, or why others recognize this. There is the issue of evaluation. Once we recognize the mastery of certain contemporary
poets, we have difficulty speaking of those individuals as facsimiles, or semiotic selves. A real self is behind the text. Certainly
the people who buy poetry books and attend poetry readings
do not think they are paying for facsimiles. The growth in the

number of poetry readings in recent years argues that authorial intention remains an important consideration in contemporary literature, and this also entails the concept of a thinking subject operating in its own "area."

A poem is what Heidegger calls a "gathering release," and in this sense it is more "the will as venture" than it is "the will to power." In the chapter "What Are Poets For?" in *Poetry, Language, Thought,* Heidegger discusses the untitled poem that Rilke wrote in June 1924. Heidegger describes the kind of poetic self-venturing that in its capacity to be forward-looking achieves the level of song: "As ventured, those who are not protected are nevertheless not abandoned. If they were, they would be just as little ventured as if they were protected. Surrendered only to annihilation, they would no longer hang in the balance."[8] For the poet engaged in the activity of writing, "balance" is the right word. The will is balanced between "power" and "venture," "gathering" and "release," limit and variation, demonstration and discovery, possession and renunciation, occupancy and relinquishment. The list could go on, but the distinction should be clear.

III

Anyone who reads poetry written since the late fifties is able to understand why it has been called *personal,* a term popular with A. Poulin, Jr., Alan Williamson, Robert von Hallberg, and others.[9] It is personal, first of all, because its truth claims are grounded mostly in an individual's testimony, which appeals to a kind of empiricism. This is in marked contrast to the method of literary or historical allusion that was so often present in modernism, where figures and diction were expected to carry cultural baggage forward from the tradition. But the subjects even a contemporary poet chooses cannot be separated from the interests that influence his or her choice, and these are informed by a whole matrix of cultural ideas brought to any subject considered. Still the exploitation of the personality of the poet who creates the text remains one of the major differences between a modernist poetics, which maintained the ideal of impersonality, and a late-modernist poetics more willing to recognize personalism. The bifurcation between impersonalism and personalism is fundamental to a poem's crossing over between speech and song, but sometimes the results are more satisfactory than other times.

The differences between James Wright's early "Mutterings over the Crib of a Deaf Child"—published in 1957 in his first volume, *The Green Wall*—and the later "Lying in a Hammock at William Duffy's Farm in Pine Island, Minnesota"—published in 1963 in *The Branch Will Not Break*, after Wright had made a major change in his poetics—are suggested by the two titles. The first evokes the strong feelings that attend a hapless child born deaf. Although those feelings are expressed at arm's length, Wright intended his "Mutterings over the Crib of a Deaf Child" as song rather than speech, which characterizes "Lying in a Hammock at William Duffy's Farm in Pine Island, Minnesota." As will become clear, Wright's earlier poem does not sing all that convincingly. It begins in quotation marks, questioning the child's future:

> "How will he hear the bell at school
> Arrange the broken afternoon,
> And know to run across the cool
> Grasses where the starlings cry,
> Or understand the day is gone?"

> Well, someone lifting curious brows
> Will take the measure of the clock.
> And he will see the birchen boughs
> Outside sagging dark from the sky,
> And the shade crawling upon the rock.

Wright's details ("curious brows" and "the measure of the clock") recall the tone of a Ransom poem; for example, "In one house we are sternly stopped / To say we are vexed at her brown study / Lying so primly propped." The reader may feel that the stanzas alternate between question and answer a bit like an Arthur Murray ballroom exercise. Wright shifts between direct speech and quoted lines that, in the guise of some public voice, ask about the child's future: What will the child " 'do if his finger bleeds' " or if " 'a bobwhite . . . flutes like an angel' "? The direct sections are spoken by a person who responds to the questions, eventually saying he will take responsibility for the child. Wright's speaker says he will sing when the child needs him to, song here suggestive of unity, but the rhetorical questions that drive the poem do not produce singing, although Wright writes with many of the formal elements used to generate the effects of song. "Mutterings over the Crib of a Deaf Child" is a little too self-conscious. It is a dialogue more concerned with the idea of what a poem, and indirectly a poet, should be than with the deaf child. There is something staged and impersonal about Wright's performance here, with Wright looking over his shoulder at the audience, or at his modernist mentors.

Written after he had distanced himself from the New Critics, "Lying in a Hammock at William Duffy's Farm in Pine Island, Minnesota" is at first glance just the opposite of "Mutterings over the Crib of a Deaf Child," neither polished nor impersonal and very direct. Yet these two poems share a common trait; in their different ways they speak rather than sing. The view in the second poem contradicts a chordlike understanding of unity that might inform song. Here is a familiar anthology piece, "Lying in a Hammock at William Duffy's Farm in Pine Island, Minnesota":

> Over my head, I see the bronze butterfly,
> Asleep on the black trunk,
> Blowing like a leaf in green shadow.
> Down the ravine behind the empty house,
> The cowbells follow one another
> Into the distances of the afternoon.
> To my right,
> In a field of sunlight between two pines,
> The droppings of last year's horses
> Blaze up into golden stones.
> I lean back, as the evening darkens and comes on.
> A chicken hawk floats over, looking for home.
> I have wasted my life.

In this poem the surroundings of a limited *here* and *now* dominate; they are the particulars of the Duffy farm—a "bronze butterfly," "cowbells," "the distances of the afternoon," "sunlight," animal "droppings," "A chicken hawk." In the presence of these, Wright feels he has wasted his life; that is, he finds himself drawn into question such that his only means of response is to enumerate the things around him. They, rather than Wright, are primary. They have a wholeness and ontological status that Wright does not share; thus he does not sing wholeness but only enumerates the externals that draw him and what he has done with his life into question.

On one level, Wright's procedure appears to be highly objective. He recounts what he has seen, then makes one generalized remark about it. However, his realistic description has the limitation of not allowing him to go beyond what he happens to see around him one afternoon at the Duffy farm. In its temporal and spatial restrictiveness, Wright's is a condition reminiscent of the observing scientist mentioned earlier who must concentrate on tree frogs within the limited framework we think of as objective scientific method but that begins with radically subjective decisions about what he will look for, where he will look, how long he will look, and so forth. The results of Wright's observations here are not achieved with scientific rigor, but the sense of realism the poem generates for its authority borrows from the popular sense that description can provide information with a detachment and precision similar to those of scientific procedure. Poets obviously do not practice scientific methods, but it is important to recognize where certain popularized notions about science and objectivity serve either as modes of thought in poetry or as justifications for certain practices—here supposedly accurate description that concludes with a kind of coda. Description is used to create at least the appearance of objectivity; then at the poem's conclusion it is turned to expressivistic purposes.

There is the question of metonymy in Wright's poem. Can the Duffy farm be taken as representing nature? Or is it more accurately understood as being a part of nature, human manipulation of the environment being a part nature also? If the farm represents nature metonymically, then we have a picture of harmony between humankind and the environment. The "cowbells" placed around the cows' necks so that the farmer can locate his animals denote location, a bit of human reason, but they also make a kind of music out of the "distances" that Wright perceives; we should remember that the perception of such "distances" is an anthropopathism. Does the poem work metonymically or is it a bit of anthropopathism?

We are told that "The droppings of last year's horses / Blaze up into golden stones," a strained figure that has the misfortune of creating the bathetic pun that concludes the poem—"I have wasted my life." Also, for some the "chicken hawk" appears at the poem's end as an unintentionally comic figure distracting readers with visions of William Duffy's chickens scurrying under a gliding shadow; these visions will remind some of a cartoon, others of the idiomatic expression "to chicken out." If we read this poem as working metonymically, we get a huge mismatch. The homely cycles of the Duffy farm name a world different from the larger, often uglier, more violent, and much more complex cycles that we call nature . . . unless we sentimentalize nature. "Lying in a Hammock at William Duffy's Farm in Pine Island, Minnesota" fails to deal with the complexities of nature adequately in large part because it avoids the short poem's techniques for balancing several competing perspectives at once—irony, paradox, and ambiguity. The brevity of this favorite anthology piece, as well as its tendency to oversimplify questions about wholeness and anthropopathism, causes it to end on a vague, sentimental note.

The particulars of the Duffy farm stand in marked contrast to the particulars enumerated in a poem such as Richard Wilbur's "Love Calls Us to the Things of This World," where the figurative match rests more happily:

> The eyes open to a cry of pulleys,
> And spirited from sleep, the astounded soul
> Hangs for a moment bodiless and simple
> As false dawn.
>
>   Outside the open window
> The morning air is awash with angels.

Success with figurative language requires that one veer neither too far in the direction of thing, as Wright does, nor too far in the direction of idea. In part, "awash" is meant as the morning laundry, which seems to overflow from the clothesline; it is also meant figuratively, in the sense of physical and spiritual bounty. With both Wright and Wilbur, we believe what is said because some-where the poem's details and the author's intentions converge in the guise of a perhaps fictional but nevertheless serious person. The choice of details adds up to the establishment of character and authority. Wilbur describes laundry hanging on a line; there is nothing more spectacular about it, in and of itself, than the things that Wright finds at the Duffy farm. Yet Wilbur goes be-yond the literal world that Wright, in his sincerity, cannot and would not wish to slip. Wright's imagery is literal because that is a large part of the point he wishes to make—the world around us raises questions about the value of our concerns. In contrast, Wil-bur's physical details take on human dimensions from the outset. Having clothed "the backs of thieves" with "clean linen"—that is, having urged us to respond charitably to others' failures—Wilbur concludes with "lovers" going "fresh and sweet to be *undone*" (italics mine), and, in his humorous exuberance, he wishes to allow "the heaviest nuns [to] walk in a pure floating / Of dark habits, / keeping their difficult balance." For Wilbur, the world is an array of likenesses. It is real, contradictory, and metaphorical, and it urges us into new names for it and, reflexively, for our-selves. For Wright, the world is literal to the point of sentimen-tality, and nothing short of personal transcendence will satisfy. Wright's own interest in transcendence may be substantial, but that is something other than his poem.

In "Year's End," Wilbur tells us that "winter downs the dying of the year / And night is all a settlement of snow." Here, "set-tlement" operates as a legal term used in dealing with an estate, as the physical action of the snow gathering on the ground, and as any sort of agreement—all three of these in contrast to the "wrangling" of the bells (an auditory pun) in the poem's last line. Wilbur gives us a "settlement" made orderly by human interven-tion: "From the soft street the rooms of houses show / A gath-ered light, a shapen atmosphere." It is a light that is collected, harvested, picked up gradually until we have a "shapen atmo-sphere," "shapen" in the sense of the wholeness Wilbur finds, a rather delicate wholeness. The year's end is commonly called New Year's Eve, but Wilbur has chosen to talk about the other side of the coin, not what is coming but what has passed. The two events, one year's ending and another's beginning, back up to each other and exploit the play of similitude. They work the way a simile works in order to compare two things. Wilbur launches into a whole series of implied comparisons by way of a simile introduced in the line five of the first stanza. The "light" is "gathered" into "a shapen atmosphere / Like frozen-over lakes whose ice is thin / And still allows some stirring down within."

The second, third, and fourth stanzas catalog leaves "Graved" (engraved and buried) in ice as "dancers in a spell," "ferns" fossilized and "mammoths" preserved in ice from "their long sojourns, / Like palaces of patience," and a "dog" plus various people "incomplete" and "random," as they have been buried by the ashes of Pompeii before they have had the time "To do the shapely thing they had not done." Having cataloged some of the ways we are frozen in time and found incomplete, Wilbur directs us to the way New Year's Eve makes us an "afterthought," as it balances between past and future and catches us "incomplete" in its moment. The poem concludes:

> These sudden ends of time must give us pause.
> We fray into the future, rarely wrought
> Save in the tapestries of afterthought.
> More time, more time. Barrages of applause
> Come muffled from a buried radio.
> The New-year bells are wrangling with the snow.

The second half of line one, which is from Hamlet's soliloquy (3.2.68), provides one more example of the way time doubles in the mind such that we exist in the present and somewhere else at once. Here time doubles as the opposites of the year's end and New Year's, disputing an ancient dispensation that is at once lawful and lawless—the "night" becoming "a settlement of snow" versus "The New-year bells" that wrangle "with the snow." Put differently, the past presents itself "in the tapestries of afterthought," but the present and future, through which we must "fray," are where we unravel and attack, as best we can. Year's end and New Year's occur simultaneously. They are opposites that constitute each other and also opposing perspectives focused on the same moment.

"We fray into the future" and are "rarely wrought / Save in the tapestries of afterthought," with "rarely" meaning "infrequently" or "excellently" and "wrought" meaning "formed," "shaped," "elaborated," "ornamented," and "wrought-up" (as in "deeply moved"). We do not live in the present tense but "fray into the future"—that is, scare, separate, unravel "into the future"—and it is only later, in "afterthought," that we begin to understand ourselves as there we find raveled together and re-presented what itself came to us by unraveling. But the melodic articulation that Wilbur projects into the future does *not* fray; it rounds past and future over a groundless present. The play between old and new in the objects cataloged and in the different, old and new, sometimes contradictory meanings of particular words ("Graved," "monument," and "Barrages" are other good examples) implies not only that the past, present, and future are brought together by the suspensions of ice, stone, ash, and the event of the New Year's celebration but also that time is condensed by language, which weaves our "tapestries of afterthought." That being the case, the greater the skill Wilbur has with language, the greater his plumbing of our central riddle, time, which on New Year's Eve we lament by celebrating in a manner as absurd as the "random hands" of "the people" of Pompeii, who were found "incomplete," having not done "the shapely thing." "Year's End" is an articulation of the way we mistake things completed (leaves, fossils, the people of Pompeii, and New Year's Eve itself) for tapestrylike wholeness, in which time and space are represented together.

Numerous poems by Wilbur balance opposing meanings and apply a melodic curve to time. Their unity is partly due to the internal oppositions carried by words such as "wrought," "fray," and "barrage," the last of which yokes a man-made dam with the release of concentrated gunfire. Aesthetic unity also comes from the opposition of stressed and unstressed syllables. But it primarily comes from Wilbur's sense of the "difficult balance" we must maintain in the face of time and the various casualties that accrue, one example of such balance briefly occurring between year's end and New Year's. If we report back like honest empiricists in the Lowell Thomas tradition, then we give up the balance between what we know from our culture and can imagine about that knowledge and what we happen to experience at one moment in one place; we forget the cultural past even as it applies torsions to the present, and in the emphasis we feel obliged to give to experience we pretend to a kind of objectivity that results from narrowing our perspective, which is a highly subjective thing to do. Wilbur's work is fully confrontational. It refuses to let one side of choice preclude the other merely for the sake of aesthetic closure. The songster's possibles and the realist's probables are kept on equal terms, neither ruling out the other. Wilbur's complex diction reminds us that the chance to mediate between experience and what we bring to experience is always present, waiting for us in the language we inhabit.

Many of James Wright's poems speak with memorable specificity (for example, "Autumn Begins in Martins Ferry, Ohio," "Two Postures beside a Fire," "Ohioan Pastoral," "Mantova," "Two Hangovers," and "Stages on a Journey Westward"). The last of these, "Stages on a Journey Westward," opens with a personal catalog:

1

I began in Ohio.
I still dream of home.
Near Mansfield, enormous dobbins enter dark barns in autumn,
Where they can be lazy, where they can munch little apples,
Or sleep long.
But by night now, in the bread lines my father
Prowls, I cannot find him: So far off,
1500 miles or so away, and yet
I can hardly sleep.
In a blue rag the old man limps to my bed,
Leading a blind horse
Of gentleness.
In 1932, grimy with machinery, he sang me
A lullaby of a goosegirl.
Outside the house, the slag heaps waited.

The subject of Wright's catalog is the world surrounding him when he was a child, that world read as an analog for Wright himself. His father sang to him, but Wright does not sing now. The idea of a child being sung to by his father in his father's house suggests the concept of wholeness. In "Mutterings over the

Crib of a Deaf Child" Wright promises to sing, saying he will "lift" the child into his "arms and sing / Whether" the child "hears [his] song or not." For Wright, song finally serves not in a positive vein but in contrast to his situation, as a reminder that wholeness has been lost. Fair enough. But the confrontation that waits for us among our many alternatives, which Wilbur makes us recognize, is passed up by Wright's two poems. Wilbur's aesthetic closure opens up to possibility; Wright's aesthetic openness in a poem such as "Stages on a Journey Westward" closes off possibility. There is a dramatic effectiveness to his insistence that the "Journey" be only "Westward," but it unfairly precludes our freedom to choose other directions on the compass—something that in another poem, the second part of "Two Hangovers," Wright recognizes *is* available to him when, waking with a hangover, he and a blue jay both know that "the branch" on which the "jay is springing up and down," and on which Wright is reentering the world, "will not break." But elsewhere he handles a similar attempt at affirmation less convincingly. Here is the beginning of another anthology piece, "A Blessing":

Just off the highway to Rochester, Minnesota,
Twilight bounds softly forth on the grass.
And the eyes of those two Indian ponies
Darken with kindness.
They have come gladly out of the willows
To welcome my friend and me.
We step over the barbed wire into the pasture
Where they have been grazing all day, alone.
They ripple tensely, then can hardly contain their happiness
That we have come.
They bow shyly as wet swans. They love each other.
There is no loneliness like theirs.
At home once more,
They begin munching the young tufts of spring in the darkness.

In "A Blessing," Wright's own gentleness and generosity have betrayed him into taking a familiar poetic device, the pathetic fallacy, too far. We are told "the eyes of" the "two Indian ponies / Darken with kindness." The horses "come gladly out of the willows." They "welcome" Wright and his friend. We are told "they can hardly contain their / happiness" as they "bow shyly," and we discover that "They love each other" and that "There is no loneliness like theirs." By this process of additive characterization, Wright moves from the acceptable understanding of the ponies as being kind, glad, contented, and shy to his claim that "they love each other" and that their "loneliness" is unlikened by any other. These last two assertions go too far. And they are not brought back by the self-consciously poetic "tufts of spring" that the horses munch two lines later.

Those who would defend this well-known poem may wish to stress that it is about ecstasy. At the end Wright says, "Suddenly I realize / That if I stepped out of my body I would break / Into blossom." But Wright's assertion of his own ecstasy and the poem's aesthetic achievement of it, actually the poem's failure to achieve ecstasy, are different matters. The poem relies on Wright's testimony, but that testimony is flawed by Wright's assertion of love and a unique loneliness for two reasonably well-fed, contented horses. Wright may have felt as he tells us he felt, but we are not convinced of the horses' love and loneliness. Here there is too much emotion with too little reason for such emotion, and sentimentality creeps in.

Wright seems to desire wholeness; the very idea makes him ecstatic. If he achieves unity on a personal level, he does so in the sense that unity is concord, as described earlier—concord in a musical sense, a chord that is temporal and has harmonic effect, to the point of ecstasy perhaps, but that does not require resolution, is whole but not complete. But while Wright himself may have experienced unity, wholeness, ecstasy, and the experience of these may have led to his writing "A Blessing," the poem itself does not contain these. This is because the poem must exist within a social and linguistic context that requires stronger evidence than the reported love and loneliness of ponies. The claims of authorial intentionality are very important, but they are only part of the formula. The failure here is that in a poem that proceeds at the concentration of speech there is not enough unity in the experience described to convince the reader of the songlike conclusion Wright wishes to make.

The thrust of "Mutterings over the Crib of a Deaf Child" is to entertain the idea of wholeness in the form of song, but not to find wholeness. The child will remain deaf and will "learn pain," although the adult speaker will remain vigilantly at hand to "sing." Later, in "Stages on a Journey Westward," Wright is even further away from song. He merely alludes to his father's having sung to him as an example of a once-felt sense of unity. Wright's reference to song is similar to the way ecstasy is meant to work at the end of "A Blessing." Were he to step out of his mortal body, he would "break / Into blossom," or, elsewhere, "break / Into" song. The ideal of a chordlike unity is retained in these poems and others so that it may stand in contrast to description, the appropriate mode of thought for a poetry contending with yet reliant upon the conventions of realism. The need for contrast is why Wright would have to "break" in order to blossom, or sing. The ideals of "blossom" and "song" are employed in these two poems not only for expressive reasons but also to help define the realism of a world that in its erosive multiplicity only answers to speech. But Wright has contemporaries who name the world differently, and who thus receive different answers.

A poem can play experience against thought, and, as Vaught cautions, can do so "without subordinating" either one to the other. How this is done reverts to basic choices made while writing. Experience arrives piecemeal. A poem is a mode of thought which assimilates experience. If a poet selects one mode, material is appropriated one way; a different choice brings a different appropriation. And, as with all thought, poetry not only absorbs experience but also effects it. Poems that speak do one thing with experience; those that sing do another. Poems that do both hold the alternatives of speech and song in a mutually articulating balance, like a problem held next to its answer but incapable of being replaced by it. Here is the beginning of a poem that elevates its speechlike catalog to the wholeness of song. It is Robert Pack's "Waking to My Name," the title poem of his *New and Selected Poems* (1980):

> Behind me the woods fill with the clashing
>   of fresh bird calls—
> phoebe, chickadee, robin, wren—
>   as the June sun

angles in as if to render visible
    the faint tart scent
of the red pine and the white pine, the cedar,
    the hemlock and the fir;
and behind me as I wake hungry for my own
    flowing, slow arising,
the names keep pouring in—my grandmother,
    Ida, my mother,
Henrietta, my sister, Marian; Patty,
    my wife, Pamela,
my daughter: their faces mingle and separate,
    age and grow young,
as their vowels on my lips, their consonants
    blunt on my teeth,
pluck them back into themselves, into
    the certain image
chosen by my heart again to remind me
    something of each one
has not been left behind, and will not change.

Pack sings out of an assumption that he is a unitary subject (he has a *name* to wake to) and that those he sings about are unitary also, identifiable by the names he lists. In this poem, the person who catalogs the world around him knows that "most of the full of [his] life is behind [him]." "Behind" as in past, but also "behind" in the sense of backing him as well. The ultimate thrust of this enumerative poem is to sing wholeness, not number fragments. Having called into presence the members of his family and the natural surroundings he welcomes as he wakes, Pack concludes this way:

And the June sun dawns upon my hand—
    nails and knuckles,
fingers, veins and thumb—which reaches
    out to the scented woods
and the visible names that merge in the lifting mist
    of my wakening age,
as I fly forth to the radiant green field
    with phoebe and chickadee

clashing, and robin and wren, and my name pulsing,
    repeating with my blood
that most of the full of my life is behind me.

Why such song in the face of "wakening age"? Because Pack is
writing out of the will as venture. The vehicle for such venture is
trope. The "names" he recites "merge in the lifting mist / of [his]
wakening age" because they operate metaphorically; Pack wakes
to his "Name" by waking to his names. This is identity born
out of the multiples that grow from the metaphorical aspect of
naming, which argues for the extensiveness of being. In Pack's
understanding, identity is no more autobiographical than it is biographical, no more subjective than it is objective. He is the aging
autobiographical man who wakes to spring and knows he is getting older; he is equally the biographical man who is a father,
son, husband, brother, and who lives beyond himself or any one
season in the relations he has built with others.

Pack's understanding of wholeness circumscribes process, and
it originates from his having combined the stubborn particularity
of the catalog with the metaphorical extensiveness of the naming
process. The speaker knows "that most of the full of [his] life is
behind [him]," in the double sense mentioned earlier; thus he is
at once "full" with the fullness of the past and "full" with what
that past has given him, which extends outward from him in ways
that, unlike the discrete self, are not time-locked and linear. When
Pack chooses, his poetry is able to sing because it results from his
complex understanding of the multifaceted self, which cannot be
comprehended in isolation either from other people or from the
world we share with others. With Pack, one name becomes a complex gathering for many other names.

IV

For every poem with a heavy emphasis on unity and song, there
seems to be an equally honest reckoning suitable only for speech
made by a poet who thinks on the basis of the presuppositions
carried to experience. And in post–World War II poetry, many
poets' presuppositions have led them to create work that out of

necessity speaks rather than sings. The enumerative way these poems have been constructed has often served as an analog for the self. If poetic discoveries in part constitute the poet (fragmentary or unitary), the poet who takes in experience in turn heavily influences what those discoveries will be. Here is a plainspoken poem that I believe most readers would agree is a respected anthology piece, William Stafford's "Traveling through the Dark":

Traveling through the dark I found a deer
dead on the edge of the Wilson River road.
It is usually best to roll them into the canyon:
that road is narrow; to swerve might make more dead.

By glow of the tail-light I stumbled back of the car
and stood by the heap, a doe, a recent killing;
she had stiffened already, almost cold.
I dragged her off; she was large in the belly.

My fingers touching her side brought me the reason—
her side was warm; her fawn lay there waiting,
alive, still, never to be born.
Beside that mountain road I hesitated.

The car aimed ahead its lowered parking lights;
under the hood purred the steady engine.
I stood in the glare of the warm exhaust turning red;
around our group I could hear the wilderness listen.

I thought hard for us all—my only swerving—
then pushed her over the edge into the river.

The diction is flat and the syntax is direct. The poem is reticent about its intensity, and operating behind this surface is a reclusive Stafford, reluctant to make any assertions beyond practical advice. This reluctance to say much about what has happened turns out to be the poem's means for making two of its most important points, that language does not control events and that we are all subject to casualty. We all must drive through the dark. Accident is without motive and thus impersonal. Because it is purposeless, the subject of the accident, the victim, is, within the terms of *accident,* nonessential. Equally vulnerable, Stafford's speaker would be wrong to describe what has happened to the doe and her fawn in any but the most guarded manner. His method of address is appropriate to the minimal news he bears.

We are expected to recognize our own mortality in the doe and her fawn, who are victims of "a recent killing," and in the speaker who comes upon the doe and finds himself so severely limited by what he can do. As he tells us, "to swerve might make more dead." His only choice is to throw the doe and her fawn "over the edge into the river." Otherwise, he or some other driver could go over the same edge. The speaker has "thought hard for us all," and he calls this his "only swerving"; that is, to think of alternatives is dangerous. There is something deterministic about the options available to the speaker, and this quality is yoked with the contradictory randomness of the accident that killed the doe and that is killing her fawn. This yoking of contraries dramatizes what is finally an irrational event. We are free in our vulnerability to accident but determined in our ability to respond to it. The multiplicity of natural forces at work around us makes nature as a whole free in comparison to our limited powers for response as individuals. Surrounded by nature, we appear determined.

Stafford leaves the fawn alive to open up the event, to give his reader time to consider ways of avoiding another death. Were both the doe and fawn already dead, then the only response would be to remove the doe. But by having us find the fawn alive Stafford takes the accident to its fullest implications. (He also risks sentimentality. Given that we are all only mortal, what is the fawn's role, beyond serving as an expression of futility and grief?) The speaker tells us he "hesitated." Originally meaning "to stick fast, stammer," this term is the right word. The speaker does not want to go over the edge himself; he wishes to stick fast, and his indecision about the fawn amounts to a stammer in his thinking. In order for one life *not* to go over the edge, another *must* go over. However, because it is still in the womb, the fawn is more the potentiality of life than an instance of it, and here Stafford puts a hook into his reader. Were the poem strictly about a doe and her fawn, it would be sentimental. Instead, we are encouraged to think of living in the broadest understanding. To the extent this works, the potential for something to live waiting in the doe's belly is the subject of concern more than the fawn is. Meanwhile the cold process that informs all life is running inevitably downhill in the dark river below.

The word "hesitate" concludes the third stanza. The first three stanzas have employed literal imagery. The fourth stanza, which represents that time the speaker hesitates, is composed of figurative imagery. For the first time we leave the literal world the driver has stopped to confront and gain a glimpse of what that world suggests. The automobile is "aimed ahead," its lights "lowered" as though they were eyes. The engine purrs, and the "exhaust" turns "red" in the taillights as though they and the doe's blood were one. The animal attributes given to a machine are appropriate because here the car is seen as an extension of the will. In Stafford's understanding, human intelligence, which designed the automobile, is the one characteristic that separates us from animals, but in this instance it has brought Stafford's speaker to a place where he is stopped and made to confront the inadequacy of human understanding. The car carries the speaker ahead down a dark road, then idles, matching his hesitancy as he thinks "hard for us all."

Traveling through the dark, human thought must constantly mediate between the will to drive on, to go on living, and the inevitable alternative to going on represented by the obscured vision that comes with nightfall, the curves in "the Wilson River road," a steep drop to the river, and at least one road hazard in the form of the doe. In part, we are treated to an example of frontier logic which Charles Darwin would have applauded. The doe and fawn are thrown into the river. The life process represented on the individual level by them is sacrificed in favor of life represented on a general level by the numerous travelers who must navigate the winding road, and finally by the river itself. The road and the river are the only means for traveling through the dark. But each is linear, finally. And once you start out, your way, if not your end, is determined.

Because of this sense of determination, Stafford would have us feel we are stillborn in some way. The fawn "waiting, / alive, still, never to be born" finally represents what we feel has happened to the possibility for some end to "the Wilson River road" and all the other roads we are apt to navigate over a lifetime. They are

not followed to their ends but are interrupted by one kind of physical accident or another. And to think too hard about this is to
"swerve," to run the risk of going over the edge.

The waiting fawn opens up an alternative that is always available—the opportunity to doubt, or hesitate, as the poem's speaker
tells us he did. If the archaic meaning of *hesitate* was "to stick
fast," "to stammer," the contemporary meaning is "to hold back
in doubt." It is here, in this contemporary sense of hesitation, that
we see why Stafford had to write a poem that speaks. The understanding he brought to his subject required it. In a poem about
coming to the edge of mortality and either stepping back or going
over, Stafford comes to an intellectual edge, one that divides hope
for the possible from his reckoning of the probable, and it is here
that he really elects to step back. The intensity we associate with
lyrical poetry is usually found in a poem's melody, metrical co-
herence, particularity of image, and the fusion of idea and image.
In Stafford's poem, intensity is primarily achieved by restraint,
that pitted against the pathos we experience for the unborn fawn
waiting in its mother's belly. The poem is at once explicit and reserved. It speaks plainly.

In another example of a poem that only speaks, but that is not
plainspoken and that does its speaking with an intensity as great
as or greater than that of song, Anthony Hecht employs restraint
similar in degree to Stafford's guarded language, but Hecht's major technique for objectifying what he wants to say is the use of a
historical event, the martyrdom of Hugh Latimer. That, and an
even bleaker form of martyrdom presented in a grim drama acted
out near "a German wood" by "two Jews," "a Pole," and a German officer with his "Lüger settled back deeply in its glove." The
second event is a slightly altered account of something described
in Eugen Kogon's *Theory and Practice of Hell.* " 'More Light!
More Light!' " follows:

Composed in the Tower before his execution
These moving verses, and being brought at that time
Painfully to the stake, submitted, declaring thus:
"I implore my God to witness that I have made no crime."

Nor was he forsaken of courage, but the death was horrible,
The sack of gunpowder failing to ignite.

His legs were blistered sticks on which the black sap
Bubbled and burst as he howled for the Kindly Light.

And that was but one, and by no means one of the worst;
Permitted at least his pitiful dignity;
And such as were by made prayers in the name of Christ,
That shall judge all men, for his soul's tranquillity.

We move now to outside a German wood.
Three men are there commanded to dig a hole
In which the two Jews are ordered to lie down
And be buried alive by the third, who is a Pole.

Not light from the shrine at Weimar beyond the hill
Nor light from heaven appeared. But he did refuse.
A Lüger settled back deeply in its glove.
He was ordered to change places with the Jews.

Much casual death had drained away their souls.
The thick dirt mounted toward the quivering chin.
When only the head was exposed the order came
To dig him out again and to get back in.

No light, no light in the blue Polish eye.
When he finished a riding boot packed down the earth.
The Lüger hovered lightly in its glove.
He was shot in the belly and in three hours bled to death.

No prayers or incense rose up in those hours
Which grew to be years, and every day came mute
Ghosts from the ovens, sifting through crisp air,
And settled upon his eyes in a black soot.

Although we feel intensely about the death of the doe and her
fawn, we feel even more so about the suffering of our own kind,
especially when our own kind is also the cause of that suffering
and we are thus drawn directly into question as a species. In the
Stafford poem, we are merely one form of life among many forced
to confront mortality. " 'More Light! More Light!' " argues we
are our own mortality, physically and spiritually. Stafford's speaker
renders firsthand experience. What he has to tell us is at once
graphic and restricted because he remains on the road where he

found the doe. Hecht's speaker ranges over several hundred years, from when Latimer was burned at the stake to sometime during World War II. While the description is as powerfully graphic as we could wish, the lasting force of what Hecht's speaker tells us comes from the contrast drawn between two very different types of martyrdom. The first was carried out in the name of the church. Latimer could at least call for "Kindly Light." Paintings of Christian martyrs often depict ecstatic subjects. However realistic or unrealistic this is, compared to the actual event, it reveals the hope brought to martyrdom by a Christian understanding of it, something quite different in intention from the Nazi practice of extermination. Had the gunpowder gone off as it was supposed to do, those watching Latimer would have been confident that he had arrived in heaven early.

This is not true of what happens several hundred years later "outside a German wood." (The events described took place at Buchenwald.[10]) Hecht has counterposed two martyrdoms that are horrible and yet otherwise unalike. They reflect two opposing views—wholeness and fragmentation—and by doing so carry out their own crossing over between the assumptions behind poetic speech and song. Although both martyrdoms are utterly gruesome, the contexts in which the two events take place are totally different. One carries metaphysical presuppositions; the other does not. The martyr burned at the stake for his religion has hope of heaven. The Jewish prisoners have lost hope long before, from too much "casual death," which has "drained away their souls." The Pole who "in three hours bled to death" from a gunshot wound in the belly loses the hope that enabled him to refuse to bury the others because they demonstrated that they were willing to bury him. Again, the self is found in a kind of "similitudo" reminiscent of what Gilson and Lewis describe, but it is a lateral rather than vertical likening.

The Pole sees his skeptical self in the other two men, who are willing to bury him alive although before he was unwilling to do the same thing to them. More than by causal reasoning and other logical structures, we make the world familiar and find ourselves through similitude, including various devices for mirroring and doubling; thus the simile-like structure Hecht invents to liken two events, two kinds of martyrdom. They are the same yet different.

Seeing them this way initiates thought about them and delivers us from the numbing shock that comes with our initial recognition of what has happened. The simile-like structure is our means for constitutive play, which frees us to rearrange relations, to change things. Sequence, which makes causality possible, also makes similitude possible temporally, rather than just spatially. This allows Hecht to play similar actions against each other in order to dramatize the radical differences that exist between the two cultural contexts in which these grim deaths occurred. The moral horror behind Hecht's poem is that the Pole was made to believe that he could *not* change things, that his refusal meant nothing. This little bit of terror happens every day. Likening is a way to fight it.

There is considerable difference between the opening description of Hugh Latimer's death and the remainder of the poem. In the opening stanzas, while the subject is horrible, the language is baroque, and the lines are noticeably longer than they are elsewhere in the poem. Both of these characteristics are meant to suggest the elevation of Elizabethan speech, which here is close to song. Also the confidence of the poem's baroque opening carries with it the assumption that language, and by implication human reason, works. This assumption is put to ironical purposes, we feel, as we read the first three stanzas. But upon finishing the poem and returning to its beginning, we realize that whatever the particulars that accompany the awful blindness to so many religious differences, the not-so-selective blindness of a twentieth-century totalitarian state is even worse. The poem's baroque opening is, on rereading, pulled back from some of its ironical possibilities because of the context created by the modern horrors that follow it.

As Hecht says "We move now to outside a German wood," he contracts his speech to something closer to Stafford's plainspoken medium. His diction and syntax straighten into a steady hammering of events that need no embellishment, that in fact make embellishment impossible. No one is capable of imploring his "God to witness," and there is no "Kindly Light" left "in the blue Polish eye" after the Pole has been buried alive by those he refused to bury alive. Instead, we are left with the "mute / Ghosts from the ovens" settling on the Pole's "eyes in a black soot." Hecht's language, which in the beginning was close to song, has tightened. The terse conclusion of " 'More Light! More Light!' " places it among a large number of contemporary poems that must speak, and can only speak, because the poets writing these poems see nothing to sing about.

When he wants to, Hecht sings masterfully, but " 'More Light! More Light!' " was not written to sing because its subject cannot sustain even the hope for human wholeness. We are drawn into radical question by the world Hecht describes. It is worth noting that this is partially because in the past Hecht himself had been drawn into question. As a young soldier during World War II, he had experiences similar in their brutality to the one he describes. He was an early witness to the concentration camps. Thus " 'More Light! More Light!' " speaks rather than sings in part because it is tied so directly to experience, especially to what Hecht saw in one instance. He was the interpreter for an officer who shot a German sergeant in the stomach so that the man would die slowly, and did so after the sergeant had surrendered. The American officer falsely claimed that while he was disarming himself the German sergeant attempted to throw a grenade.

Another poem that speaks a good part of the time is Nemerov's "To D——, Dead by Her Own Hand." It is a plainspoken address to Nemerov's sister, the photographer Diane Arbus, who committed suicide in 1971. Childhood is invoked in a discussion of unity and fragmentation:

> My dear, I wonder if before the end
> You ever thought about a children's game—
> I'm sure you must have played it too—in which
> You ran along a narrow garden wall
> Pretending it to be a mountain ledge
> So steep a snowy darkness fell away
> On either side to deeps invisible;
> And when you felt your balance being lost
> You jumped because you feared to fall, and thought
> For only an instant: That was when I died.
>
> That was a life ago. And now you've gone,
> Who would no longer play the grown-ups' game
> Where, balanced on the ledge above the dark,
> You go on running and you don't look down,
> Nor ever jump because you fear to fall.

Nemerov's child and the grownups run "along a narrow garden wall" much the way Stafford's motorist travels along "the Wilson River road." The motorist travels above the dark river below; those on the wall move "on the ledge above the dark." The hand-me-down notion that childhood enjoys a measure of wholeness which adulthood lacks serves as a foil in Nemerov's hands. Nemerov does not romanticize childhood. The child running along the wall would rather jump than fall, just as the adult running through the paces of her life chose suicide over a breakdown. Control always, continued life maybe. The poem's last line works two different ways at once. Adults "never jump" out of fear they might fall; they maintain the appearance, at least, of control. But adults also "never jump" because they know that jumping is just another way of falling, and they "fear to fall." In part, Nemerov is getting at the riddle implicit in suicide: a person cares so much about herself or others that she finally wishes not to go on caring. Suicide performs its own grim role in similitude. Jumping gets rid of anxiety about falling but at the same time duplicates the source of anxiety.

There is a linear character to the lives described in poems that speak. What unity the people can claim, they gather from a temporal understanding of themselves. The primary thrust of poems that speak is that the self is fragmented, but this understanding continues to take its significance from opposites—unity, wholeness. This is the beginning of Nemerov's "View from an Attic Window":

1

Among the high-branching, leafless boughs
Above the roof-peaks of the town,
Snowflakes unnumberably come down.

I watched out of the attic window
The laced sway of family trees,
Intricate genealogies

Whose strict, reserved gentility,
Trembling, impossible to bow,
Received the appalling fall of snow.

Nemerov goes on to say that "among many things / Inherited
and out of style" he "cried, then fell asleep awhile." Meanwhile,
the "snowflakes" fell "from darkness to darkness." Then, as the
second section of the poem sings, he tells us why he responded
this way:

2

I cried because life is hopeless and beautiful.
And like a child I cried myself to sleep
High in the head of the house, feeling the hull
Beneath me pitch and roll among the steep
Mountains and valleys of the many years
    Which brought me to tears.

The poem ends:

But what I thought today, that made me cry,
Is this, that we live in two kinds of thing;
The powerful trees, thrusting into the sky
Their black patience, are one, and that branching
Relation teaches how we endure and grow;
    The other is the snow,

Falling in a white chaos from the sky,
As many as the sands of all the seas,
As all the men who died or who will die,
As stars in heaven, as leaves of all the trees;
As Abraham was promised of his seed;
    Generations bleed,

Till I, high in the tower of my time
Among familiar ruins, began to cry
For accident, sickness, justice, war and crime,
Because all died, because I had to die.
The snow fell, the trees stood, the promise kept,
    And a child I slept.

This is a poem about the way our sense of multiplicity erodes
individual identity. From his attic window, the speaker watches

the "Snowflakes unnumberably come down" among bare branches. His attic is a "cemetery of spare parts / For discontinued men," and the snow outside falls "in a white chaos from the sky," equivalent in number to "the sands of all the seas, / As all the men who died or who will die." Anyone who watches the evening news is reminded daily of what Nemerov is talking about—the casual starvation and disease in drought-stricken countries, mass murders, bombings, and all our continuing Third World brush wars. Multiplicity, let alone disaster, erodes the significance of the individual. That we as a country sometimes possess the solutions to some of these problems but never seem to put an end to them only exacerbates our sense of futility and meaninglessness.

Nemerov also says "we live out of two kinds of thing." The trees he describes thrust "into the sky / Their black patience . . . and . . . branching / Relation" and show us the way "we endure and grow." They represent connection, "As Abraham was promised of his seed." In contrast to connection, however, there "is the snow," which is featureless in its hopeless multiplicity. We understand ourselves two ways. On one level we are the momentary products of probability—the dying doe that Stafford must jettison, the Polish prisoner dying "outside a German wood," or the adult "balanced on the ledge above the dark" who goes "on running" and does not "look down" for fear of falling. Each of these is a subject appropriately described by speech.

On another level, however, there is reason for song. We are like "The powerful trees" with their "branching / Relation" in the sense that our kind can choose to endure, from generation to generation. The individual dies, but the tribe continues. Thus Nemerov concludes—"The snow fell, the trees stood, the promise kept, / And a child I slept." Childhood and unity appear again, but this time not in the spatialized/metaphysical understanding of the self that we associate with certain modernists. Instead, the speaker in the poem represents the temporal/existential self of late-modern poetry, an individual who answers the contingencies of identity first of all by admitting they exist. The fleetingly unified speaker—who sleeps, like "a child," at the end of "The View from an Attic Window"—has discounted the self's claims to permanence, and his wholeness comes from recognizing limits to existence, the "venture" that he is. Those limits fleetingly delimit the imaginative free play necessary for song.

As I have already suggested, this balance between the trees "thrusting into the sky / Their . . . branching / Relation" and "the snow, / Falling in a white chaos from the sky" is one way of describing Heidegger's idea of "the will as venture," with those "ventured . . . who are not protected . . . nevertheless not abandoned." Knowing that he does "hang in the balance"—for one thing, that he is mortal—"man goes with the venture," and his doing so increases *Being,* in Heideggerian terms. "Balance" means a number of things, and Heidegger's usual intention is to make words do multiple duty. Here what is suggested is that there is such a thing as a balance, a kind of scale, in which we are held; judgment is also suggested, as are counterbalance, stability, aesthetic harmony, physical equilibrium, mental and emotional steadiness. But more than anything else, "balance" is a relational term. As with trope, it holds two things, two forces, apart and together. Movement is allowed to continue because the two things are not fused. Were they fused, we would be lessened by one. Nature is not nominative but active; identity is not a fixed property, but at the center of a process that starts with *like* or *as.* We are *beings* who occasion *Being.* Poetry, or poetic thought, is a nonutilitarian use of language that occasions our turning to and into what Rilke calls "the Open" and Heidegger calls "the pure draft," with poetry as a likening that holds things in relation, simultaneously off and near.[11] Through poetic thought, we are able to get beyond, however briefly, the individual will that holds the world over against itself.

Here is "Where You Go When She Sleeps," which concludes T. R. Hummer's first collection of poetry, *The Angelic Orders* (1982). The speaker first asks, "What is it when a woman sleeps, her head bright /In your lap," and, untroubled, dreams a dream "That does not include you"? The answer begins indirectly with a simile: "you are like the boy you heard of once who fell / Into a silo full of oats, the silo emptying from below." Then a short narrative describes the boy forgetting "his father's warning," leaning too far over the edge of the silo and falling in, "arms . . . out, too thin / For wings" of either a Daedalus or an angel. The narrative finally serves as a metaphor. Here is the entire poem:

What is it when a woman sleeps, her head bright
In your lap, in your hands, her breath easy now as though it had
    never been
Anything else, and you know she is dreaming, her eyelids
Jerk, but she is not troubled, it is a dream
That does not include you, but you are not troubled either,
It is too good to hold her while she sleeps, her hair falling
Richly on your hands, shining like metal, a color
That when you think of it you cannot name, as though it has just
Come into existence, dragging you into the world in the wake
Of its creation, out of whatever vacuum you were in before,
And you are like the boy you heard of once who fell
Into a silo full of oats, the silo emptying from below, oats
At the top swirling in a gold whirlpool, a bright eddy of grain,
    the boy,
You imagine, leaning over the edge to see it, the noon sun breaking
Into the center of the circle he watches, hot on his back, burning
And he forgets his father's warning, stands on the edge, looks down,
The grain spinning, dizzy, and when he falls his arms go out, too
    thin
For wings, and he hears his father's cry somewhere, but is gone
Already, down in a gold sea, spun deep in the heart of the silo,
And when they find him, his mouth, his throat, his lungs
Full of the gold that took him, he lies still, not seeing the world
Through his body but through the deep rush of the grain
Where he has gone and can never come back, though they drag him
Out, his father's tears bright on both their faces, the farmhands
Standing by blank and amazed—you touch that unnamable
Color in her hair and you are gone into what is not fear or joy
But a whirling of sunlight and water and air full of shining dust
That takes you, a dream that is not of you but will let you
Into itself if you love enough, and will not, will never let you go.

In one of the poems discussed earlier, "In a Dark Time," Roethke speaks of the "Death of the self in a long, tearless night." Hummer sees loss of the self in a quite different vein, partly as a recovery of the self. Proceeding by a simile that leads into a narrative that then is a metaphor, the focus of "Where You

Go When She Sleeps" moves among the speaker, the sleeping woman, the boy who dies, his father, the farmhands, and then concludes with the woman and, through her, plus all those named before, addresses the speaker again. But now the speaker is much larger because each person named serves as a metaphor for the others listed, as they progressively lead into each other. The extensiveness of being implied by this process takes the notion of unity to a new level. Hummer holds out for the "unnamable"— both what Nemerov calls "a white chaos from the sky" and the promise "Abraham was [given] of his seed."

It is tempting to call what Hummer does a heightening of lyrical intensity, but while such a summary is in part accurate, it misses the poem's main point. The title of Hummer's book is *The Angelic Orders,* and "Where You Go When She Sleeps" is the book's concluding poem. Hummer is after something beyond the empirical bias of poems that speak, and his effort to name it results in the poem's lyrical intensity and metaphorical extensiveness. The poem has a melodic wholeness, which derives from the willingness to let go. The speaker's response to what he sees in the woman sleeping opens into a major key for him.

Rather than operating by a series of observations taken from the external world, as "Traveling through the Dark" does, Hummer's poem stands on the ground of its own, immediate conviction, which is a gathered tradition of thought and belief. The success of the poem rests in its own concentrated projection of wholeness, as Hummer has learned to understand wholeness, rather than in an event on a dark road at night or some other particular circumstance rendered by description. The difference between Stafford's method of apprehending the truth and that used by Hummer is a matter of what scale was used to make these two poems.

"Traveling through the Dark" is the acting out of an idea, actually the acting out of a set of presuppositions. It is a stage on which we can watch the conclusions to certain givens that go with the understanding behind the poem. The understanding that directs Stafford's aesthetic choices amounts to a literal-mindedness, which we often mistake for accuracy and objectivity. In this spirit, Stafford fails to liken and differentiate as much as he might. A large part of the minimalist character of the poem results from its reliance upon what appears to be an empiricist's strictures for what can be said to be true. The truth claims for Stafford's poem are based upon a poetics of objectivity, but objectivity here is restricted to a limited area. All the things described by Stafford's poem exist in a small place for a brief time. We feel that the poem is a realistic treatment of experience and therefore credible. What we forget is the question of scale. Stafford has written what in many ways is a compelling poem, but, finally, are those truth claims made empirically or anecdotally?

"Where You Go When She Sleeps" uses several poetic modes of thought to arrive at a heightened lyrical moment, something we usually think of as strikingly subjective, and yet the appeal Hummer makes is ultimately outward, to "a dream that is not of you but will let you / into itself." It is something external, and to that degree objective, and it "will never let you go." It is close to what Heidegger calls the self's "gathering release," and something similar to the way a song is experienced by the person who sings it.[12] Hummer sings out of a concentrated gathering of prior knowledge, as well as prior relations embedded in the language. His method is not limited to events at one spot along a road at night, but uses the poetic modes of thought of simile and metaphor to liken and differentiate what he finds over a wide field of human experience and understanding.

Stafford's traveler who must hesitate on the "Wilson River road" means to be as objective as possible, but, insofar as his consciousness is limited to a *here* and *now,* he is highly subjective in his thinking. Hummer's modes of thought, his movement from simile to narrative to metaphor, open up the possibility for *more* experience than the occasion itself, one person's experience of a woman sleeping, would otherwise offer. Hummer's exploration, through the variables introduced by simile, narrative, and metaphor, provides the reader with a basis for considering possibilities beyond the speaker's immediate situation. Stafford's mode of thought tends to do just the opposite; out of its skepticism and reserve, it closes off variational thought that might lead to new possibilities. Poems that sing insist on a connection between unitary selves and a unitary world; poems that speak proceed out of a sense of disjunction between the self and its surroundings. One mode of writing opens out; the other tends to close off.

There are, of course, many examples of the way unity, identity, and wholeness are achieved to one degree or another in late-modern poetry. In the conclusion to the highly lyrical "A Cast of Light," Hecht summarizes our stake in these three goals this way:

> And the heart goes numb in a tide of fear and awe
> For those we cherish, their hopes, their frailty,
> Their shadowy fate's unfathomable design.

Our fate is "unfathomable" because we "fray" forward "into the future," as Wilbur would say. We are forever in a historical process, part of a Heideggerian unraveling, yet the idea of "design" is not given up. As Heidegger says, we hang "in the balance," are "retained . . . upheld." Design and venture are equally important because there is something that we have hopes for but never entirely possess, something "we cherish" that, as Hummer says, "will never let [us] go"—those others who make us whole in the extensiveness of what Pack repeatedly finds to be our constantly developing autobiographical/biographical identities. We are a unity as venture that survives on whatever scale we wish to use for measurement. We have the freedom to move between the reportorial gray areas of our best empirical efforts articulated by poems that speak and the projections of wholeness that we make through lyrical poems. Amid the fragmentation, there *are* highly predictable morphologies, of thought—"branching / Relation," as Nemerov says, or "design," as Frost and Hecht say, but "Relation" and "design" can be either beautiful or more terrifying than fragmentation. We can have it either way at any time we want—because of the mind's power to differentiate and posit itself by negating; also because of another thing, existing out ahead in the mind's capacity for relation and teleological promise, like the completions to the first bars of melodies, or the opening lines of poems that sing.

4

Howard Nemerov:
Mimicry and Other Tropes

I

What poets believe about their subject matter and themselves determines their modes of thought. Poems that sing result from one set of beliefs; poems that speak result from another. Of course, as was the case with the examples taken from Frost, Hecht, Nemerov, Pack, Mariani, and others, both sets of assumptions may meet in the same poem. Lowell's shift from his early high-modernist poetics to a late-modern poetics that shared ground with a phenomenologist such as Husserl argues not so much for a phenomenology of poetry, though there is that to be considered, as for a change in belief on Lowell's part. Before anything else, this led him to adopt a set of minimalist assumptions in place of his Catholic understanding. Changes in his poetry followed.

The appearance of what in chapter two I call the emaciated poem resulted from an intellectual defensiveness and minimalism that dominated a significant number of poets who were reacting against the influence of modernism. Despite serious limitations, the emaciated poem did seek to apprehend the world, especially through the eye, without cluttering up the view with a lot of what some during the late fifties and the sixties considered to be the academically self-conscious cultural baggage of modernism. It seems clear now that dissatisfaction with modernist baggage was at times the result of that movement's overshadowing success, not the inauthenticity of traditionalism or of what purported to be an impersonal poetics.[1] The belief during the late fifties, however, that there was a need for departure from some of the tenets of modernism was a significant factor in the aesthetic choices made by a variety of poets, and it eventuated in the employment of less encumbering, more plastic tropes.

The preference for tropes that make use of similitude, rather than equivalence or correspondence, continues to distinguish contemporary poetry from modern poetry, but, while the tradition may no longer be spoken of in the lofty terms we associate with Eliot, neither is it now seen as an object for rebellion. Many poets once again seem to regard the tradition as a practical source, especially as it exists in poetry written in English.[2] For a significant number of poets who were of the same generation as Lowell but who came into their own a decade or two after he received the Pulitzer Prize for *Lord Weary's Castle,* aesthetic decisions have been much less influenced by immediate elders, either in imitation or in rebellion, because by the time these poets reached maturity in their work there was considerable distance between them and the modernists. And many of the poets who commanded a great deal of the attention given poetry during the late fifties and the sixties (Lowell, Schwartz, Ginsberg), and who might have been a source of influence, were not father figures but more like siblings. Also, their work had not achieved the scope of that done by the modernists; therefore they could not be a comparable source of anxiety.

Although their birthdays are scattered throughout two decades, Lowell, Snodgrass, Schwartz, Berryman, Ginsberg, and Wright are contemporaries of Nemerov, Bishop, Hecht, Van Duyn, Wilbur, Pack, and Hollander. But the first group came to oppose their modernist elders and in their opposition remained influenced by modernism, whereas the second group looked both more and less to their predecessors and benefited from a sense of freedom about what they could do. That is in no way meant to argue for the temporal provinciality of Lowell, Berryman, and company. They knew the tradition as well as anyone. It is only to suggest that the first group felt the pressing need to follow the modernist mandate to make poetry new and thus, ironically, rebelled, but the second group pursued what we can see now was a more independent course. Rebelling is not as independent as simply doing what one thinks is best, especially when for twenty years of doing so one pays for the independence of not displaying the latest fashions by appearing to be out of step. It is as if having received plenty of orders, thanks to their military service during World War II, Nemerov, Hecht, and Wilbur had confronted all the authority figures necessary for a lifetime. In their different ways, the Oedipal paradigm was less persuasive for them because they had found their riddling murders in a wider theater. Of course, Jarrell, James Dickey, and others also saw the war, and poets who share strong affinities with Nemerov, Hecht, and Wilbur were never close to the war. The point is not the firsthand experience of combat, totalitarianism, the holocaust, and the atom bomb, but the way different writers have responded to modernism and to the increased skepticism brought home by the solemn summary that followed World War II.

In a skeptical era such as this one, some modes of thought seem more reliable than others. As they have been associated with theism, symbolism and allegory have been seen as problematical. Change has come with their replacement by less extensional tropes, which have made it possible to think variationally about different levels of order all over again. One such change has been the use of mimicry as a trope. As with metaphor with slippage, simile, metonymy, and synecdoche, mimicry provides a means for deflection and displacement. In synaposematic mimicry, the defenseless animal that mimics another animal because it has some strong defense does so in order to survive. The contemporary poet who in his or her poetry mimics the god—in action, trace, or absence—performs a similar function. Defenseless in the face of a decentralized metaphysics, a poet such as Nemerov employs the displacement of mimicry as a deflecting shield, and the thing displaced is the thing feared. Such a slanted reiterative gesture relies on the poet's use of figurative language to articulate a problem and in doing so to swerve outside that problem, however briefly. The writing of a series of synaposematic poems, therefore, can provide poets a sequence of epochés which holds off the judgment handed them of their individual insignificance and which holds open the possibility of discovering some new sign inscribed by the act of a swerving mimicry. When, as Howard Nemerov does, we confront the vast multiplicity of our kind, which goes unanswered by a decentralized metaphysics, a sense of the erosion of the self becomes inevitable. A poetic mode of thought applied to this problem both sights and deflects it. The reader's benefit from the poem's deflection is a brief ataraxy. But the process is not simply an analgesic respite from our one big headache.

The deflections and swerves inherent in a mimicry that uses figurative language open areas we have not seen. Before anything else, a certain amount of distance is created. To mimic not only means to imitate, simulate, or resemble in a biological sense, but also to ridicule by imitation. The use of mimesis by poets is a gesture that can reveal the distance between them and the objects they wish to reproduce. Just as mimics, in order to be intelligible and effective, must position themselves separately but close enough to be associated with their subjects, poets' use of mimicry at once retains an object and places it at a distance. The one who ridicules says, "I am *not* that other," simultaneously showing us the other and difference from the other.

Put another way, when we mention mimicry we think "of" a thing imitated, but "of" is a middle term that both holds a thing off and holds it close. It may indicate a point or direction by which one reckons, a derivation, a cause, the constitutive material of a thing, belonging or possession, a separation, an object of some action, the place in time of a particular action. There is both overlap and distance created by the polynomial function that "of" introduces between a subject and its object, or between an object and its copy. The relationship between the contemporary poet who employs synaposematic mimicry and the object imitated involves all these meanings. The poet's mimicry carries these meanings the way a primitive shepherd's notched bone was used for reckoning his sheep or the way a Mesopotamian egg-shaped envelope with clay balls inside it was used for the same purpose. At first mimicry carries us through an ordinal sequence of particulars; taken in the aggregate, however, it becomes a cardinal summary that is both inclusive and separative. I wish to take Nemerov's poems on their own terms first, then consider how by synaposematism and other modes of thought they investigate, separate, deflect, make safe, and generate wholeness.

II

In the title poem of his seventh collection of poetry, *The Blue Swallows* (1967), Nemerov says, "helplessly the mind in its brain / Weaves up relation's spindrift web" and "Imposes with its grammar book / Unreal relations on the blue / Swallows." He concludes:

> O swallows, swallows, poems are not
> The point. Finding again the world,
> That is the point, where loveliness
> Adorns intelligible things
> Because the mind's eye lit the sun.

The "spelling mind" imposes what is in many ways an arbitrary order and limit, but in doing so the Platonic cave behind the "mind's eye" delimits and occasions the sun's real light. The objects of Nemerov's art, here the swallows, are "evanescent, / Kaleidoscopic beyond the mind's / Or memory's power to keep them there," but Nemerov "Weaves up relation's spindrift web." He writes a poem in order to make a continuum of the nominalistic details (thus the reference to "William of Occam" in line twenty) that the swallows create and that an individual experiences while standing alone on a bridge that crosses a stream. Just as the bridge on which Nemerov stands is a man-made object that spans (both to measure and to extend across) that area the stream divides from the land, the poem he writes spans the way the "swallows divide the air." "Poems are not / the point," because they are the means for mediation, an interpretation by which the consciousness returns to the world it inhabits. The use of mimicry here helps Nemerov deflect the swallows through the mind's "grammar book" into "relation's spindrift web." As in many of Nemerov's poems, the troubling other (here "shapes" that in their multiplicity are beyond the mind's powers of thought) is displaced by an act that not only mirrors but is also interpretive and constitutive. The "swallows . . . Kaleidoscopic beyond" our mental powers are mirrored and thus displaced by the poem. But there is also an action contributed to the scene that goes beyond mirroring: "the mind's eye" lights "the sun."

In *Figures of Thought: Speculations on the Meaning of Poetry and Other Essays* (1978), Nemerov says that "the whole art of poetry . . . consists in getting back that paradisal condition of the understanding," a condition "that says simply 'yes' and 'I see' and 'it is so.'" Discussing the way "the words subjective and objective" entered our language, he summarizes the shift from when subjectivity was attributed to God's mind to its contemporary role in the human mind. He is troubled by our modern insistence that the world be divided into objective and subjective parts. Tracing that insistence back to Galileo's and Locke's "division of the qualities into primary and secondary," Nemerov considers the scientific use of such a distinction to have been to reduce "the primary qualities to quantity, or number, alone, so that only what is enumerable is effectively regarded as real."[3] His concern echoes Hannah Arendt's observation that scientists have adopted a "'language' of mathematical symbols" which was initially intended "only as an abbreviation for spoken statements" but which "now contains statements that in no way can be translated back into speech." Scientists "move in a world where speech has lost its power. And whatever men do or know or experience can make sense only to the extent that it can be spoken about."[4]

Nemerov believes the role of literature is to serve as the one place where the distinction between subjective and objective does not apply, where things the scientist reduces to number the poet articulates without being reductional. However, that role is more ideal than factual because of our historical moment, as Nemerov acknowledges. We *do* live in a world of numbers. That is where our intellectual history has landed us. And we are now "much too concerned to turn our experience into a result."[5] Or, to borrow from Arendt again, "knowledge . . . and thought [may] have parted company." We have been much too willing to exchange "knowledge" for "know-how."[6] Poetry's task of taking us back to what Nemerov calls a "paradisal condition" of assent, the "'yes' and 'I see' and 'it is so'" mentioned earlier, is the substance of the recognition made at the end of "The Blue Swallows," where "loveliness / Adorns intelligible things." Within that poem, of course, intelligibility is a matter of contention as much as it is a realization. The poet as deflecting mime and constitutive speaker does not finalize what he sees. The problem of the intelligibility of experience in the face of the world's multiplicity is a difficulty for the mind, which Nemerov's poetry engages by using the relational devices of simile, metaphor, synecdoche, metonymy, and mimicry.

Nemerov calls the problem of quality and quantity "a slow collapse in the idea of meaning which [has] progressed simultaneously with . . . the rate at which knowledge" has been gathered. His use of "knowledge" here is equivalent to what Arendt means by "know-how." We have quantities of facts without meaning, too many "swallows" for "the spelling mind" to arrange. For Nemerov, "language is an abstract and utterly arbitrary but totally articulated system of relations," at once anthropomorphic and thus outside the physical world around us yet vitally necessary to our existence in that world. He objects to "the public language of . . . the media" because, to reverse Frost's "luminary clock against the sky," it "is neither right nor wrong." That is, it is not a "totally articulated system of relations" the way, for example, a poem can be.[7]

As a statement of purpose, Nemerov says in his poem "Lion & Honeycomb" that he writes "for the sake of getting something right / Once in a while." The poem is a thing that stands "On its own flat feet to keep out windy time," yet it is no more than "a moment's inviolable presence . . . in integer / Fixed in the middle of the fall of things." Or, to return to "The Blue Swallows," the "mind's eye" may light "the sun," but it winks in doing so. In an interview, Nemerov is quoted as saying that the major impact literature has had "is to make people believe . . . that the world is a story." There are Platonic archetypes, "the idea comes first," but at the same time the world ravels (both comes together and unravels) itself "over the ruins" in an ongoing story of presencing and absenting. In the same interview, Nemerov describes the world's raveling as being "like a fountain that flowers in its fall; it's always going on." Yet he asserts that "there *is* a logos and it's up there" (italics mine). And a poem stands on "flat feet" in opposition to "windy time."[8] Understood this way, poetry balances the static idealism of the Platonic form with a profound sense that the world is all process. Despite "flat feet," the poet's logos is more verb than noun, and a poem that in its mimicry deflects process, however briefly, is itself a process that shields poets from the world's and their own raveling.

The central problem for such a time-ridden poetics is to find permanence in process, the static reflection on running water. The title poem of another Nemerov collection, *The Western Approaches* (1975), begins:

> As long as we look forward, all seems free,
> Uncertain, subject to the Laws of Chance,
> Though strange that chance should lie subject to laws,
> But looking back on life it is as if
> Our Book of Changes never let us change.

The paradox reflected here is that change is concomitant with permanence; "Chance" is "subject to laws," and "Changes" fail to "let us change." These antinomies constitute each other. Looking forward, there is possibility. But looking backward produces the opposite view; thus toward the end of the poem Nemerov says he knows

> How a long life grows ghostly towards the close
> As any man dissolves in Everyman
> Of whom the story, as it always did, begins
> In a far country, once upon a time,
> There lived a certain man and he had three sons.

Again the idea of story, a continuum, is here invoked with the logos reconciled to process.

III

As a mode of thought, a poem splits into a double hermeneutic. The reader interprets the finished poem; but the poet writes in order to interpret the particulars of personal and cultural experience, to articulate a "system of relations," as Nemerov says. In addition, there is a split within the poetic mode of thought itself, a split between the conventional properties of language and the unique, briefly appropriate figurative language necessary for what the writer wishes to grasp variationally by using tropes. You can only be an interpreter when you are working between two or more languages. As with geography, poetry can, through figuration, be a kind of earthwriting. It also can be skywriting and any number of other kinds of writing. As Nemerov says, "men now begin to see that they may invent other languages for other purposes—indeed, they do so already." Nemerov is keenly aware of how a poetic mode of thought always functions between two or more languages, two or more systems of relation, joining them by its own relations, which are always figurative and slanted. This process is dynamic to the point that a poem is not *a* mode of thought but many modes working at once. To Nemerov's understanding, in its interpretive role poetry possesses the "power . . . to be somewhat more like a mind than a thought."[9]

When he considers an object, Nemerov stands to one side and approximates the dimensions of the thing. He views it from various aspects. There is an angularity to his method; as much as it discovers new perspectives, it also reshapes relations. In another essay, "The Swaying Form," he responds to Montaigne's assertion that "there is no man (if he listen to himselfe) that doth not discover in himselfe a peculiar forme of his, a swaying forme, which wrestleth against the art."[10] The goal of such wrestling is "that art, by vision and not by dogma, patiently and repeatedly offers the substance of things hoped for, the evidence of things unseen."[11] But art itself, the mediating process between the desired object and the desiring subject, pivots and deflects as much as it mediates. The interpretive act passes through stages. Both the poem and the object to be interpreted are "protean" forms:

> The form, that is, is simultaneously ruling and very variable, or fickle; shifting and protean as the form of water in a stream, where it is difficult or impossible to divide what remains from what runs away. The passage [Montaigne's], read in this way speaks of something in us which is double in nature, on both sides of things at once or by turns. And I would identify this "forme" with the impulse to art, the energy or libido which makes works of art. It is no paradox to say that the artistic impulse fights against "the art," for anyone who persists in this business knows that a part of his struggle is precisely against "the art," that is, against the accepted and settled standards of art in his time.[12]

Each mode of thought employed in a poem is subject to sedimentation, a covering over that separates it from the object it is meant to apprehend. This results from changes in the cultural context within which meaning takes place. Thus the hermeneutic enterprise not only always goes on but also must do double duty, because writing the text is an interpretive act dependent on certain modes of thought, the same way that reading the text is an interpretive act dependent on modes of thought.

In the interview cited earlier, Nemerov begins by commenting that "it's always remarkable to [him] that one thing should follow another." He considers that "the most remarkable feature of thought."[13] In interpreting experience, he employs various modes of thought. These are means by which things *do* follow one another. But the mode of thought that carries him ahead most frequently is mimicry, contained in major controlling images, such as rivers, snowfalls, the change in seasons, seeds, trees, leaves, snow globes, and newspapers—things that balance form and process by asserting or by denying circularity. Of course, there are myriad other objects as well, such as dandelions, gulls, a quarry, mirrors, a loon, a dial tone, turtles, lobsters, goldfish, gulls, striders, football, pets, and joggers. These and too many more to list generate in Nemerov's imagination various mirrorings that at once articulate and displace what threatens.

An example of one of Nemerov's poems doing not just double but multiple hermeneutic duty is "Runes," which exploits the various meanings of *rune:* the characters used in the runic alphabet, a charm or spell, a secret or mystery, and a poem or song in Finnish or old Norse. In the poem, these meanings represent the problem of human understanding pitted against process. The exact meaning of runic writing is a mystery to us now; reading runes is like trying to decipher a secret, or a charm or spell whose purpose we no longer comprehend. These problems with intelligibility parallel the hermeneutic difficulties one has with a text read out of context. Thus Nemerov's poem at once tries to interpret the significance of earlier writings, both those found in the landscape and those man-made, yet mirrors the fact that it, too, is subject to a historical process that will eventually sediment its meaning. Articulating such a process temporarily reflects and deflects it and opens up a new area from which Nemerov can regard it. It creates the play of similitude that simile provides, allowing us to liken and to differentiate at once. Here is the opening stanza of "Runes":

> This is about the stillness in moving things,
> In running water, also in the sleep
> Of winter seeds, where time to come has tensed
> Itself, enciphering a script so fine
> Only the hourglass can magnify it, only
> The years unfold its sentence from the root.
> I have considered such things often, but
> I cannot say I have thought deeply of them:
> That is my theme, of thought and the defeat
> Of thought before its object, where it turns
> As from a mirror, and returns to be
> The thought of something and the thought of thought,
> A trader doubly burdened, commercing
> Out of one stillness and into another.

Whether addressing thought, language, poetry, seed, or running water, Nemerov regards the same predicament: that which appears static paradoxically owes its existence to something always in process. The best mode of thought for grasping what we perceive under this condition is the simile-like trope, because while it likens it does not try to establish correspondence, or equivalence. It allows things to keep moving. Nemerov's special contribution to this modality is his use of mimicry.

"Runes" concludes by saying first that "To watch water . . . / Is to know a secret," or "to have it in your keeping." Finally, however, it is neither knowing nor keeping, "But being the secret hidden from yourself." The poet who considers the nature of runes is made to confront "the thought of thought," because the ultimate rune, riddle, charm, and hermeneutic maneuver for a poem is a reflexive one. Poised between interpreting experience (watching "running water") and being interpreted itself, the poem occupies a no-man's-land of similitude where understanding travels like "A trader doubly burdened, commercing / Out of one stillness and into another." The double hermeneutic, the "stillness" of the poem poised between two readings, is like the "stillness . . . in the sleep / Of winter seeds," a script that is passive and waiting to be read but also capable of regenerating a living structure all over again. Viewed another way, we celebrate recurrence in time, "the stillness in moving things," the high predictability of the morphology among what "winter seeds" finally produce, for example, yet we must lament the individual loss that such a process dictates. Because we are part of a process, we can neither contain it nor encompass its meaning. What we can do is identify pattern by likening particulars. If not forms in this science-minded era, then the interpretation and reflection of formulas.

In "One Way" Nemerov approaches the double hermeneutic in poetry by narrowing his gaze to what "a word does when / It senses on one side / a thing and on the other / A thought." The two go "deep / Together . . . like sunlight / On marble, on burnished wood." The light "seems to be coming from / Within." If the poem implicates both reader and writer, a word used in the poem implicates both idea and thing, which join and separate in their own play of similitude:

> One's being in a world
> Whose being is both thought
> And thing, where neither thing
> Nor thought will do alone
> Till either answers other.

The poem performs an act of mediation between thing and thought. Because each needs the other, "neither thing / Nor thought will do alone"; the meaning of one entails the existence of the other. "Two lovers" are given as further evidence for the doubleness Nemerov sees. "Each" sighs the "other's name / Whose alien syllables / Become synonymous." The function of a poem as a double hermeneutic results, therefore, from its most basic stuff, the words it uses. When we see that the words which double for the poet are in turn doubled again by the reader who matches the poet's intention with his or her own, we step into a quadratic arrangement. The poem becomes polynomial. The shift can be something like the move from ordinal to cardinal numbers, as suddenly we have both succession *and* relation. We would have succession and correspondence within a mathematical system, but the slippage in meaning that goes with the use of simile-like figuration is not exact enough to give us correspondence, or equivalence. The mystery of things following in sequence is the ordinal power necessary to get beyond the world of mere quantity, which Nemerov says we have fallen into. Once sequence is established, relation and quality again become possibilities.

A poem gathers objects by various forms of relation, including the mirroring-deflecting process of simile-like figuration. This is the activity by which "the mind's eye" lights "the sun." This process is at work again in the first two stanzas of "Figures of Thought":

> To lay the logarithmic spiral on
> Sea-shell and leaf alike, and see it fit,
> To watch the same idea work itself out
> In the fighter pilot's steepening, tightening turn
> Onto his target, setting the kill,
> And in the flight of certain wall-eyed bugs
> Who cannot see to fly straight into death
> But have to cast their sidelong glance at it
> And come but cranking to the candle's flame—
>
> How secret that is, and how privileged
> One feels to find the same necessity
> Ciphered in forms diverse and otherwise
> Without kinship—that is the beautiful
> In Nature as in art, not obvious,
> Not inaccessible, but just between.

This poem, published in *The Western Approaches,* shares its title with *Figures of Thought,* Nemerov's collection of critical essays. The recurrence of the title reminds us of the central role that figuration plays in Nemerov's poetry. The "logarithmic spiral" combines logos (a word, proportion, ratio) and arithmos (number). Thus we have *word-number-spiral, proportion-number-spiral,* or *ratio-number-spiral.* Logarithms are used for shortening mathematical calculations, and in this they facilitate things the way cardinal numbers do. A word-number spiral gives concision to process. It shows us what has happened and what will happen by the shape of its figure, which reveals "the same necessity / Ciphered in forms diverse and otherwise / Without kinship." But what does cipher give us? It is a naught, a zero; a person or thing without importance or value; a nonentity; secret writing, code, or the key to a code; letters woven together intricately. To cipher is to solve a problem or to express secret writing. One way of combining a number of these meanings for cipher is to say that it is a likening. The likening itself is a kind of naught, zero, something without value, and it is a kind of secret writing. It disappears behind the things it likens. Simile-like tropes direct attention away from where they rest, the way a Janus does. They look in two directions at once, which positions two views relative to where the figure rests in between. We come to things the way "wall-eyed bugs" pursue light. Obliqueness captures beauty; truth is, perspectively, off-center or skewed in one way or another.

In the two stanzas quoted from "Figures of Thought," the succession generated by Nemerov's figurative catalog is pushed through relation to "logarithmic" power as the hermeneutic task given the poem takes us back into the polynomial world of process. The world is "always weaving itself over the ruins." The logos is a verb, and figuration is both spatial and temporal. As with the fountain Nemerov describes as flowering "in its fall," the world is constantly raveling into and out of existence, and our means for reading this process is not by quantification but by the constitutive act of figuration.

IV

Nemerov's remark that "only what is enumerable is effectively regarded as real" translates into one of the major themes in his poetry: multiplicity. This concept is represented variously—swallows, seeds, seasons, snow, sand, and so forth. The most common image for multiplicity in Nemerov's poetry is snow. He uses this image to articulate and then deflect the erosion of individual significance. We exist in such numbers that on an individual basis we are insignificant. Here the scientist's reduction of the primary qualities to quantity seems depressingly justified. We know roughly how many millions of human beings have been exterminated just in this century; during the evening news we see those suffering from starvation; we have had a war brought into our living rooms, where we could consider on a daily basis how flimsy our rational powers often are, especially when dealing with lives depersonalized by geographic remoteness; in large cities we encounter in one year more people than someone living in a small town of the last century might have seen over a lifetime; the media and modern travel expose us to vast numbers of people; a Darwinian sense of our history suggests we are only one installment in a nonanthropomorphic process. The list goes on, but for the moment we shall consider one major controlling image, snow, which appears in numerous poems by Nemerov.

In "The View from an Attic Window" the "Snowflakes unnumberably come down." The snow is "appalling" and falls "until all shapes" go "under . . . as the snow- / flakes from darkness to darkness go." "We live in two kinds of thing." One is "the powerful trees," which generate "branching relation" showing us "how we endure and grow." But "the other is the snow," which falls "in a white chaos from the sky":

> As many as the sands of all the seas,
> As all the men who died or who will die,
> As stars in heaven, as leaves of all the trees;
> As Abraham was promised of his seed;
>   Generations bleed.

The vast multiplicity of the snow blanks everything as it falls from a featureless sky, the indifferent cosmos that reigns over a world devoid of symbols. The trees offer their "branching / Relation," which fits with the promise given Abraham and, remotely, Nemerov, but the main feature seen both from the attic window and inside the attic itself is number beyond distinction, or quality. The family's many personal effects, which are stored in the attic, in their datedness parallel the impersonal process of the snow, which causes "all shapes" to go "under."

"The Snow Globe" describes a child's toy played with when the speaker was sent to bed at night and "They left [his] light on while [he] went to sleep." Shaking the globe, he watched the snow "rise up in the rounded space / And from the limits of the universe / Snow itself down again." The poem concludes:

O world of white,
First home of dreams! Now that I have my dead,
I want so cold an emblem to rehearse
How many of them have gone from the world's light,
As I have gone, too, from my snowy bed.

Again, the multiplicity of those who have gone before is related to the "cold . . . emblem" of the snow, which in its whiteness holds all the colors of the spectrum, all the particulars of experience. The child's renunciation of his parents, his isolation and loneliness, when he is sent to bed is acted out by covering the small world in the globe when he shakes up the snow and lets it fall. This miniature act of deflecting renunciation takes on its adult form later when Nemerov has his "dead" and by writing the poem mimics what causes him grief. Deflecting, he stands behind "an emblem," safe for now in a place where he is free to go on looking simultaneously ahead and back over his shoulder in a combined attitude of renunciation and retention. As a child, he shook the globe and obscured the world as much as his coming sleep would obscure it, but the snow settled and that world always returned, just as he always woke from his sleep. As an adult, things are different. The snow really is cold and does not always settle to the same world. Unlike the globe, the real world is more temporal than round. The snow melts and things are different. People do not always return, or wake up in the morning.

The use of snow to represent the depersonalization that results from multiplicity is stated succinctly in the short poem "Snowflakes":

Not slowly wrought, nor treasured for their form
In heaven, but by the blind self of the storm
Spun off, each driven individual
Perfected in the moment of his fall.

The power of this passage results from our recognition of ourselves in what Nemerov describes. Doubt makes it difficult for us to believe we are "treasured . . . In heaven," or have a human version of a "form," a soul. The vastness of the evolutionary process erodes our sense of individual significance. "Each driven individual" is "Perfected in the moment of his fall" because identity is the product here of limit and loss rather than futurity and gain. Skepticism reigns. That is, because of the enormity of our evolutionary past, identity comes not from our joining but our separating from the herd, the ultimate separation being death; thus, identity results from deletion rather than addition. Nemerov's view here contradicts the traditional Christian promise that each individual has a soul and is known by a name given in baptism. The emotional power of this brief poem stems in large part from our recognition that it functions in counterpoint to Christian consolation. The significance of "Snowflakes" resides in the dialectical opposites presented by the poem, the bald opposites of quantity and quality.

The experience of oblivion on the individual level is represented by snow in a somewhat different manner in "Again." Consisting of one long sentence, the poem describes the return of winter. The headlong pace of Nemerov's rhetoric dramatizes the equally headlong return of death and dormancy:

> Again, great season, sing it through again
> Before we fall asleep, sing the slow change
> That makes October burn out red and gold
> And color bleed into the world and die. . . .

The process continues, as Nemerov catalogs the sequence of events which brings on winter, the dead time of the year. He even has the snowflakes "drown," their geometrically brief but perfect arrangements passing "down the intervale" and dissolved by the impersonal "slow black flood" of the "river." But his arrangement of these changes adds up to something quite different from what they alone represent. The ordinal events add up to something cardinal. Someone does the cataloging, and this stands counter to the enumerative and erosive character of the process described. As with "Snowflakes," this poem has a lyrical intensity that argues wholeness rather than a list of discrete particulars. The sense that winter's dormancy has come "Again" tells us that the speaker is operating out of a different set of standards from those that nature provides and that the poet must enumerate in order to accurately describe the change in season he has observed. The change has come "Again" because by mirroring and displacing the coming of winter the speaker has moved from succession to relation. He has bent what he sees in order to see something else, that there is not only "change" but also periodicity. The loss that here literally *is* winter holds in its bleak meaning its opposite, a return. Nemerov's enumeration adds up to the metrical numbers of a poem. Read straight through, "Again" sings wholeness out of the changes that come with winter and that characterize loss. The poem's title tells us that this end to things has happened before; therefore, we can assume that later there will be a return, a beginning somewhere in the future.

"The Mirror," "The Winter Lightning," "Winter Exercise," "First Snow," and "The Unexpected Snow" are other poems in which snow suggests the loss of self. In "First Snow" we are told:

> Always the solemnest moment of the year
> Is this one, when the few first flakes
> Come falling, flying, riding down the wind
> And minute upon minute multiply
> To being blind and blinding myriads.

Once more we have number in conflict with qualitative distinction. The flakes "multiply" and do so "minute upon minute" until they become "blind and blinding myriads." That is, they are innumerable, quantities that defy intelligibility. Similarly, in "The Unexpected Snow" the snow represents the way identity is eroded, and this generates "thoughts / About the cold and murderous world, and how / We managed in it for a little while."

Multiplicity is played in a different key in "The Goose Fish," in which a "hugely grinning" fish head whose "moony grin" is both "peaceful and obscene" suggests the ludicrousness of "Two lovers" who have "prized / Themselves emparadised" along "the long shore, lit by the moon / To show them properly alone." Rather than snow, the lovers' condition is the "sand," in its multiplicity. "The long shore" is made up of sand, which sifts down the evolutionary hourglass that has drawn the lovers into question. How significant can it be that they "embraced / So that their shadows were as one" when they find themselves in company with a fish whose appearance suggests something prehistoric—that is, a thing outside human reckoning of time—which therefore makes a grotesquerie of their sense of personal importance?

What the lovers are forced to confront is that their highly personal act actually participates in an impersonal process that is wide of human value or individuation. In part this realization is dramatized through a shift in diction. In the first stanza, the lovers have "embraced," are "as one," feel "graced," and finally have "prized / Themselves emparadised." Let us assume people in love *do* feel this way, to varying degrees. But starting with the lovers' "stage-fright," the diction that follows implies a movement away from the lovers' invested view of things to the omniscient author's tilting humor about the scene.

The lovers are drawn into question at first by "The goose fish," then by all the other details surrounding them. Standing in the "hard moon's bony light," they share with the dead fish the sand and stars. These are quantities rather than qualities. The moon, often associated with life cycles, here gives off a "bony light" and a "china light." It reveals the absurd grin of "The goose fish," "a wide and moony grin / Together peaceful and obscene" and altogether uncaring. The moon finally goes "down to disappear / Along the still and tilted track / That bears the zodiac." The whole scene rests under a heavenly arrangement that is at once "still and titled." Order is askew. The fish is "So finished a comedian" because there is no basis for certainty. We often laugh at incongruity and at what we partially fear. Here Nemerov provides us both. The fish with "picket teeth" that leave "their mark," presumably from someone having been goosed, is a "rigid optimist"; that is, no optimist at all. He is the reduced lovers' "patriarch, / Dreadfully mild in the half-dark," rather than half-light, and he appears choked by the sand they share. The purpose of Nemerov's humor is not primarily to make us laugh but to articulate a seriously held view. In "The Goose Fish" our laughter echoes what in Nemerov's understanding has already happened to us, a joke. "The joke / That so amuse[s]," the fish is the contradiction between the way we pursue our individual lives with absolute care and seriousness and the larger world we inhabit, which in its arrangement argues against human significance. As with Nemerov's other comic moments, his mirroring such a situation is an act of synaposematic mimicry. Our laughter deflects, setting the threat outside our immediate circle. That other element of mimicry, ridicule, also plays a role in Nemerov's wit and humor.

V

Wit and humor are major elements in Nemerov's insistence that poems pass judgment on (which means they in some way make statements about) experience. They are the means by which he carries out a type of mimicry that does not quite equal ridicule but that distances us from incongruity with an energy worthy of ridicule. *Inside the Onion* (1984) offers a number of examples of wit and humor, the common ground of these siblings being Nemerov's practice of working incongruity against form. "Poetics" follows:

> You know the old story Ann Landers tells
> About the housewife in her basement doing the wash?
> She's wearing her nightie, and she thinks, "Well hell,
> I might's well put this in as well," and then
> Being dripped on by a leaky pipe puts on
> Her son's football helmet; whereupon
> The meter reader happens to walk through
> And "Lady," he gravely says, "I sure hope your team wins."
>
> A story many times told in many ways,
> The set of random accidents redeemed
> By one more accident, as though chaos
> Were the order that was before creation came.
> That is the way things happen in the world,
> A joke, a disappointment satisfied,
> As we walk through doing our daily round,
> Reading the meter, making things add up.

Here Nemerov once again questions the intelligibility of experience. His questioning takes the shape of an incongruity he has discovered. He mimics what he has found in a deflecting manner that allows us to laugh and leaves us momentarily shielded. The second stanza of "Poetics" demonstrates an insistence that poetry make things understandable. Instead of giving his reader a personal testimony, Nemerov gives a concrete situation and then likens it and says something about it. "That is the way" functions as *like*. Meaning results from similitude, from counterposing the particulars of a situation with abstract thought about that situation. In addition, the absurdity of the things that happen to the woman in her basement is counterbalanced by the poem's formality and rational conclusion. These contraries are part of the joke, the "disappointment satisfied," as the poem opens up by means of a pairing between the first and second stanzas which balances sameness and difference. The woman's absurd experience is contrasted with the second stanza's rational summary of our state, but the contrast ends by yet another turn that asserts sameness. As a deflection of the incongruity it represents, the poem "adds up" in cardinal answer to an ordinal incompleteness we all must face.

Viewed somewhat differently, "Poetics" describes a predicament of mind then concludes with a statement about the way the mind works. In its articulation of the intellectual accidents to which we are always susceptible, the poem mirrors and deflects them and thus shields Nemerov and his readers from them, at least momentarily. There are other poems by Nemerov that operate similarly. Also found in *Inside the Onion,* "First Light" gives us a speaker who, "wanting to see the world made new / In every weather," walks "out of darkness and into first light." What he finds are "An early worker, a late-returning drunk," some "joggers . . . fleeing Death," and the objectification of all this in the form of a newspaper being delivered, "The Harvester delivering The Globe." "Striders" describes water bugs "Like mariners . . . committed to the deep" who "cannot swim." These insects walk "atop the water's thinnest skin," and if "Caught in a breaking weather, they will drown." The surface tension of the water that holds them up is comparable to the linguistic surface tension that holds meaning up. "Wintering," "A Grain of Salt," and "A Blind Man at the Museum" work similarly. The last of these concludes: "A dumb show of predicaments untold / Moving familiarly among the worlds." By mimicking predicaments Nemerov deflects an area that is wide of them.

Nemerov's use of wit and humor demonstrates an intellectual rigor reminiscent of the modernists, yet his subjects reflect an increased skepticism about multiplicity and the intelligibility of experience, which is common in postwar writing. His decision to sometimes use wit but at other times use humor, with informal diction, even slang, played against formal poetic structures, is the result of an essentially bleak view of experience and the traditional means we employ to explain experience. At the same time, an insistence on form and reason in his poetry argues that Nemerov certainly holds out for something more than absurdity or meaninglessness.

Here is part of "Adam and Eve in Later Life":

On getting out of bed the one says, "Ouch!"
The other "What?" and when the one says "I said
'Ouch,' " the other says "All right, you needn't shout."

Deucalion and Pyrrha, Darby and Joan, Philemon and Baucis,
Tracy and Hepburn—if this can happen to Hepburn
No one is safe.

The comic poem's movement from "bewilderment [to] illumination" mirrors and displaces a threatening incongruity. And it makes an implicit statement. Just as comedians must gauge their audience in order to get a laugh, poets writing comic poems also must recognize their readers' presuppositions. They must calculate what their readers, in effect their culture, assume about some incongruity in order to displace that assumption with some surprise. Once Nemerov shows us Adam and Eve in old age rather than the youthfulness of their lives in the garden, a return begins that sums up, implicitly states, the values which originally made that incongruity humorous. The poem ends with the two talking over coffee and studying "the backs of their hands." They conclude that "they are slowly being turned into lizards," although "nothing much surprises them these days."

Many contemporary poems are written out of the conviction that it is more honest to render the appearance of things with realistic imagery than it is to risk making statements that carry cultural baggage. Nemerov recognizes the conflict between reason and the senses, alluding to it as "empiric and its theory" in the title poem of *Inside the Onion*. He also sees the limitations of either side of the argument, as well as the problems that occur when both sides are brought together. In "Gnomic Variations for Kenneth Burke," he says that "The senses and the mind deceive each other." Such deceptions can be exposed, however, by the mind's comic bent.

In "Acts of God" we are told that God's behavior amounts to "exhibitions of bad taste on a scale / Beyond belief." Where God is concerned, Nemerov argues that events have more than questionable causes. He is full of back talk about *last things* (the title of another poem). "Total Immersion," "Calendars," "Prayer of the Middle Class at Ease in Zion," "Epiphany," and "Facing the Funerals" are some examples of his metaphysical sass at its best. The ultimate incongruity for Nemerov is mortality. For him the cosmos is like half a ball, the overhead half missing. Time is a weakening mainspring. "Facing the Funerals" ends: "Men have their faiths as coffins have their handles, / Needed but once but handy to have then." In "Gnomic Variations for Kenneth Burke" Nemerov wryly concludes that "dialectic . . . Remains . . . Unbeatable and obvious as language." For him the "Godelian and Delphic word has ever been / *Don't look under the hood while driving the car—.*" "Inside the Onion" pursues the same problem:

> Slicing the sphere in planes you map inside
> The secret sections filled up with the forms
> That gave us mind, free-hand asymmetries
> Perfecting for us the beautiful inexact.

Whether comic or serious, humorous or witty, Nemerov's statements of incongruities round off into balanced opposites: "the forms / That gave us mind" seen as "free-hand asymmetries," or, elsewhere, "space / Geometrized resisting its geometry." Nemerov's opposites are the divisions by which he thinks, by which he moves between the noisy world of experience and the silent world of thought. Such balance starts with the material world—for example, an individual gazing at an onion until his eyes weep. Here Nemerov's brand of empiricism becomes a mode of thought that accounts for two perspectives: one narrowed to the physical onion, the other free of the onion's particulars. The onion exists both on a physical level and on the level of amused reflection, as experi-

ence and also as abstract meaning. We are shielded by the poem's
mirroring gesture, which brings order through "the beautiful in-
exact" and opens new areas, "free-hand asymmetries."

VI

In "The Human Condition," included in *The Blue Swallows,* Nemerov mimics the problems with subjectivity and objectivity which
he describes in *Figures of Thought.* He is in a "motel room where
[he] was told to wait." His orders have come from an impersonal
source such that he finds himself facing a comic and somewhat
Godot-like predicament in which, not knowing where he is, he
paces "the day in doubt / Between [his] looking in and looking
out."

> In this motel where I was told to wait,
> The television screen is stood before
> The picture window. Nothing could be more
> Use to a man than knowing where he's at,
> And I don't know, but pace the day in doubt
> Between my looking in and looking out.
>
> Through snow, along the snowy road, cars pass
> Going both ways, and pass behind the screen
> Where heads of heroes sometimes can be seen
> And sometimes cars, that speed across the glass.
> Once I saw world and thought exactly meet,
> But only in a picture by Magritte.
>
> A picture of a picture, by Magritte,
> Wherein a landscape on an easel stands
> Before a window opening on a land-
> scape, and the pair of them a perfect fit,
> Silent and mad. You know right off, the room
> Before that scene was always an empty room.
>
> And that is now the room in which I stand
> Waiting, or walk, and sometimes try to sleep.
> The day falls into darkness while I keep
> The TV going; headlights blaze behind

Its legendary traffic, love and hate,
In this motel where I was told to wait.

The title for the poem is taken from a painting by René Magritte, *The Human Condition,* of which Magritte has said:

In front of a window seen from inside a room, I placed a painting representing exactly that portion of the landscape covered by the painting. . . . For the spectator [the scene] was both inside the room within the painting and outside in the real landscape. This is how we see the world. We see it outside ourselves, and at the same time we only have a representation of it in ourselves. In the same way, we sometimes situate in the past that which is happening in the present. Time and space thus lose the vulgar meaning that only daily experience takes into account.[14]

This method of doubling creates its positive out of the negative made by the two frames, which contradict each other. Rather than sealing off meaning with a forced closure, the method of double parentheses opens meaning up to thought, where it may continue moving back and forth between image and frame, thing and idea. The speaker has a "television screen" set before a "picture window," and this double framing doubles his mental reflection; scenes are generated from looking in as well as looking out. Outside the window, "along the snowy road, cars pass/ Going both ways," while on "the screen" still more traffic, "heads of heroes . . . and cars," appears. Nemerov's is a Cartesian room in which doubt rather than reassurance results from what he encounters. The room without location, the window, and the television screen are presentations of the world, which operate by the contradictions they generate between "looking in" and "looking out." Neither view permits the other, wholly, but each serves as a commentary on the other, so thought must oscillate in a not quite geometric manner between the disclosure given by one surface and, to a degree, the contradictory and covering-over evidence of the other surface.

The resemblance between the "television screen," which provides pictures of people in cars, and the "picture window" full of real traffic places them in comparison such that they function as contraries, the one "in" and the other "out." Nemerov has said that "thought proceeds to create the world by . . . opposites" and that "a world of opposites is impossible, intolerable." The opposites we find "must be mediated and shown to be one; because . . . in the world as experienced they *are* one."[15] The task created by the opposition of screen and window is to take what thought has divided, ultimately the separation of the speaker from the world, and see whether that gap can be mediated.

The television has been placed directly in front of the window. The speaker faces in the same direction in order to look in and to look out. One point of view produces two seemingly opposed views. And the room in which he stands becomes a container for what he sees of the world through these two views; the television screen inside shares what passes on the road outside the same way that Magritte's two frames, by one's placement inside the other, duplicate one view. An important part is played by the overlap of what is seen on the screen and what the window reveals, the overlap in the repetition of "landscape" (lines fourteen to sixteen). Equally important is the synaphea that occurs during the likening of the speaker's view to Magritte's painting—"Before a window opening on a land- / scape, and the pair of them a perfect fit" (lines fifteen and sixteen).

The synaphea between these two lines is imperfect but insisted on by dividing "landscape" with a hyphen and by not capitalizing the first letter of "scape." Simile is medial; it stands between likeness and difference. The hyphen is also medial. It can be used either to divide or to join words, to make different or make the same, just as the screen and window simultaneously divide and join their "legendary traffic, love and hate," which in turn are themselves contraries capable of compounding and dividing into a meaningful free play. The physical break in the previously compounded "landscape" suggests first division and second that either the land is in the "scape" or the "scape" in the land, both finally. This matches the contradictory predicament of the speaker, who by analogy is trapped in his mind (as he is trapped in an anonymous room), although his mind is nevertheles capable of articulating the room and even its own entrapment: the room is in the mind and the mind in the room. The speaker is divided from the world outside; thus, things are seen through a window or a screen, never directly. By his re-cognition, he also brings the outside world inside. As Magritte says, "We see it outside ourselves, and at the same time we only have a representation of it in ourselves." When is the world in the speaker, or he in the world? The place where he has landed provides him a view, a "scape," which is at once a thing seen passively from inside and a way out to an alternate place promising "scape" in another sense: escape. This doubling from opposites, divisions, and compounds adds up to a predicament of mind and a question about right action, what to do once the waiting is over.

Told to wait in an unknown place, the speaker nevertheless watches people capable of "love and hate," even heroism. At least he *sees* our re-presentations of "love and hate" and heroism. But the underlying problem in all this is one of action. The speaker has been made completely incapable of action. He has the order to wait from a remote authority, which in its remoteness takes on greater authority. And he lacks something particularly useful to action, "knowing where he's at." Thus the source for action is present on the screen in the guise of the opposing passions "love and hate," and the individual capable of action, the hero, is present, but, in one more contradiction, the ability to act has been removed, drawing the entire process by which one progresses from motive to action into question. We are back to "The Blue Swallows," in which Nemerov says, "Ah, poor ghost / You've capitalized your Self enough." But we are brought to such a point this time by Magritte's frame for the mind, rather than Hamlet's.

The inability to act because of an intellectual predicament is the poem's most important consideration, as its title, shared not only with a painting by Magritte but also with a famous book by Arendt, makes clear from the outset. Although failure to consider the question of right action would trivialize the predicament of mind which the poem describes, the first task for the reader is to grasp the dimensions of the mental room in which the speaker finds himself halted. There is movement within that room, and we do not want to render a fictive stasis to what is a constant play between alternatives that continuously qualify each other. Nevertheless, more clarity as to the dimensions of the motel room is needed, and Magritte's painting provides the key to what otherwise remains only a partial interior.

Various paintings by Magritte contain the double perspective

Nemerov is talking about. In viewing Magritte's *Going Towards Pleasure, Pandora's Box, Clouds, The False Mirror, Homage to Shakespeare,* and others, we find ourselves at once "looking in and looking out," thus constantly moving about in the gap that has been created by doubling. A similar kind of gap occurs out of tautology. In Magritte's oeuvre, a painting's title and image are often tautological, yet in part it is this tautology that enables us to think about the work. The overlap in tautology turns into a contradiction that generates the thought, which is where the meaning of the work lives; the meaning is not in the representation of an image but in some contradiction in that image. As Nemerov was quoted earlier, "thought proceeds to create the world by dividing it." When someone says, "You're always from where you're from," we move beyond the initial sense of a meaningless tautology to similitude, in which suddenly an individual's formative hometown is carried forward once more into meaningful play and interpreted all over again in light of the present.

Nemerov's "Human Condition" begins and ends with the same idiomatic line, "In this motel where I was told to wait." His repetition does not create circularity and closure for aesthetic effect; it causes a tautology that turns into a thought-provoking contradiction. What the line means at the opening of the poem is different from what it means at the end. The contradiction between the meanings of a repeated line opens the poem to thought, just as Magritte's doubling of title and object opens his painting. The implications of the room where the speaker has been told to wait broaden as he turns his reflection to "where he's at," duplicating his location with his "doubt" about it. The enumeration of objects in the room reminds us of their questionableness: insofar as the mind is concerned, "the room . . . was always an empty room." Founded upon contradiction, the human condition mimicked by this poem is one of acute dislocation handled by an equally acute sense of the angularity in the language we use, thus the slang in the poem's diction. The figurative word standing between thing and idea is imprecise and thus skews and displaces what it names; it exemplifies why the speaker cannot know "where he's at."

When he is idiomatic, Nemerov is working his diction against the condition he is describing. Along with the line that opens and closes the poem, the use of "stood," "where he's at," and "right off" remind us of this sort of angularity. They are precisely imprecise in order to match the situation described. An idiom has a meaning that cannot be derived from the sum of the meanings of its elements. Its meaning results from an ordinal series that defies any cardinal summary. This mimics the "condition" Nemerov describes. A condition can be a stipulation, a prerequisite, a provision, a restriction, a condition of being. All of these apply to what Nemerov has in mind, a various entrapment; thus "where he's at" rather than where he is. The use of "at" suggests someone who has been thrown into a predicament, rather than someone with the freedom to choose his situation. Mimicking that predicament with slang displaces it so that the speaker can stand outside what otherwise threatens him.

In "The Backward Look" Nemerov combines his sense of dislocation and entrapment with his reservations about the technological requirement that quality be reduced to quantity. The poem's setting is one of "the first motels in space." The astronauts who have reached the moon look back upon earth "As once in heaven Dante looked back down / From happiness and highest certainty," but what they have brought with them is not the knowledge of hell and purgatory but "the golf / Balls and the air." They possess things and their "immense power / Of being bored," rather than understanding. A sort of existential ennui results from the meaninglessness of their location. "From earth" man "prayed to heaven." Now the direction is reversed, and man prays "Earth of the cemeteries" and "Earth mother of us" to "grant us safe return . . . to generation, death, decay." In sum, man prays to be returned to meaningfulness, to be allowed to "take" the moon's "dust and rocks," which "the heaven of technology" has given us but which cannot be parsed within human terms, and to "start back down" to the earth, where meaning and mortality still pertain, because, despite our adventures beyond them, the limits that define our being remain earthbound.

The vast depersonalization represented by snow, outer space, and time is one thing when presented to us by nature but quite another when we cause it. We make our contribution through technology in "The Backward Look." In Nemerov's poem about the suicide of his sister, "To D——, Dead by Her Own Hand," the individual, rather than a technological society, chooses "deeps invisible." Either way, we are forced to confront the abyss over which we continually ravel and unravel ourselves. Nemerov addresses this problem in "Holding the Mirror Up to Nature":

> Some shapes cannot be seen in a glass,
> those are the ones the heart breaks at.
> They will never become valentines
> or crucifixes, never. Night clouds
> go on insanely as themselves
> though metaphors would be prettier;
> and when I see them massed at the edge
> of the globe, neither weasel nor whale,
> as though this world were, after all,
> non-representational, I know
> a truth that cannot be told, although
> I try to tell you, "We are alone,
> we know nothing, nothing, we shall die
> frightened in our freedom, the one
> who survives will change his name
> to evade the vengeance for love. . . ."
> Meanwhile the clouds go on clowning
> over our heads in the floodlight of
> a moon who is known to be Artemis
> and Cynthia but sails away anyhow
> beyond the serious poets and their
> crazy ladies and cloudy histories,
> their heroes in whose idiot dreams
> the buzzard circles like a clock.

The tragedy we face is a limitation of mind confronted with a "freedom" so vast that it is the source of terror as much as it is of opportunity. Nemerov questions the ideal, ranging from Plato through the eighteenth century, that the mind and art can mirror the world. Some shapes exist outside the purview of mimesis. Our tropes fail: "Night clouds / go insanely as themselves" in a world where synecdoche no longer likens part and whole. Not only poetry but also philosophical thought suffers from the failure of metaphor. The analogues that constitute our understanding of something new fail to help us. Or at least they fail in certain circumstances.[16]

This is a skeptical treatment of some of our oldest notions about the intelligibility of the world. In part, Nemerov is in dialogue with the Platonic separation of ideas, the things in this world which reflect those ideas, and the works of art which reflect the reflections. He does not reject the level of ideas the way Aristotle does but questions order on all levels. The ideas may be there, and we with our mirrors are incapable of seeing them. Or in certain circumstances the ideas may *not* be there. The "poets" have "crazy ladies and cloudy histories," while "their heroes" have "idiot dreams" in which "the buzzard circles like a clock." Time is a carrion beneath which human action and ethics, "histories" and "heroes," demonstrate randomness rather than choice.

Nemerov says, *"as though* this world were, after all / nonrepresentational" (italics mine). This is a variation on simile, and in particular the *as if,* which I shall discuss in chapter five. The expression "as though" at once likens and qualifies. Re-presentation occurs, but it is a limited mode of apprehension, as, we are told, is metaphor. Both are imperfect devices for handling sameness and difference. One problem with mirroring nature is that nature itself can be read as mirroring some larger order. But how does one mirror a mirror without entering an infinite series of smaller and smaller images of the same objects? And what reference is there to frame the oversized synecdoche that nature provides us? Here the tautology of the doubled mirrors can leave us knowing "nothing," a place where "We are alone" and "die / frightened in our freedom." This is a location more desolate than that which the astronauts find in "The Backward Look" when they land on the moon's "desert" and gaze back to earth, which does not meet them with a reflection of their reflection but is itself and waits like a welcome.

One problem Nemerov discovers in "Holding the Mirror Up to Nature" results from a redundancy in our use of the looking-glass. But there is an opening here as well. We do not have to crack the glass to break through the surface, but only pair it with another glass, because from our perspective pairings are always slightly askew, as if the mirrors were at an angle to each other, rather than perfectly matched. Our "freedom" reveals not only the things that can "be seen in a glass" but also the multiplicity that results from a digression of shared objects and the admission of new objects through the swerve created by the imperfect points of view from which mirroring occurs. "Night clouds / go insanely as themselves" because no two are ever quite identical.

Another problem with holding a mirror up to nature is that what we mirror through a synchronic picture we make static when the character of nature is to remain in process. This is the riddle of "Painting a Mountain Stream," discussed in chapter two. The essence of a stream is that it streams, but a painting must represent its object in static terms. Thus Nemerov tells us to "paint this rhythm, not this thing." Moving us beyond the limitations of mimesis, he gives us an abstract statement. But the mirror continues to be a major mode of apprehension. A problem with using the mirror is that it reduces a three-dimensional object to two dimensions. The depth behind what the mirror faces can only be interpreted. That which stands in the distance behind the mirror's image is never brought forward. In "Holding the Mirror Up to Nature," which concludes his fourth volume, *Mirrors and Windows* (1958), Nemerov turns a reflexive gaze on reflection itself, finding "Some shapes" evade reflection. The tool for gathering experience and deflecting it, the mirroring poem, proves inadequate. Yet human value persists.

"Some shapes" *can* "be seen in a glass," and some *do* "become valentines / or crucifixes." There is still "the vengeance for love." Imitation is relational, but process goes beyond relation, into a "freedom" past our ken. That is why "the heart," which is powered by relation, not only "breaks" but also must break. Once asked about the dialogue he maintained with a Christian God, Nemerov replied that as a good Jew he could not respect a God who became sentimental about what his people did. This kind of mismatch between human perception and what we are able to posit as ultimate truth exists on various levels in Nemerov's thinking. In "Holding the Mirror Up to Nature," it settles upon "the floodlight of / a moon," rather than the moon itself. And we call what we see "Artemis / and Cynthia but" it "sails away anyhow / beyond the serious poets." The object of our attention here is the moon's light, a reflected light suggestive of reflective thought. Even "serious poets" cannot grasp it. The one reflection cannot grasp the other reflection; thus "the clouds go on clowning / over our heads," wide of our understanding.

In his essay "The Swaying Form: A Problem in Poetry," in *New and Selected Essays* (1985), Nemerov considers the reflexive character of language and poetry all over again. Calling language "the marvelous mirror of the human condition," he goes on to outline the way mirroring both limits and delimits experience. "Language," we are told, is "a mirror so miraculous that it can see what is invisible, that is, the relations between things. At the same time, the mirror is a limit, and as such, it is sorrowful; one wants to break it and look beyond. But unless we have the singular talent for mystical experience we do not really break the mirror, and even the mystic's experience is available to us only as reflected, inadequately, in the mirror. Most often man deals with reality by its reflection." And reflection occurs in language. For Nemerov, "Civilization, mirrored [likened] in language, is the garden where relations grow; outside the garden is the wild abyss."[17] But humanity is capable of being an abyss as well as a garden. The opening poem of *Mirrors and Windows,* "The Mirror," begins: "O room of silences, alien land / Where likeness lies." Nemerov questions, "how should I understand / What happens here." And he concludes, "in the leaden glass / I watch with observed eyes the stranger pass." The Platonic notion of the reproduction of the idea or thing in art functions better with objects in the world than it does when reflexive art is matched against a reflexive gaze. Even the objects of the world are rendered as "quivering duplicities," suggesting not only doubleness but also deception. When the mirror is turned to the self, Nemerov describes "the snow" that "drifts down" in the "coming night"— multiplicity found inside as well as outside.

"Storm Windows" begins, appropriately enough, with "People putting up storm windows," until a "heavy rain" forces "them indoors." Walking home, Nemerov notices the way the "windows lying on the ground" are "Frame-full of rain." Thanks to the framing that holds the water in and presses the grass beneath, he sees "through the water" standing on the "glass . . . the crushed grass, how it" appears to be swept "in lines like seaweed on the tide." But of course what sweeps here is what the frames hold still and press down. The contrast between the static frame, which

holds the water on the glass, and the grass underneath, stream-
ing "away," mirrors the relation between the person who sees all
this and the world of "memories," which, like the "crushed grass,"
seems to "stream / Away." The poem concludes:

> Something I should have liked to say to you,
> Something . . . the dry grass bent under the pane
> Brimful of bouncing water . . . something of
> A swaying clarity which blindly echoes
> This lonely afternoon of memories
> And missed desires, while the wintry rain
> (Unspeakable, the distance in the mind!)
> Runs on the standing windows and away.

The windows frame their own mirroring, here an activity that can
deflect, give back, or run away with the objects presented. If "the
mirror is a limit," as Nemerov asserts in "The Swaying Form," it
is one that while "sorrowful" to us because of what slips past it
also delimits meaning.

VII

"The Loon's Cry" is a watershed for Nemerov's thinking about
the intelligibility of experience and what multiplicity does to
meaning. It is a meditation upon the "signatures" that "In all
things are" and that "may by arts / Contemplative be found and
named again." It is also one of the poems in which Nemerov
stands toe to toe with the best of twentieth-century poetry and
confronts the movement in this century from the use of symbol
and allegory to the use of tropes that are more fluid in the way
they handle meaning. Because I wish to end with a close reading of
"The Loon's Cry," I quote it in full:

> On a cold evening, summer almost gone,
> I walked alone down where the railroad bridge
> Divides the river from the estuary.
> There was a silence over both the waters,
> The river's concentrated reach, the wide

Diffusion of the delta, marsh and sea,
Which in the distance misted out of sight.

As on the seaward side the sun went down,
The river answered with the rising moon,
Full moon, its craters, mountains and still seas
Shining like snow and shadows on the snow.
The balanced silence centered where I stood,
The fulcrum of two poised immensities,
Which offered to be weighed at either hand.

But I could think only, Red sun, white moon,
This is a natural beauty, it is not
Theology. For I had fallen from
The symboled world, where I in earlier days
Found mysteries of meaning, form, and fate
Signed on the sky, and now stood but between
A swamp of fire and a reflecting rock.

I envied those past ages of the world
When, as I thought, the energy in things
Shone through their shapes, when sun and moon no less
Than tree or stone or star or human face
Were seen but as fantastic Japanese
Lanterns are seen, sullen or gay colors
And lines revealing the light that they conceal.

The world a stage, its people maskers all
In actions largely framed to imitate
God and His Lucifer's long debate, a trunk
From which, complex and clear, the episodes
Spread out their branches. Each life played a part,
And every part consumed a life, nor dreams
After remained to mock accomplishment.

Under the austere power of the scene,
The moon standing balanced against the sun,
I simplified still more, and thought that now
We'd traded all those mysteries in for things,
For essences in things, not understood—

Reality in things! and now we saw
Reality exhausted all their truth.

As answering my thought a loon cried out
Laughter of desolation on the river,
A savage cry, now that the moon went up
And the sun down—yet when I heard him cry
Again, his voice seemed emptied of that sense
Or any other, and Adam I became,
Hearing the first loon cry in paradise.

For sometimes, when the world is not our home
Nor have we any home elsewhere, but all
Things look to leave us naked, hungry, cold,
We suddenly may seem in paradise
Again, in ignorance and emptiness
Blessed beyond all that we thought to know:
Then on sweet waters echoes the loon's cry.

I thought I understood what that cry meant,
That its contempt was for the forms of things,
Their doctrines, which decayed—the nouns of stone
And adjectives of glass—not for the verb
Which surged in power properly eternal
Against the seawall of the solid world,
Battering and undermining what it built,

And whose respeaking was the poet's act,
Only and always, in whatever time
Stripped by uncertainty, despair, and ruin,
Time readying to die, unable to die
But damned to life again, and the loon's cry.
And now the sun was sunken in the sea,
The full moon high, and stars began to shine.

The moon, I thought, might have been such a world
As this one is, till it went cold inside,
Nor any strength of sun could keep its people
Warm in their palaces of glass and stone.
Now all its craters, mountains and still seas,

Shining like snow and shadows on the snow,
Orbit this world in envy and late love.

And the stars too? Worlds, as the scholars taught
So long ago? Chaos of beauty, void,
O burning cold, against which we define
Both wretchedness and love. For signatures
In all things are, which leave us not alone
Even in the thought of death, and may by arts
Contemplative be found and named again.

The loon again? Or else a whistling train,
Whose far thunders began to shake the bridge.
And it came on, a loud bulk under smoke,
Changing the signals on the bridge, the bright
Rubies and emeralds, rubies and emeralds
Signing the cold night as I turned for home,
Hearing the train cry once more, like a loon.

This poem is a complex example of synaposematic mimicry. Nemerov catalogs his surroundings to imitate that which threatens, not because something in his surroundings possesses a means for defense, as would be the case in biological mimicry, but because by likening himself to what he sees he makes himself indistinguishable from the landscape he must inhabit. In addition to Magritte's observation that we see the world "outside ourselves" even as we "have a representation of it in ourselves," Nemerov mirrors the world's representation back to it—making himself invisibly present. At least that is the initial gesture of his likening; the final gesture is a slanted metaleptic act in which the train's "cry" is substituted for that of the loon. The sound of one thing is likened to another, and that act of translation becomes a sign for "the cold night." The nonanthropomorphic cosmos "balanced" overhead, in which human time is always running down, is represented by a protective mimicry intended to hold it at arm's distance. The forbidding structure that threatens is mirrored by an aesthetic structure that seeks to slip the threat. Behind such mimicry, what balance is possible comes from similitude, created by the speaker's position as he stands on a bridge that spans the alternatives provided by two different kinds of water, the one (the estuary) cyclical and thus promising renewal, and the other (the river) bleakly linear.

In its act of mirroring, "The Loon's Cry" serves as an antistrophe for survival, directed against the "cold evening" with "summer almost gone." As a species, we are defenseless in the face of a "Chaos of beauty, void, [a] burning cold, against which we define / Both wretchedness and love." The extremes of "wretchedness and love" provide additional motive for a poet's synaposematism, because they balance the extremes of relation: the threat of exile (the Old English for *wretch* is *wrecca,* "outcast," "exile"), as opposed to the promise for continuance with others through "love." Defenseless before what he hears and sees, the speaker articulates his surroundings and by doing so mirrors back in a deflecting gesture that which otherwise he feels will annihilate him. But his own act of synaposematic mimicry is itself a response to other reflections that inform the world around him.

Nemerov describes having confronted a "balanced silence" that "centered where [he] stood." Balance comes from two opposing objects that mirror each other: here, the sea and setting sun "answered" by "The river" and "the rising moon." He has found himself at a loss, "naked, hungry, cold." But for his poetry that is a place of origin where he is "Again, in ignorance and emptiness / Blessed beyond all that we thought to know." For a moment he becomes another Adam, "Hearing the first loon cry in paradise," and the poem turns into an elaborate naming process in which "nouns of stone / And adjectives of glass" are less powerful than "the verb / Which surge[s] in power properly eternal / Against the seawall of the solid world." Nemerov is preoccupied with time and process. For him, the logos remains verbal rather than nominative. But "respeaking [is] the poet's act," and there are "signatures / In all things . . . which leave us not alone." It is the poet's task to find by his "Contemplative" art the "signatures" that may be human projections but that reflect who we are, and then to name them all over again. Through poetic thinking, figures are read, modified, and repeated. That is the only balance that can be brought to the "two poised immensities" between which Nemerov finds himself standing as a "fulcrum."

The location for the poem is, as with "The Blue Swallows," a bridge. Nemerov's rule is that thought begins with division, and here he stands, having included himself in the information he records, as a "fulcrum" to "two . . . immensities," whose particulars appear as follows. Over the "railroad bridge" that "Divides the river from the estuary," the sun and moon function as paired opposites; "God and Lucifer" are paired in "debate"; "mysteries" are "traded" for "things, / For essences in things"; Nemerov compares himself with Adam; and "a whistling train" is paired with the cry of the loon. As in "The Human Condition," the pairings argue both sameness and difference. The river and the estuary are both bodies of water, but the former is fresh-water while the other is where salt water begins. The river is directional, flowing in a way that suggests linear time and that urges us toward measurement. The estuary is where boundaries become indefinite and where time becomes cyclical as the water widens into one body, the ocean, whose tides are governed by the moon. The river is surrounded by land; the ocean that the estuary leads to is surrounding rather than surrounded.

On one level, what is immense about the sun and moon is their physical presence, not what they might signify. Having "fallen from / the symboled world," Nemerov is forced to confront "Reality in things," a here and now that erodes meaning. Thus the loon's cry is "a savage cry" given in answer to Nemerov's "thought." As the sun disappears, reflection replaces direct light, and a "voice" that seems "emptied of . . . sense" reduces mental reflection from the status of cognition to a nominalistic red now, blue now, green now. In this situation, only by division does meaning have a beginning. Lacking traditional symbols to comfort him home, Nemerov must posit his own spatial arrangement the way that early navigators posited a description of the world at once inaccurate and useful. Adam also lacked symbols and had to begin by being the center for experience and then by naming things. Naming is a process that not only identifies but also divides. Insofar as A is A, it is not B. And so forth.

Another pairing is made up of God and Lucifer, a division that Nemerov, having set aside "Theology" and "fallen from / The symboled world," entertains but does not embrace. As a part of this pairing, "mysteries" of a metaphysical ranking are traded for the physical world of "essences in things" in an intellectual fall that takes us from when God's immanence in all things "Shone through their shapes . . . as fantastic Japanese / Lanterns are seen" to a concept of "Reality" which exhausts the "truth" of previous dualistic systems. We no longer enjoy the Platonic notion that the planets possess souls, or the Aristotelian idea that the planets give us the harmony of the spheres. Indeed, Nemerov precludes the idea of a fixed order with truth depending from that order. There is no traditionally received level of meaning; thus Nemerov likens himself to Adam "Hearing the first loon cry in paradise." And in this likening there is another pairing and another division: the historically self-conscious Nemerov set against the prelapsarian Adam still innocent of our first act of division.

Because Nemerov believes things cannot be explained in absolute temporal and spatial terms, order is perspectival. And it begins with pairing and figurative thought. The most important pairing in "The Loon's Cry" is the one that is most simple: the sound of the train whistle and the sound of the loon. Here Nemerov divides and unites as he goes beyond ordinal thought into a cardinal prolepsis that not only both mirrors and deflects but also throws the dialectic he has been wrestling with out ahead, where for the moment it no longer threatens. At first Nemerov hears the loon; then he is uncertain whether he hears the loon or the train; then he feels "the bridge" begin to "shake" and knows that now he hears the train whistle. The sources for the same sound are radically different—the one a bird, the other a locomotive. Yet they are brought together in the consciousness of someone capable of likening them. Nemerov has fallen from "The symboled world," but he can still liken the world—by using simile-like modes of thought.

The loon cries out of all the physical surroundings that Nemerov finds so threatening, and what he hears is "Laughter of desolation on the river, / A savage cry"—the loss of self caught in the linear time of "the river." The loon represents to him the absolute alienation that human beings face in a world governed by nonanthropomorphic laws. Humanity is outcast. But then the man-made train has the same sound the loon has. And by simile Nemerov can identify the two as at once different and identical, suggesting an overlap between two sounds and also an overlap between mind and world. Perhaps the world is a "home" after all, or capable of being made into one. If so, we "seem" "Blessed beyond all that we thought to know." But as Nemerov leaves things, even this may be just one more likening on our part, a projected fiction by which we comfort ourselves with nothing more than the hope that there are things out there "Signing the cold night" and thus we may liken our way to a provisional "home."

The poem is organized around a set of mental and physical actions by the speaker. Listed, the actions provide a summary of the internal debate that brought Nemerov to what he recognizes in the loon's cry. He begins by saying that near the end of the warm season he "walked alone" and "could think only" of the particulars of experience, not of any higher and more comforting interpretations they might have been given in the past. He has fallen from the "symboled world" that "in earlier days" offered "mysteries of meaning, form, and fate / Signed on the sky," and he envies the past with its metaphysics and dualisms, in which he no longer believes. In contrast, he has a physical world of dualisms invented by the mind's ability to liken and divide. But this understanding of realism and the way the mind works precludes the truthfulness of anything on a higher level, such as "Theology"; thus the loon gives "A savage cry . . . emptied of . . . sense." The world of symbols has been replaced by a realism that restricts Nemerov to freer but shorter-ranged tropes.

Nemerov says of the loon, "I thought I understood what that cry meant," not "nouns" or "adjectives" but "the verb," at once building meaning and battering the fixity of any one meaning it might build. "The moon, I thought, might have been such a world / As this one is, till it went cold inside. . . . / And the stars" no longer "Worlds, as the scholars once taught" but "Chaos of beauty, void, / O burning cold." Contrary to Plato, the planets do not have souls; Aristotle's belief in the harmony of the spheres is a bit of dated wishful thinking. Now, we "define" the human extremes of "wretchedness and love" by setting them "against" the "Chaos of beauty," rather than the harmony of beauty. Again, thought is by division, rather than by deduction from some higher order based upon reason and belief. The haunting cry of the loon is a denial of home; the matching whistle of the train is equally denying. But when overlapped in the mind of the listener, they join in sameness and difference, making an arrangement out of sequence. The succession of their moments, of their soundings, is transposed from an ordinal chain (as linear as the river or as Nemerov's understanding of time) into a cardinal moment fleetingly outside succession.

VIII

Our fall from "The symboled world" results from doubt, which on one level seems to function as a negative but on another level is a positive response. In their skepticism, Nemerov, Lowell, and others replaced symbol and allegory with less extensional tropes, but their doing so at that time was a necessary move away from a mystification left over from the symbolists of the nineteenth century and continued to a degree by some modernists. Rather than precluding the possibilities of experience (as, for example, Paul de Man would tell us a symbol can do by insisting upon identity, or allegory can do in reverse manner by insisting upon difference), less extensional tropes open up an area in which there is a constitutive free play.[18] At this point in what has been a dialectical exchange between several poetic strains—romantic-symbolist, surrealist, expressionist, the empirical-realist poetics of imagism and phenomenalism, and (as demonstrated by many of the poets discussed here) a projective-constitutive poetics—less turns into more.[19]

At the same time, contemporary poets remain in dialogue with the tradition, shaped as it is by the metaphysical assumptions of earlier centuries; thus while their tropes may displace earlier beliefs, they also retain those beliefs in an imaginative free play that never lets them disappear. What has been displaced remains related. When in the eighth stanza of "The Loon's Cry" Nemerov says, "For sometimes, when the world is not our home," he introduces that state of mind in which poetic venture, a departure from "home," takes place. Rilke talks about a state "outside all caring" where there is a "safety" that results from "unshieldedness."[20] This is a kind of gathering ekstasis, something more than the abandonment of self. For Heidegger, it is relational. It is our means for occasioning otherness.

The tradition is not rejected by a trope's venture of displacement, but retained by it. An earlier belief now drawn into question is more alive for the questioning it receives. It is brought forward. Identicals have nothing left to say; thus symbols that equate fail while lesser tropes become, in their differentiation, the occasion for a speaking back. A doubting Thomas reminds us not only of his empirical needs but also of the wounds he wishes to touch, along with all they may re-present. To question a belief is not exactly an act of mimicry, but both the doubter who questions and the mimic who mirrors operate by a displacement that also moves in a one-to-one homeomorphic mapping. The way back to the previous object and the object itself are retained as an initial displacement finally settles into an oscillation that points to two places at once. Things previous and things present exist in the double-pointing gesture of displacement.

Today, the symbol has become problematical to the extent that the higher object it is meant to represent no longer can be embodied. Heidegger would say that this is because the gods have fled, that we live "in a destitute time."[21] But the slippage in the lesser tropes allows the object named a measure of free play that not only grasps things absent but also makes return possible. In this sense, when Nemerov says, "This is a natural beauty, it is not / Theology," we are better off. His having "fallen from / The symboled world," and recognized that fall, leaves the future of the meaning of that world open to constitutive free play. The imperfect trope never becomes one with its object, but it allows movement and signs the way home for that object. It serves as both sentinel and guide. In its completeness, the symbol restricts the movement necessary to bring an object back into presence.

In this century, an early example of loss of "The symboled world" is provided by "Sunday Morning," where Wallace Stevens is in dialogue with the Christian tradition and certain Neoplatonic ideas. "Sunday Morning" examines the world behind symbols, and it arrives at its conclusion by way of a considerable amount of Socratic jockeying of positions, an act that mimics much of what the poem questions. The movement generated by mimicry is a major feature of "Sunday Morning." By writing about a traditional set of beliefs in a way that "ventures" them, and thus does not let them go but keeps them in play, Stevens holds before us what he at the same time tells us is missing. The issue is: For how long does something missed remain missing? Is it really lost, or just covered over instead? To venture through trope is not to abandon but to put into play, a play that according to Heidegger is necessary for *Being*. The lesser tropes start from the ground up; they do not depend from heaven like "ripe fruit" that "never fall[s]," or like "boughs" that "Hang always heavy in [a] perfect sky." The ambition for that kind of stasis may be left to a theism read through symbolism and allegory. Once the "fruit" and the "boughs" lose credibility in the face of realism, which functions as a form of skepticism, deduction from a cosmology becomes impossible; poets must abandon symbol and allegory and project upward through the constitutive process of lesser tropes.

Stevens presents a mix of Neoplatonic and Christian ideals, without accepting any of them. He plays these ideals against our skepticism and does so partly in terms that overlap with Plato's *Phaedrus*. From the list of books sold out of Stevens's library after his death, we know he owned more than one copy of the Jowett translation of *The Works of Plato*. Plato describes the soul as a pair of wings which, as translated by Jowett, once it has "begun the heavenward pilgrimage may not go down again to darkness."[22] This image of the soul as a pair of wings resembles the closing image of "Sunday Morning," where the birds "make / Ambiguous undulations as they sink, / Downward to darkness, on extended wings." And Stevens's use of the four birds throughout the poem echoes Plato's notion of the winglike character of the soul.

Discussing the erotic form of divine madness, Socrates says that the soul, seeing "the beauty of earth, is transported with the recollection of the true beauty; he [the soul] would like to fly away, but he cannot; he is like a bird fluttering and looking upward and careless of the world below."[23] Both descriptions leave their subjects balancing in a midair gesture of desire, generated by that Platonic staple, beauty. Stevens catalogs earthly beauty throughout his poem. In the last stanza, just before the "Ambiguous undulations" begin, or what Socrates would call the "fluttering" as the soul looks "upward . . . careless of the world below," Stevens describes the "Deer" that "walk upon our mountains . . . the quail" that "Whistle . . . spontaneous cries," and "Sweet berries" that "ripen in the wilderness." This may be viewed as hedonism (Winters's description of it) only if we rule out the understanding of beauty embedded in the Neoplatonic and Christian traditions, which are brought into play again as Stevens mirrors the world his protagonist inhabits.[24]

Putting one of Stevens's phrases to work, A. Walton Litz describes "Sunday Morning" as "a rehearsal for that 'great poem of the earth.' " Litz continues:

> The revolutionary aspect of "Sunday Morning" lies in its sharp break with the nineteenth-century tradition of poems on faith and doubt. Unlike the typical nineteenth-century poet who found himself, in Arnold's lines, "Wandering between two worlds, one dead, / The other powerless to be born," Stevens did not feel the tug of traditional faith. In his view, we live in "an age of disbelief," a space of time between the death of one great coordinating mythology and the birth of another; the poet's job is to record our lives and make them tolerable by supplying "the satisfactions of belief" (Op 206). For Stevens, the "death of God" is not a subject for debate but a premise from which to begin. It is this perception of what has now become our accepted lack of faith that makes "Sunday Morning" still the most "modern" of poems.[25]

An important part of the aesthetic balance between "disbelief" and "the satisfaction of belief" is the playing out of despair. The "Complacencies of the Peignoir," the "Coffee and oranges," and the "green freedom of [the] cockatoo" on the rug *do* "dissipate" what Stevens calls "The holy hush of ancient sacrifice." But in response to what? Our finitude, the "old catastrophe" of death, as it contrasts with the infinite. Stevens's interests include "the earth" and hedonism, but they go beyond these to the origin of our despair, the discrepancy between our knowledge of the infinite and our experience of our own finitude. Kierkegaard argues that "in order to will in despair to be oneself there must be consciousness of the infinite self." This is the hypothetically Platonic self that "Sunday Morning" explores. Finally, it is a self pushed to the point of becoming what Kierkegaard would call "an experimental god":

> So the despairing self is constantly building nothing but castles in the air, it fights only in the air. All of these experimental virtues make a brilliant showing; for an instant they are enchanting like an oriental poem: such self-control, such firmness, such ataraxia,

etc., border almost on the fabulous. Yes, they do to be sure; and also at the bottom of it all there is nothing. The self wants to enjoy the entire satisfaction of making itself into itself, of developing itself, of being itself; it wants to have the honor of this poetical, this masterly plan according to which it has understood itself. And yet in the last resort it is a riddle how it understands itself; just at the instant when it seems to be nearest to having the fabric finished it can arbitrarily resolve the whole thing into nothing.[26]

There are "ambiguous undulations" over nothing. Hedonism, a fascination with "the earth," possibly aestheticism, may be regarded as forms of despair. But despair is a condition, not an end. And, in the Kierkegaardian scheme of things, the articulation of despair is the first step one takes to overcome it. There is no "tug of traditional faith" upon Stevens, but he demonstrates an acute awareness of our finitude. "Death is the mother of beauty" because our relation to a metaphysical system (which could encompass the good, the true, and the beautiful) exists now by negation. But, as Heidegger says, the negation of a metaphysical statement remains within the realm of metaphysical thought. Having the "death of God" as "a premise from which to begin" means that Stevens holds the opposite proposition near, within the realm of recovery. The emptiness of the symboled world that Stevens articulates is easily recognized as absence—absence of the god, or of meaning. It also resembles an entrance hall. Along with echoes from a metaphysical tradition, the poem's language itself opens the central problem of absence. Words may call missing things into presence, but prior to that they take the place of what is missing, and this is the first step taken toward calling something back into presence. Gesturing simultaneously toward similarities and differences, trope figures forth a return. Similitude and difference become the boundaries within which meaningful free play can take place.[27]

In the *Phaedrus,* Socrates describes the four kinds of divine madness that the soul experiences: prophetic, initiatory, poetic, and erotic. These are matched with four gods who watch over them: Apollo with the prophetic, Dionysus with the initiatory, the Muses with the poetic, and Aphrodite and Eros with the erotic.[28] Stevens appears to have had some such categorization in mind when starting "Sunday Morning." Following Plato's image for the soul as a pair of wings, the four species of birds in the poem (parrot, swallow, quail, and pigeon) outline the protagonist's understanding of herself. The birds work as an imprecise organizing device, an arbitrary limit perhaps suggested during a rereading of *Phaedrus,* and at one time employed in a way more associative than governing. Used suggestively, the birds are vital for the slippage they create, a series of deflections that opens new areas.

The "cockatoo" and the "pigeons" work against the myths that Steven's protagonist entertains. The first of these helps "to dissipate / The holy hush of ancient sacrifice." The second closes the poem not with an assertion of faith or disbelief, either of which would allow a counterposition, but with "Ambiguous undulations," leaving all the matters of faith and philosophy that the poem raises wavering in a poetic midair. The "quail / Whistle . . . spontaneous cries." In the *Dictionary of Symbols and Imagery,* quail are associated with resurrection, lasciviousness, fertility, and, "according to some Greek lyric poets," are "sweet-voiced."[29] Such a combination of attributes fits the complex tone and argument of Stevens's poem, as all the while it proceeds on the assumption that symbols are hollow. The "spontaneous cries" become a synecdoche for the tragic Dionysian opposites of death and resurrection brought out of ecstasy, exercises in freedom, and the brutality of the Maenads. They also remain literal "cries." That is, within the context of the poem the spontaneity of a *cry*—a call, lament, inarticulate expression of distress and here of despair—is enough of a synecdoche to call into question, to venture, the myths Stevens is considering.

The swallow, which Stevens associates with "desire for June and evening," is linked with spring (rebirth) and fertility, the cycle of the year; is sacred to the "Great Goddess of Fertility and War"; is associated with the dew, with domesticity, with hunger; and in this capacity is related to prayers. In Christian usage, "a young swallow symbolizes one crying for spiritual food." In terms of hunger, it is related to "contentment in poverty." Wantonness, hope, diligence, instability, and thought are some of the other things associated with the swallow.[30] The associations the bird carries are consonant with the mixed attitudes of the poem, which pivot over doubt, where "death is the mother of beauty" because it demarcates the line between our finitude and our ideas about the infinite. The image of "awakened birds" in "misty fields" and the protagonist's "desire for June and evening" work synecdochically to represent some measure of hope. The quails' "spontaneous cries" and the protagonist's "desire" being "tipped / By the consummation of the swallow's wings" provide, through a troping more fluid than the traditional use of symbolism allows, the movement necessary for a full display of the knowledge of hope and the condition of despair that characterize the winged soul that circles through "Sunday Morning." It is a soul flying through disbelief; therefore the particulars of the world gathered by metaphor, simile, mimicry, metonymy, and synecdoche are used where symbolism and allegory cannot be. The first five methods tend to work in a way that the contemporary mind, in its skeptical empiricism, or in its realism, finds acceptable. In contrast, to be understood, the traditional forms of symbolism and allegory questioned here must depend from a higher order, requiring deduction from a system of faith that no longer works for Stevens.

Although we are still "modern" and the importance of Stevens's poem for us has in no way lessened, perhaps now, at the end of the century that Stevens and others of his generation began, we are really further along in what Litz calls the "space of time between the death of one great mythology and the birth of another." Today, we are late modern, or postmodern. (Either term derives its significance from modernism.) We know we are somewhere beyond modernism, and now it seems "the poet's job is" *not* "to record our lives and make them tolerable" in a gesture that comforts us with facsimiles of myth, especially through symbol. Instead, the task today is to stand outside myth and to explore possibility by playing language variationally against experience. Poetic language provides various systems of observation by which we may do this. Our goal is the "satisfactions" gained from poetic likening; but, rather than a likening downward out of the tradition's hierarchies, our task is a likening upward through tropes that work with few preexisting structures.

Stevens, writing from early to mid-century, and Nemerov, writing from mid-century to the present, share subject and method. But they do so at different times and therefore within different contexts for us to interpret them—and for them, in the act of writing, at different times to perform their own interpretations. By means of mimicry, they both deflect an inscrutable metaphysics. The absence of the god and the sense of meaninglessness which results from this are mirrored back in a gesture that both protects and opens up new areas. Stevens ends with ambiguity; "maybe yes and maybe no," he tells us. Nemerov, because he comes later in the dialectic, focuses not on the question of a metaphysics itself but on the means by which we think about the physical as well as the metaphysical. For him, our ability to liken a train's whistle to a loon's cry is our first constitutive step back into order—certainly not the beginning of a "great coordinating" myth, but a place to start. Heidegger would say that here belatedness has the advantage because it occurs at a point when the chance for a return or uncovering has presented itself. Such a step back into a likened world that approaches order is made possible by first abandoning symbol and allegory, which are emblems of that highest order, myth, and taking up less structured but more fluid and, at this point, more constructive tropes.

We are accustomed to thinking of realism as being at odds with the desire for some higher order. Roman Jakobson has told us that metaphor is dominant with romanticism and that metonymy goes with realism.[31] The shift I have described does not fit Jakobson's paradigm, but it is similar to it. Such a shift is not the movement from metaphor down to metonymy but the movement from symbol and allegory down to metaphor with slippage, simile, metonymy, synecdoche, and mimicry. When we say the mind is God, we both mean that statement and recognize all that it precludes, that it is simultaneously possible in some senses and impossible in others. The imprecision we bring to the metaphor by questioning it makes it a simile-like structure. Metaphor in this condition produces the *as if* rather than the *is*. At the same time, it is a positive step toward more meaning, not a falling off into a reduced realism. The slippage in the less extensional tropes amounts to a clearing, an open space where meaningful free play can take place again. In their fluidity, these tropes allow a return. Meaning is not imported but built where, as Nemerov says, "word . . . senses on one side / a thing and on the other / A thought." Thought and thing engage in a dynamic play, and word is where they play.

Earlier meanings are latent in the modes of thought considered here, because of the words used; those earlier meanings are never completely lost. They are played or ventured—a process by which having become covered over they once again can be uncovered. As it grows out of the tradition, symbol and its legman companion, allegory, work better the more they seal themselves off from indefiniteness, the covering-uncovering movement of meaning. But mimicry, metaphor, simile, metonymy, and synecdoche—each warps its object such that an opening occurs, the new occasion for something not quite new. In "Sunday Morning," Stevens is the master of what he sees, finally a system of vacant symbols. In "The Loon's Cry," Nemerov is the master of seeing, the modes of thought which constitute new places and the objects of thought to fill those places.

5

Patterns of Similitude in the Poetry of Justice, Hecht, Van Duyn, Bishop, Wilbur, Hollander, Pack, and Pinsky

I

At the same time it likens, similitude opens a gap between two objects, or a gap between an object and its appearance. In *Being and Time* Heidegger remarks that "an entity can show itself from itself . . . in many ways, depending in each case on the kind of access we have to it." He adds that "it is possible for an entity to show itself as something which in itself it is *not*. When it shows itself in this way, it 'looks like something or other.' " He then uses disease as an analogy for what he means. The difference between the disease itself and its symptoms exemplifies the gap between a thing and the appearance it gives us.[1] But even a misleading symptom can provide a trail back to what is causing it. Heidegger is concerned with the Kantian idea of phenomenon, and he has a complex understanding of what he terms "appearance," which, like a symptom, may by revealing itself also reveal something that does not appear, that may stand in place of the thing not seen, or may simply veil the thing.[2]

John Hollander's discussion of the way that literary echoes are modes for figuration suggests one means for the play of similitude, in which a figure turns variously. Discussing William Carlos Williams's "Spring and All," he suggests that "blue" and "surge" in the poem's third line are echoes of Shelley's "Ode to the West Wind," "spread / On the blue surface of thine aery surge." When Williams repeats these words our attention is turned briefly back to Shelley's poem; but Williams reverses the order of the words, "under the surge of the blue / mottled clouds." Shelley's "mode of revelation is prophetic; it turns one way. And Williams's is almost epistemological"; it turns another way. But "the great epiphany of process is engendered in both cases."[3] With Williams's allusion in "Spring and All" to Shelley's poem, we see the way that, similar to the relation symptoms have with a disease, echo "represents or substitutes for allusion as allusion does for quotation." Echo marks a gap between the original sound and its later occurrence.

The tradition modifies the process of Williams's writing his poem, even as Williams saw himself in opposition to much that was traditional. Williams's opposition was not abandonment, but relational. The emphasis given to things, with which we like to tag Williams, and the opposing emphasis given to abstract thought, with which Winters has been tagged, are two sides of one currency. (Nemerov's answer to that debate is to say that "neither thing / Nor thought will do alone.") A red wheelbarrow and a statement such as Jonson's "O could I lose all father now!" represent two poetic turns available. If we hold them both in mind, thing and thought form a dyad. As Magritte uses titles that name the objects represented in his paintings in order to create tautologies (which then break into the play of sameness and difference), the physical and the abstract in poetry can create a similar play. Similar to disease and diagnosis, thing and idea face each other from either side of figuration, or symptom.

Skepticism about the tradition and about meaning in general makes epistemological questioning appear much more reliable than prophecy, and this increases the value of simile-like structures and lessens the worth of symbols. Because of the less "prophetic," more localized intentions of "Spring and All" or of many of the poems that I shall discuss later in this chapter, the turns that are made possible by simile, metonymy, synecdoche, chiasmus, anacoluthon, apostrophe, and so forth seem more reliable than other devices. As with echo, allusion, and quotation, they liken but do so locally. Simile-like structures work on a scale smaller than allusion entails or prophecy projects, but at that level they are constitutive.

The revisionary practices of many contemporary poets have run counter to what appeared to be the fixity of New Critical readings of poetry. Although the principles of New Criticism were designed to invigorate the tradition, over a period of time they also became turned away, as to varying degrees they themselves began to look like what they were originally designed to overcome, forms of prescriptive thought. When we survey the cycles of so many schools in recent poetry, what appears to have been the most revolutionary process occurring in postwar poetry has not been aesthetic systems of one group or another but language itself and, in particular, modes for exploring similitude, the rhetorical patterns that make simile-like tropes possible. And the contemporary poets most gifted with language appear to have made the major contributions with these figures. Avoiding prescriptions, they have found various ways to pattern the exchange between like and unlike.

Another change that has occurred in postwar American poetry has been the lessened use of foreign borrowings. An obvious difference between high-modernist work and the work of the generation that came to maturity after the war is that now we are less apt to run across a contemporary poem that uses learned allusions taken from various languages, ancient and modern—a technique typical of Pound, Eliot, and Tate—in order to establish its authority. And we seldom find a poem that employs a stand of quotations from other languages, something that was characteristic of Pound and sometimes present in Eliot and Tate. The tradition of English poetry contains a long list of profitable borrowings from other literatures, and, as part of their interest in the tradition, the modernists did not overlook such a resource. More recent poetry does not reflect the same degree of foreign influences, yet many contemporary poets write translations. Thus, the interest in other literatures appears to be as great as ever, but the sense of the appropriateness of allusions to other literatures as a means for authority has changed in a way similar to the shift away from symbol and allegory, figures for correspondence.

In *Being and Time* Heidegger discusses the way we find ourselves immersed in a world horizon we cannot see. That horizon is handed down to us in the form of tradition, with which we must enter into a sort of genetic philology, for the first meaning of a thing remains an arche. Because of the uses to which symbol and allegory have been put in a literature embedded with theistic assumptions, as well as the fixity that irony, paradox, and ambiguity seem to have acquired from our expectations about them, since the war these primary tropes have tended to be seen as agents for controlling meaning in a way that disguises things. As these modes have moved from written to read tropes, they have turned into figures that cover their subjects. In the extensional readings given them, they have tended to move from the play with which they were written to the correspondence with which they have been read. Add the author's use of allusion as a means for a poem's authority, and this tendency only increases.

For poets working after the dominance of the New Criticism, such modes are often understood as a hearkening back rather than the means for presencing. They are like misleading symptoms. In his discussion of the logos as letting-something-be-seen, Heidegger says, "everything depends on our steering clear of any conception of truth which is construed in the sense of 'agreement.'" (Elsewhere, he objects to theories of correspondence, as well as to judgment as "a way of 'binding' something with something else, or the 'taking of a stand.'") Truth must be uncovered, *"discovered";* thus, in Heidegger's view the problem with an overdetermined trope is its precision, its lack of the slippage that would enable it to explore similitude, to take part in the covering/uncovering process within the shared horizon of discourse.[4] Where similitude is concerned, the position of Heidegger is opposite to that of Aristotle, who preferred metaphor to simile because of metaphor's precision—A *is* B, rather than A is only *like* B.

As a result of the precision with which some tropes have been read, their apparent fixity has led poets to use more local devices, which start, but do not end, with experience rather than allusion. Some of these devices have been idiosyncratic to the individual poet, but all of them have provided the movement of meaning necessary for individuals facing what to them has often looked like a self-reifying tradition left over from the modernists, one that Heidegger would describe this way:

> When tradition thus becomes master, it does so in such a way that what it "transmits" is made so inaccessible, proximally and for the most part, that it rather becomes concealed. Tradition takes what has come down to us and delivers it over to self-evidence; it blocks our access to those primordial "sources" from which the categories and concepts handed down to us have been in part quite genuinely drawn. Indeed it makes us forget that they have had such an origin, and makes us suppose that the necessity of going back to these sources is something which we need not even understand.[5]

In order to write, poets have to find a way of beginning all over again in a state that is somehow prior to the received "categories and concepts" Heidegger cites. In response to their skepticism about the tradition and meaning, many poets turned to experience, something less than a "primordial 'source.' " Various changes were made in an attempt to stand outside what to many appeared to be a received body of sedimented thought. The most rewarding option, however, was the rather unsystematic use of the less extensional tropes, not so much for their apparent realism, I would argue, as for their variational power where similitude was concerned. Rather than rebelling against and thus reinforcing the tradition as "master" or throwing away the tradition's structures (by which meaning might have become hidden to a degree, but also by which it had been handed down and kept within the bounds of play), the lesser tropes were able to continue displacing, deflecting, covering, and uncovering. They were not locked in an oppositional tug-of-war that stalled movement. Through use of the less extensional tropes, the "hardened tradition" could "be loosened up, and the concealments which it [had] brought about" could "be dissolved." In part, it could be deflected. The move away from symbol and allegory and the less extensional use of irony, paradox, and ambiguity meant the employment of modalities that were not pre-structured and allowed an exploration of possibilities, including even the "possibilities of [the] tradition." The present was freed, and the past could once again be appropriated and the future moved into.[6] The Janus could once again enjoy its double vision.

For those poets who consciously rebelled against the modernists, opposition to the hierarchical past was not just a matter of rejecting certain tropes or contradicting one's literary elders. Existentialism encouraged questions about the tradition. Yet, in one interesting way, the existential thought of the fifties was a problematical source of principles for poets. The most influential proponent of existentialism was Sartre, but his assessment of the movement had its blind spots. His misreading of *Being and Time* and his categorization of Heidegger as an existential philosopher was corrected by Heidegger in his "Letter on Humanism," published in 1947: "All that man is, i.e. in the traditional language of metaphysics the 'essence' of man, rests in his ex-sistence. But ex-sistence, so thought of, is not identical with the traditional concept of *existentia,* which signifies actuality in contrast to essentia as possibility."[7] And then shortly after: "Sartre formulates . . . the basic principle of existentialism as this: existence precedes essence, whereby he understands *existentia* and *essentia* in the sense of metaphysics, which since Plato has said *essentia* precedes *existentia.* Sartre reverses this phrasing. But the reversal of a metaphysical phrase remains a metaphysical phrase. As such it remains with metaphysics in the oblivion of the truth of Being."[8]

Sartre's reversal seems very much like the reaction of Lowell and other poets against the theistic and hierarchical interests of some of the most influential modernists. Lowell's departure from the church and assumption of the confessional mode paralled the exchange of a metaphysical understanding for an existential one, as Sartre defined existentialism. After *Life Studies,* confessional tactics flourished as the poetic pursuit of a number of the tenets of existentialism—for example, the absurdity of many of the details that characterize Lowell's evening in "Skunk Hour"; his sense of meaninglessness even as the poem is dedicated to his friend Elizabeth Bishop, who in kind dedicated "The Armadillo" to Lowell; the question of suicide, which in "Skunk Hour" seems always waiting just ahead in the next sentence; the affirmation at the end of the poem; and the way that affirmation is conveyed without denying any of the incongruities previously described. One problem with the ideas shared by existentialism and confessionalism was that the metaphysical proposition did not thus go away. By reversing the modernist "phrasing" of hierarchies, metaphysical and aesthetic alike, poets of the younger generation continued what they sought to supersede. Their shift in the kinds of figures they preferred seemed corroborated by such a reversal, but, insofar as they fell into an oppositional tug of war with the ideas that preceded them, both confessionalism and existentialism failed to bring about the change they intended. They remained attached to what they obscured or denied.

The existential principle that life is absurd is grounded in a tradition of reason. If we characterize something as absurd, out of what body of thought do we do so? Saying something is absurd is a statement that appeals to reason. It stems from an existing body of logical thought, just as Heidegger tells us that the reversal of a metaphysical phrase remains a metaphysical phrase. Existential philosophy and confessional poetics were intended to break free of the tradition and to be authentic in thought, utterance, action. But in both cases the tradition continued to cast its shadow as an opposing "master," blocking "access to" the fluid " 'sources' " behind the "categories and concepts" that govern thinking. An example of the modernist shadow is the emaciated poem. The poets who wanted most to break free of modernism retained modes of thought that employed varying degrees of agreement, equivalence, judgment that binds, correspondence—all of which describe an economy that inherits and depends from the preexisting structures of the tradition.

II

Likening is a process in which things do not come to rest. With simile-like arrangements things are seen as similar even as their nearness reveals difference. The turning is the main matter. Neither likeness nor unlikeness suffices. There is a gap between the extremes of uncovering and covering over in which similarities and differences oscillate. This is the movement we gain from a simile-like arrangement that makes a dyad dynamic. Two objects are never wholly separated; they are never wholly joined. But by their polarity, they create movement in a variational free play that simultaneously covers and uncovers things.

If we are to continue to find the fluidity of meaning similitude provides, it is necessary that the various figures we use not freeze their subjects. The reason for the change in postwar poetics was not just the anxiety of younger poets over modernist domination but that, within the context of the time, certain devices as they were then read *did* freeze their subjects. Considering the critical climate of the early fifties, we can see how irony, paradox, and ambiguity had been used dynamically, but then, due to expectations about them, came to shape meaning and to miss its fluidity. The read trope seemed to have overtaken the written trope, even as increasingly poets turned to the academy for patronage, where techniques for reading were the major enterprise. In the poetry of an Eliot, Pound, Tate, or Ransom, irony, paradox, and ambiguity were intended to uncover and to further the dynamic play of meaning; in the hands of later close readers, who required stasis in order to conclude effectively, these tools appeared to stabilize meaning. Reading the tropes rather than writing them tended to leave them within fixed rather than fluid margins. The emaciated poem resulted from a recognition of this problem. Although it was the result of an aesthetics much more problematical than that of the New Critics, it, along with confessionalism and other attempts at renewal, did nevertheless serve as a barometric indicator that many poets felt a change was needed. Symbolism was the point of departure.

Discussing the decline of symbolism, Peter Fingesten says that our "discovery of the objective character of symbols as formal rather than psychic configurations destroys their so-called magic aura." The same destruction happens to allegory, because it draws its truth claims from the same basis that symbol does: "Allegory is a symbol for a symbol." Reflecting the kind of skepticism that also influenced postwar poetry, Fingesten says that "a symbolic world view . . . is synonymous with a magic world view." Magic entails "belief in the numinous content of nature." By "the theory of correspondence," we can read from nature "patterns, designs, or purposes of higher origin." Such a process was employed by

Copernicus, whose failure to discover the elliptical shape of orbits resulted from his adherence to "Plato's symbolic interpretation of the circle," which was believed not only to have corresponded to the universe but also to have informed it. Belief in a higher order, Platonism, led to a misapprehension of the physical world, of reality. Fingesten continues:

> The destruction of the symbolic world view was accomplished gradually, with the Neolithic separation of the world into the Sacred and the Profane, the Hebrew prophets' attacks upon the alleged powers of symbols, criticism by certain Christian philosophers such as Clement of Alexandria, and philosophical schools such as Skepticism and Nominalism, culminating in the experimental scientific method. Following the lead of science, the vestiges of symbolic interpretations of phenomena will yield to descriptive and analytical techniques in all fields. One may assert, therefore, that insofar as any symbolic elements are part of the study, description, or observation of phenomena, those parts, and any conclusions based thereon, will be false.[9]

This summary would have been acceptable to Lowell around the time he was changing his poetics shortly after the war. Fingesten's account was published in 1970, at the close of the sixties. My purpose here is not to trace the history of symbolism before or since the war, but to think about why, after the nineteenth-century symbolist influence in the work of Yeats, Eliot, the believing Lowell, and other poets, symbolism lost standing. We know that the erosion of the credibility of symbolism in this century has resulted partly from ideas about the objectivism of scientific method, which has shared ground with a literary interest in realism and naturalism. And we know that scientific method and our concepts of realism in turn have been drawn into question by modern and contemporary literature informed by principles of relativity and indeterminacy. Not only symbolism has been displaced, but some of the scientific modes of thought that displaced it have themselves been questioned. Paul A. Bové summarizes this movement from demystification of belief to decentralization of thought as a "threat" brought by "Modern and Postmodern literature . . . to the habitual interpretations of the entire myth of Tradition." The myth he has in mind is the idea that the tradition reflects the "decline of the west"—the loss of the "metaphysical imagination," including the "medieval metaphor of correspondence and the hierarchical Image of the Great Chain of Being."[10]

What seems destructive is actually an uncovering, but the uncovering of something that will challenge the tradition, as well as the critical methods derived from it. Bové says that "both the New Criticism and its antagonists can be called Gnostics 'interested' in establishing the priority of word over world." Citing Walter Jackson Bate and Harold Bloom as examples, Bové continues:

> Both Bate and Bloom . . . create theories of poetic interrelationships which protect the "existence" of a sacrosanct "tradition" that is continuous and unchanging. The New Critics and their adherents likewise insist upon a poetics of "unmastered" irony which allows the individual poem, as artifact, to interpose itself as Image between the reader-poet-critic and the world. . . . Brooks, Tate, Ransom, Wimsatt, and all the rest also insist upon a continuous, unchanging tradition maintained by the exclusive definition of poetry as ironic, closed form.[11]

Giving an analysis of the blind spot in Bate's understanding of the relation "Modern poets and readers" have to the past, Bové argues that "the burden of the past is not psychological illusion," as Bate would have it, "but unexamined, habitual, linguistic assumptions," assumptions such as "rhetoric, and analogues such as [the] genetic model" by which Bate reasons that the past as burden is a fiction that ends as soon as we see it for what it is. "The past," and the tradition in particular, argues Bové, "reifies language into fixed patterns which seem self-evident but are, in fact, only unexamined and therefore habitual."[12] The point to this explanation for contemporary poetry is that long before Bloom's or Bové's arguments, poets of various aesthetic ilks had sensed in certain tropes the same problem that Bové identifies in the tradition and that Bloom has traced as generational. For many poets writing during the fifties, certain tropes, as they were understood by the New Critics to work within the tradition, began to feel like "unexamined" and "fixed patterns" of thought.

The idea that language "contains within itself sedimented patterns of expression . . . inherited from the past" means that tropes built out of such language, as it exists in the tradition, may "block [rather than liberate] the poet's ability to create new works." Language can be a "store-house of tropes, ideas, and interpretations," but a storehouse is a place that shelters previously known and arranged things more than it is a source for discovery.[13] Thus in the sixties echo appeared more derivative than constitutive, though echoes continued, in what we can see now is a game in which the tradition-as-opponent continues its play—serving, blocking, and returning, as well as providing the area in which play takes place.

The question of irony is another matter in the distancing process that occurred between younger poets and their elders after the war. Irony encompasses paradox and ambiguity. They are local instances of the ironic structure. Ambiguity is an irony about fixed meaning. Paradox is an ironic juxtaposition of two fixed meanings that do not cohabit. Irony as read by the New Critics and the irony of postwar poetry divide along the lines of impersonalism and personalism. The New Critics read irony in a paradigmatic way, as Brooks's "Irony as a Principle of Structure" demonstrated in classrooms for years. Brooks reasoned that through the "synthesis" of "thrust and counterthrust" irony resulted in a poem's "stability," which he likened to the stability of an arch, where "the very forces which are calculated to drag the stones to the ground actually provide the principle of support."[14] This is a more stable arrangement than most contemporary poets seem able to accept as believable. Independent of New Critics' extensional and exegetical readings, irony operates other ways. It is related to the process of division by which we think, a notion dear to Nemerov. But often in contemporary poetry there is little room for division.

The empirical realist of plainspoken contemporary poetry seems too drawn into question to explore ironies about his or her situation. The speaker in Stafford's "Traveling through the Dark" comes to mind. The emphasis on realistic detail in Stafford's poem leaves little room for irony. As with confession, unadorned description can be an artistic pose, but when this happens we are moving back in the direction of impersonalism. A descriptive or confessional poem based on the sincerity generated by personalism, or the lack thereof, is not particularly opened to irony. Some of Wright's poems discussed in chapter three seem appropriate examples here. The line between a Brooksian irony and an irony of personalism is one of the places where modernism stops and something else takes over. But even here the line we draw must be a crooked one.

Berryman's great humor amid his confessions in the *Dream Songs* is a means for objectifying ironies. He is a confessional poet capable of the dividing thought that Nemerov prizes. Of course, another twist appears in many modernist poems, which though written out of an impersonal aesthetics contain personal ironies. Eliot and Tate come to mind first. But we can generalize and say that, in contrast to the ideal of ironic detachment of the modernists and their New Critical readers, poets following the modernists have relied, either artfully or literally, on personal experience and realism to a degree that constrains the dedoublement in irony, which their elders did not urge doing.

The emaciated poem is another example of the contraction in irony in contemporary poetry. Here irony is not just reduced by personalism and realistic detail; it is replaced by the mechanics of line breaks that disrupt the reader's syntactical expectations. Yet in the case of other contemporary poetry (for example, that of Hecht and Wilbur), irony is employed in as skilled and witting a way as the modernists ever managed it, though often not to the same *degree* and never within the same context. The juxtaposition that so often announces paradox, ambiguity, and irony (for example, in Eliot) has loosened its grip as tropes that require less structure have enjoyed greater latitude. Poets writing after the modernists have tended to be attracted to implied structures that call less attention to themselves, and this in part is the result of placing the responsibility for a poem's truth claims upon personal experience rather than cultural experience—for some, a skepticism about received knowledge; for others, skepticism about language and the intelligibility of experience in general.

Simile-like arrangements are a contemporary way to venture truth, never letting it become totally covered over and lost but never totally uncovered and held either. Because we are in constant process, all we can do is play truth, to trope it the way musicians might play variations upon a theme to keep it before their listeners. This is done by what Heidegger calls "semblance." In *Being and Time,* Heidegger says that "the uncovering of anything new is never done on the basis of having something completely hidden" (or completely revealed), but occurs "in the mode of semblance," or simile-like patterns. And the "uncoveredness" of a thing is "a kind of *robbery*." There is something *"privative"* about the way "entities get snatched out of their hiddenness."[15] Trope does such snatching. Not only does trope operate by "semblance," it also is interpretive, taking its meaning *out* of something. Trope (for Nemerov, figure played between thing and thought) is the basis for a poem's role as a double hermeneutic. Or as Heidegger describes it, "that which is *explicitly* understood—has the structure of *something as something*." And in this understanding "The 'as' [the likening term] . . . constitutes the interpretation."[16] The possibility of meaning is in similitude, trope . . . like and unlike. If we think about simile, we can get a sense of the way "semblance" and the function of the "as" operate. But first here is a variation on simile, the *as if*.

Husserl discusses the *as if*, with his attention on noetic and noematic structures of thought, the subjective and objective aspects of an experience informed by intentionality: "In the essential nature of . . . the *as if* . . . there lie possibilities for actual directings of the mental glance, which, however, never give rise here to actualities in the way of *positing*." Stating that "we do not apprehend anything real . . . as object, but an image, a fiction," his use of the *as if* suggests a means for variational exploration of the possible.[17] In his late work, Wallace Stevens used the *as if* as a means for variational thought in order to explore possibility.

In her discussion of Stevens's use of simile in his late poetry, Jacqueline Vaught Brogan says that Stevens employed the *as if* in order to hold "the gap that is both the point of fragmentation and the point of union." She believes that in this poetry "metaphor attempts to conceal the gap (with the unspoken unity of tenor and vehicle)," while "simile attempts to reveal the gap." Borrowing her expression from Heidegger, she says that simile "calls into" the gap.[18] The problem with metaphor's concealment of the gap that Brogan describes here is like the problem Heidegger has in mind when he cautions against a "conception of truth which is construed in the sense of 'agreement,' " or his objection to correspondence as "a way of 'binding' something with something else." Put to the purpose of equivalence, rather than to that of slippage, metaphor is more apt to cover over than to uncover the truth.

In its use of simile, Stevens's late poetry is one more example of the move away from extensional tropes. For Stevens, a simile-like structure allowed fluidity of meaning, and his use of it coincided with the shift by younger poets to less structured tropes. Looking to Hans Vaihinger's *The Philosophy of "As If": A System of the Theoretical, Practical and Religious Fictions of Mankind*, Brogan reads the *as if* as it functions in Stevens this way.[19] She says that "in the word 'as' there is an unheard equation that 'X is Y'. . . . Yet in the 'if' there is an unheard conditional 'If X were Y' in which there" is the implied assertion that such an equation is impossible. "The phrase 'as if' is particularly revealing for Stevens' work, for not only does it combine the movement of language toward unity in the 'as' (or unheard equation) and the movement toward fragmentation in the 'if' (or unheard conditional); it is also particularly appropriate for maintaining a recognized fiction as a formal possibility."[20]

Simile and the *as if* in particular join "the unitive and disjunctive processes of language in a precarious threshold of impossible possibility," and "in language silence is the threshold." Silence is the place where union and separation interact.[21] Brogan notes "that metaphors" can "divide as well as unite and that fragmentation joins as well as severs," especially when the finite mind is gauged against the infinite.[22] And she adds that not only do "metaphors and elements of fragmentation make 'unheard' contradictions in the way 'as if's' do," but also that "language in general . . . works like similes, both positing and displacing at once." Brogan then states:

> Simile has a certain advantage over both metaphor and fragmentation as a model for understanding certain aspects of language since it gives equal weight to both the converging and the diverging tendencies in language. For, despite the awareness of the inherent "disparities" in metaphor, most treatments of metaphor, in a kind of Romantic nostalgia for a belief in unity, tend to focus on the connections made in metaphor and to ignore the points of disconnection. Similarly, most deconstructive readings tend to emphasize the "abyss," the absence of meaning, and to de-emphasize the "capacity to mean." Simile, however, not only calls attention to both the joining and the dividing, but also exposes their inter-dependence. We should stress, however, that simile is only a model for understanding the latent tension in language: it is not that language is simile, but that it is like simile.[23]

In *On the Way to Language,* Heidegger says that poetry and thinking share a neighborhood, a "dwelling in nearness." The process of joining and dividing through similitude, by simile and other tropes, is an example of "dwelling in nearness." Simile places two things in proximity to each other, where "the essential nature of language" is "Saying." When we say, we show—"make appear, set free . . . offer and extend what we call World, lighting and concealing it."[24] Insofar as trope both uncovers and covers over again, it lights and conceals. Prior to the "unheard equation" of *as* and the "unheard conditional" of *if,* the double aspect they represent must be brought together, placed in "nearness," where it may become active. Similitude does this. A "nearness" allows the "Saying" that shows "the lighting-concealing-releasing offer of the world . . . the motion in which the world's regions face each other."[25] If we "intend nearness, remoteness comes to the fore."[26] If we hold off, nearness returns. Holding near and off at once, much the way one flies a kite, trope is the activity of language. It is where the poet can turn after other aesthetic positionings toward his or her subject have frozen. The movement of meaning requires something separative, division to a certain distance; insofar as it is static, a new poem may fail to have the separation and distance that meaning needs: "Where everything is fixed at calculated distances, precisely there, the absence of distance spreads due to the unbounded calculability of everything, and spreads in the form of the refusal of neighborly nearness of the world's regions. In the absence of distance, everything becomes equal and indifferent in consequence of the one will intent upon the uniformly calculated availability of the whole earth."[27] In its own modest way, a simile-like pattern holds things near and far at once. It introduces play, creating openness and opposing any "one will."

To oversimplify for a moment, what poets faced after two world wars, the Depression, the holocaust, and the atom bomb was a painful awareness of what technology had done to alter structures of power. They could see ways in which we had become subject to "the one will intent upon the uniformly calculated availability of the whole earth." This awareness led them to place increased value upon the "dividing" nature of human thought. Simile-like patterns provided a way to divide things yet keep them related.

Nemerov once remarked that Americans came out of World War II as the heroes wearing the white hats, but we soon learned that when we kill the killers we also walk away with blood on our hands. His observation was a dividing gesture aimed at his role in the war. When employed to explain the massive destruction and suffering that came in the war's wake, modernist tropes that were used to build architectural structures of meaning within the tradition looked like misleading symptoms. The less structured, and in that sense more independent, simile-like tropes had the virtue of offering each poem a chance at an independent start. But the new start did not require radical line breaks to disrupt the reader's syntactical expectations. And the confessional school's emphasis on personalism in poetry was not a necessary cause for poetry's continuation.

In the presence of increased skepticism following the war, the resource needed for poetry's future was contained in language. A poem that appeared relatively traditional drew its energy not from formal devices so much as from tropes, where language provided the imaginative free play of similitude. Too many free-verse poems were written on the basis of the literal-minded notion that form (or the avoidance of it) rather than figure was the major source for variational thought in poetry. The gains that accrue from language's ability to join and divide can be maintained if we rely first on the balancings offered by simile-like figures. Form plays a role, but it is a secondary one. In successful poems written over the last forty years, the play of similitude has been a matter of degree, neither blind acceptance nor rejection of either the unifying or separating, uncovering or covering-over properties of language.

III

In the title poem of *The Sunset Maker: Poems/Stories/A Memoir* (1987), Donald Justice says, *"As if . . . but everything there is is that."* What Justice has in mind is not only the problematics of experience but also the fluidity of poetic language, the way figurative language simultaneously joins and separates things. Many of Justice's rhetorical and syntactical patternings exploit semblance. Conjunctions are a frequent means by which he turns objects for his variational regard. In Justice's hands, conjunctions do not work hypotactically so much as they create dyads. Sometimes several occur in a row, resulting in a series of simile-like modifications. Another device, discussed in chapter two, is the use Justice makes of the kind of rest one experiences in music. He creates a pause in a line, letting silence separate two halves of a comparison yet hold them in proximity. The use of silence is frequently achieved by punctuation, and it often appears as anacoluthon. It is related to Justice's fondness for seeing things as contiguous rather than, say, causally related, and it also is related to his proceeding paratactically.

However, Justice has entitled a collection of his criticism *Platonic Scripts* (1984), suggesting there might be at least a propositional ideal behind the fluid surface of tropes. In an interview, he has volunteered that he has "a sort of Platonic notion that somewhere ideally exists the poem [he is] trying to write."[28] Elsewhere, he has said that he tries "to write *as if* convinced that, prior to [his] attempt, there existed a true text, a sort of Platonic script, which [he] has been elected to transcribe or record" (italics mine).[29] The key to what is being said here is in the use of *as if*. Justice is not convinced of the existence of an ideal text, or script, but he finds it necessary to operate under the belief there is one, a belief that he holds before himself for at least as long as he works on his poem. Acknowledging the importance of "subject" as a source for a poem, Justice then remarks that a poem also results from "merely fooling around. Or from thinking."[30] Thus, the subject of a poem is viewed variationally through the manipulation of certain techniques, the willingness to play things, both of these adding up to a mode of similitude; the drive to do this, long enough to create a poem of real worth, requires the belief in some order, or "Platonic script," which writing the poem will reveal.

The way Justice places himself between belief in the ideal world and the variational thought that trope provides, what he calls "fooling around" or "thinking," makes him a good example of the middle path many poets of his generation and those a bit older have taken between the hierarchies of the tradition, as it was articulated by the modernists and New Critics, and the individualism in American poetry, as it was inherited from Whitman, Dickinson, and, in this century, Williams. Justice has noted the lack of criti-

cism written by his generation and has suggested that a return to
that activity might be a timely enterprise.[31] Were Justice selecting
topics, such a return would further discussion of the way poets
have used simile-like figures to fuse both the combinative and
dividing powers of language in order to stand between traditionalism and individualism and to continue seeing their objects from
new perspectives. Although urging poets to engage in criticism,
Justice does not advocate a new school or a return to an old one
(for example, the New Criticism). For him, poetry "comes from
anywhere, and . . . there should be no hierarchy of values in the
consideration of this," except possibly Justice's own version of art
for art's sake. Put a little differently, "what matters is the result,
not the source, the origin, or the theory."[32]

Justice never becomes a complete pragmatist on the subject of
poetry. He does posit a Platonic ideal for himself when writing,
but it is an ideal-as-proposition. He is not wedded to the world
of forms. He understands rhetoric, syntax, and stanza form to be
liberating restraints, rather than the permanent structures one finds
in the world of, say, pure forms. Insisting on the role of outsider
for himself, he operates somewhere between the practical and the
ideal, proceeding *as if* both were true and false at once. If Justice's
readers find this characteristic a demanding aspect of his poetry,
that also suits his purposes. He has abandoned many of the beliefs
of his modernist elders, but not their appreciation for paradox.

Because of his circumspection, Justice enjoys the way the mind
dissolves illusion. He will not propose there is more than he sees,
but he never limits himself to literalism either. In "Villanelle at
Sundown" Justice says, "One can like *any*thing diminishment has
sharpened." In the same poem, he asks: "Or does mere distance
lend a value / To things?—false, it may be, but the view is hardly
cheapened." He claims he is unable "to tell you" the answer to
this question, but his use of tropes suggests an answer. His tropes
are pivots that enable him to gain new perspectives on what he is
considering, by turning the objects before him. His figures create
distances, diminishments, enlargements. They are constitutive and
"lend a value / To things." But, though polarity seems fundamental to his imagination, nothing stands still and no one "value"
remains fixed. Imaginative distance from an object allows for

movement, for imaginative variations on it. "Villanelle at Sundown" concludes this way:

> How frail our generation has got, how sallow
> And pinched with just surviving! We all go off the deep end
> Finally, gold beaten thinly out to yellow,
> And why this is, I'll never be able to tell you.

The echo from "A Valediction: Forbidding Mourning" and John Donne's trope on what he believed was a metaphysical relation between man and wife, "Like gold to airy thinness beat," is not made for the poem's authority but, by means of comparison, to state its lack of authority. We are not joined to one another by gold, but experience our lives as discrete individuals who only see the color of gold, "yellow," which, speaking of "Sonatina in Yellow," Justice has said suggests "decay" to him.[33] The frailty of the generation Justice is describing is a condition that becomes visible when that generation is compared with its elders. As much as a metaphysical conceit celebrated by the modernists fails to work today, the meaning of a purely physical experience, a color, fails also. Because we *are* "fallen from [a] symboled world," Justice says, earlier in "Villanelle at Sundown," that "It's nuance that counts." And nuance activates the play of similitude.

In "From a Notebook," Justice responds, jokingly, to praise for "the Adjective" by saying, "I . . . maintain that the Conjunction, being Impersonal, is the more Beautiful, and especially when suppressed." Conjunctions are a common means by which Justice pivots his subjects, sometimes to join them and differentiate between them simultaneously. As Nemerov demonstrates in his poem "Poetics," tropes are a "making." They are a way by which "things add up." With Justice, conjunctions often form the patterns in which he both joins things and divides them, creating the play of similitude.

Conjunctions are often a means for comparison so familiar to the reader's ear that, if not actually "suppressed," they at least function as understatement. In "Nostalgia of the Lakefronts," Justice recalls "Childhood . . . fading to a landscape deep with distance— / And always the sad piano in the distance." Three things

are done by these two lines. First, the opening line uses anacoluthon, something that, along with apostrophe and anaphora, appears in Justice's poetry as a means for suggesting contiguity. The
dash plus the conjunction after "distance" separate and join simultaneously, creating a similar effect. Second, there is homoeoteleuton; each line ends with the same word, "distance," which changes
its meaning as it is repeated. The third thing is related to the first
two. The slippage in syntax caused by anacoluthon and the slippage in meaning created by homoeoteleuton are extended by the
conjunction that opens the second line. "And" is inclusive; the
"landscape is deep with distance," an area of uncertainty. But we
are certain that "the sad piano" is out there. Such turns dramatize
the nuances of emotion felt by Justice as he thinks variationally
about the past, or the future. They are appropriately discrete responses, which Justice tries on and regards the way he might try
on several coats, to consider them over his shoulder in a tailor's
three-sided mirror, never ceasing to move himself and the coats,
his objects, into different perspectives. For Justice, contiguity and
parataxis are fundamental matters. And his conjunctions often balance these two patterns.

The second stanza of "Nostalgia of the Lakefronts" concludes
with homoeoteleuton in the last two lines (the repetition of "world")
and chiasmus in the last line: "At such times, wakeful, a child
will dream the world, / And this is the world we run to from
the world." These rhetorical devices pattern materials in a simile-
like way. Ideas for "world" are likened and differentiated. By
using traditional rhetorical devices to create the patterns that
occasion tropes, Justice turns from one way of regarding "world"
to another way of regarding it to yet another. The ideal behind
this method is objectivity, but what Justice does by variation and
nuance is also to posit a series of attitudes, with *attitude* for Justice meaning the emotional harmonics that are appropriate to a
particular perspective. The goal of his method seems to be an
objectified subjectivity created by turning the object of his attention around enough times that we see it from all angles and agree
with what becomes Justice's aggregative response. Conjunctions
allow Justice to turn his object so many times that we feel his perspective moves from possibility to aptness.

Justice's use of conjunctions and other devices links syntactical units. By their choric moves, their tendency to agree or disagree, liken or differentiate, these units become all the more complex. The goal of such maneuvers is accuracy, but it is carried out on the level of responses, first one, then another, until, taken in the aggregate, a series of positings by Justice adds up to a fair approximation of the nature of a situation. The "realism" of the world described is itself a chorus against which individual acts of perception are played, as the drama of getting it right proceeds toward conclusion not in the sense of "rightness" but in the sense of an individual's apperception. As Justice says at the end of "Villanelle at Sundown," *why* what he sees is the way it is, he will "never be able to tell you." But *what* he is *able to see* is a manageable matter.

In *Platonic Scripts,* Justice often uses "apprehend." He talks about the "immediately apprehensible form," "apprehend[ing] the form," "apprehensible structure," and "form which can be apprehended."[34] The choice of "apprehend" reminds us of the epistemological limits that control what Justice believes is available to him. At the same time, meaning remains additive, and conjunctions can produce pivots that uncover new perspectives, even new subjects. An object is viewed one way; additional information enables us to view it another way. To demonstrate this process, here are some lines from "Nostalgia of the Lakefronts":

> At such times, wakeful, a child will dream the world,
> And this is the world we run to from the world.
>
> Or the two worlds come together and are one
> On dark sweet afternoons of storm and of rain,
> And stereopticons brought out and dusted,
> Stacks of old *Geographics,* or, through the rain,
> A mad wet dash to the local movie palace
> And the shriek, perhaps, of Kane's white cockatoo.
> (Would this have been summer, 1942?)
>
> By June the city seems to grow neurotic.
> But lakes are good all summer for reflection,
> And ours is famed among painters for its blues,
> Yet not entirely sad, upon reflection.
> Why sad at all? Is their wish not unique—

To anthropomorphize the inanimate
With a love that masquerades as pure technique?

Here we have an example of conjunctions producing strophes, which, taken in the aggregate, add up to a complex figure for Justice's childhood. Such a figure is, like a lakefront, reflexive and static. When we talk about a lakefront, we mean what we see before us, view rather than viewer, though the viewer is profoundly present because, while what he sees is external to him, his seeing is internal. What is described is the water's reflecting surface, which may mirror us or the sky or trees. Because Justice's conjunctions make what he sees turn round and round, this kind of reflection goes beyond the polarity of subject and object. By turning things, Justice creates a roundness, somewhat the way a stick that is spun appears to be a circular object rather than a linear one. Justice moves through a series of linear arrangements which links an interior world with an exterior one. The poem itself is a kind of "stereopticon," its setting a *National Geographic* that locates the speaker, who, by recollection, would "anthropomorphize the inanimate" past. When he comes back, he returns as a "parent" for whom "the lakefront disappears / Into the stubborn verses of its exiles" or it remains in "a few gifted sketches of old piers." *Nostalgia* is a wish to return. Justice's conjunctions link together in such a way that they round into a return. He ends the poem with typical clearings of the throat: "It rains perhaps on the other side of the heart; / Then we remember, whether we would or no. / —Nostalgia comes with the smell of rain, you know." The sense of a local and personal irony created by the interruptions of "perhaps," the phrase "whether we would or no," and the dash beginning the poem's last line spins the poem's perspective through one more series of qualifying looks.

Yet the world remains linear for Justice. And the world is lineal as well, especially in *The Sunset Maker*. Parents and teachers stand in an inevitable line. The past and those who populate it constitute the primary chorus for the imagination. Justice finds in the polarity of subject and object the forces of attraction and repulsion, likeness and difference, that enable him to pivot his perspective. But his tropes, turns, or pivots stall on the polarity of before and after. For him, dislocation is more a matter of *when* than *where*. For example, the South that Justice writes about seems more temporally than geographically provincial. It exists always in the past. It remains locked in the rearview mirror, and this situation Justice does not try to turn beyond opposition, because temporal discontinuity functions as a primary impetus for his imagination. This is especially the case in *The Sunset Maker*, where Justice's treatment of time may sound elegiac or nostalgic, but he rejects resolution by catching on some local irony that turns things beyond complete resolution. The piano teachers of his childhood are good examples. In "Mrs. Snow," "stray flakes" drift from the teacher's "scalp," and she looms above her pupils "like an alp." With all the importance music holds for Justice, it is significant that he does not use it in a conventional way to suggest resolution and harmony. Instead, he says:

> And once, with her help, I composed a waltz,
> Too innocent to be completely false
> Perhaps, but full of marvellous clichés.
> She beamed and softened then.
>
> >   Ah, those were the days.

The echo of a song in the second half of the last line doubles on the poem's subject, which is a song matched and mirroring; one cliché salvages the other as the two negatives result in a positive. There are additional poems to early teachers—"Piano Lessons: Notes on a Provincial Culture," "The Piano Teachers: A Memoir of the Thirties," and "The Pupil." The figures described in these poems represent, as best they can, the conventions of music or dance, but by the oddness of their lives they also demonstrate the pitiable absurdity of the performer who is always poor compared to his or her music or dance. But Justice's early teachers primarily represent an isolation they only partly recognize, and their unawareness only adds to their vulnerability and isolation.

In addition to the discontinuity of the years that have elapsed between childhood and the present, the vividness of the scenes evoked by the three-part poem "My South" also resists resolution. What the reader experiences as the accuracy of description holds the past to one perspective. There is also the sense of fixity in a scene that has a witness who so carefully recounts its details. In the poem's first section, "Cemetery," the speaker's mother stands "so still her clothing / Seems to have settled into stone, nothing / To animate her face." The sky "Ponders her with its great Medusa eye," and then a "blacksnake, lazy with long sunning, slides" from sight in "the purpling wild verbena." The second section, "Farm," describes a bored young boy out in the country and "missing the city intensely." We are told at midpoint that *"Years later, / Perhaps, I will recall the evenings, empty and vast,"* as indeed the poem demonstrates the speaker does remember. But the turn here is not permanent. The poem shifts back out of italics and ends with the boy feeling "alone, proud, / Almost invisible—or like some hero in Homer," with a "cloud let down" to protect him. The situation and the speaker's perspective on it are not changed by the interjection of a possible view held *"years later."* In the third section, "Train," which ends with a line from Thomas Wolfe, we are told "these Southern nights / Never entirely keep— unless. . . ." And as the "unless" is produced, we pivot, and they do keep. Justice continues:

> unless, sleepless,
> We should pass down dim corridors again
> To stand, braced in a swaying vestibule,
> Alone with the darkness and the wind—out there
> Nothing but pines and one new road perhaps,
> Straight and white, aimed at the distant gulf—
> And hear, from the smoking room, the sudden high-pitched
> Whinny of laughter pass from throat to throat;
> And the great wheels smash and pound beneath our feet.

The poem's conclusion rises to a pitch it achieves not only because of the echo sounded here from Wolfe but also because what is described is something literally *from* the past. Here the displacement so often created by trope in Justice's poetry already exists in the poem's subject. The past *is* past. Justice's description and his use of echo, therefore, sound the past in another sense. They measure its depth. We can know the past by recollection and likening. The description of the train and the echo from Wolfe are matched by the play of similitude which Justice introduces in order to explore the relation between a former experience, which meant one thing when it occurred, and his later understanding of that experience.

IV

Sometimes Anthony Hecht's poems seem impersonal simply because of their accomplishment, yet frequently just below their surfaces they are highly charged with personal elements. In *Obbligati: Essays in Criticism* (1986), Hecht explains his title as referring to both "obligations" and "a musical obbligato," which is "a counterpart that must constantly strive to move in strict harmony with an intellectual counterpoint to its subject."[35] His poetry is directed by the same ethos. His precision of language fulfills the obligation to record experience accurately. And there is the sense of "harmony . . . and intellectual counterpoint," which is Hecht's response to personal experience and to the tradition as experience. With his own melodies and voices, generated by a baroque diction that always tends toward polyphony, Hecht neglects neither the world of contemporary experience nor the tradition's earlier tunes and conversations, which for him echo constantly.

Hecht's notion of literary obbligato is related to what Hollander has in mind when he says that "echoing itself makes a figure" that has its own "interpretive or revisionary power."[36] What distinguishes echo from allusion is that "allusive echo generates new figuration," just as the obbligato is both like its origin, matches it, and is different.[37] The obstruction off which the echo bounces is not fixed, unlike a musical theme, and the hearer who records the echo is not fixed either. Rather than grounding authority in an earlier text, as quotation or direct allusion would tend to do, echo pivots on an earlier meaning and brings it into play within a contemporary context. In Hecht's poetry, it is a modernist device made new again. As with new efforts at obbligato, echo will always be slightly different because the context within which it is heard is constantly changing; thus it never can be interpreted the exact same way twice. Shakespeare and Auden, two favorite sources for echo in Hecht's poetry, are the subjects of essays in *Obbligati*.

The title of Hecht's collection of poetry, *Millions of Strange*

Shadows (1977), is taken from Shakespeare's Sonnet 53. The book is dedicated to Hecht's wife, Helen. And one line in Shakespeare's sonnet is "On Helen's cheek all art of beauty set," and the final line is "But you like none, none you, for constant heart." "A Birthday Poem" considers a photograph taken of the speaker's wife long before he knew her, when she was a child admiring a new pair of shoes she had received for her birthday. An adaptation from Shakespeare's sonnet appears in the last two lines of the next to last stanza, a stanza that tells us the "picture is black and white," though what makes the little girl smile is her new pair of *red* shoes. But the "red / Has washed away in acids," and, by the process of time as a kind of acid, we are once again presented with the problem of similitude. The person in the photograph is at once the same person addressed today and someone different. In the picture she is a little girl "turned out in style." Now she is a wife and mother. The person we see in the picture turns from us as much as she turns toward us. The shoes are both the same and quite changed—there, but no longer red; thus the reason for the girl's smile is equally present and absent. And in his understanding of continuation and change, the speaker hears "A voice spent, / Echoing down the ages in [his] head." That voice is Shakespeare's: *"What is your substance, whereof are you made, / That millions of strange shadows on you tend?"* The question is a matter of essence, perspective, and will:

> And we know at once it would take an act of will
> > Plus a firm, inquiring squint
> To ignore those drunken motes and concentrate
> > On the blurred, unfathomed background tint
> Of deep sea-green Holbein employed to fill
> The space behind his ministers of state,
>
> As if one range slyly obscured the other.
> > As, in the main, it does.
> All of our Flemish distances disclose
> > A clarity that never was. . . .

The poem's argument is not just for the arbitrariness of intelligible experience, or the way figures sometimes disguise what they represent. There are real clarities. The speaker says of his wife that he knows "the live imprint / Of that smile of gratitude, / Know[s] it more perfectly than any book." The drama wrestled with here results from the difference between the singularity we find in those we love and what, on another scale, happens to all of us "with Time." The picture that both represents and misrepresents exemplifies this problem. It is the turning toward and away suggested by the contrast between Holbein's "ministers of state," individuals whose particular tasks give them identity, and the "deep sea-green" he used "to fill / The space behind" them, which suggests the eventual outcome of their lives. They may not land in a common grave, the way Mozart did, but they will be regarded from a common perspective that is impersonal, as the "range" of the living "slyly obscure[s]" that of the dead. Still, we have to remember that Hecht has only said, *"As if* one range slyly obscured the other" (italics mine). In "A Birthday Poem" he contrasts the importance that individuals have for one another with a grinding historical process judged in the abstract, "Scholars" who

> with their Zeiss binoculars descry
> Verduns and Waterloos
> The man-made mushroom's deathly overplus,
> Caesars and heretics and Jews
> Gone down in blood, without batting an eye,
> As if all history were deciduous.

The echo that operates here is both from within and without Hecht's personal experience. He knows something about the perspective of "Zeiss binoculars" from his time as a soldier in Germany during World War II, and he knows history—Verdun, Waterloo, Caesar, and so forth. But the poem ends not only with an allusion to past events but also with a trope, "As if all history were deciduous," which turns the reader's perspective one more time.

If "history" is deciduous," then by likening ourselves to leaves we are understood to fall—winding up raked, burned, and replaced next spring. At the same time, if "history" is "deciduous," then, in terms of the tree's branches and trunk, we also have another proposition—a generalized source and height from which individual leaves fall. The fragility yet uniqueness and richness of

others, as well as our relationships with them, is central to Hecht's
vision. The branch and leaf are one. He echoes Shakespeare as an
extension to a vision he already firmly possesses. For Hecht, the
tradition is part of the way we are defined, just as our connections
to others also define us.

Because we are relational beings, we are reflections and echoes
of one another in person or in text. We are defined by the shadings
others give us—the *as* of connection, or the tree and its branches,
plus an *if,* frail as foliage, that is the tenuousness of our lives, the
lives of those we care about, and the differences between those
lives. Hecht demonstrates the way figurative thought mediates between such contraries by taking his book's title from something
relatively abstract, a literary source, and in "A Birthday Poem"
applying it to a highly personal subject, his wife. As it is used here,
echo is not lineal or linear but closer to surrounding, because it
becomes polyphonic.

In "The Grapes," from *The Venetian Vespers* (1984), shadows
are exchanged between two resorts. The *"Beau Rivage"* is shadowed in the morning; the *"Hôtel de l'Univers et Déjeuner"* is
shadowed in the evening. One morning the speaker feels the "sunlight moving on [her] skin / Like a warm glacier," and she knows
that her "little life [has] somehow crested" and that the light she
has seen through the "unblemished jade" of a bowl of "green
grapes" will round over into shadow for her, with no real change
in her life; no one to love her will ever appear. That is, she will
not find the relation necessary to give her permanent identity but
will wind up like "the sole survivor / Of a crash, idly dandled on
that blank / Untroubled waste, and see the light decline." In "A
Cast of Light," also included in *The Venetian Vespers,* the significance of the light itself is its rich interruptions, themselves like
echoes, made by the "sea-green darkness," "the huge cave-roof of
giant oak and pine." Here shadows are facets not only of identity,
"those we cherish, their hopes, their frailty," but also "Their
shadowy fate's unfathomable design." They repeat the dimensions
of surrounding surfaces in a way that suggests the depth of a
future that waits out ahead somewhere but is for now "unfathomable." The shadows are uncertain, but they liken the way light
encounters the limits that cause them.

In the first poem of *The Hard Hours* (1967), "A Hill," the

speaker says, "I had a vision once," one that turns out to be re-flexive. It occurred while he was shopping with friends in a market in Italy. The vision was of "a hill, mole-colored and bare," with the weather "very cold, / Close to freezing, with a promise of snow." The speaker recalls that a branch broke nearby, like "the crack of a rifle," and made a "soft and papery crash." The hellish scene ends with this summary: "And that was all, except for the cold and silence / That promised to last forever, like the hill." Then the speaker is back in Italy, where there are "prices," "fin-gers," "sunlight," and "friends." Then both speaker and reader return to the present tense of the poem's opening. It is ten years later, and finally the hill is recognized as one that "lies just to the left / Of the road north of Poughkeepsie." The speaker stood "before" that hill "for hours in wintertime" when he was "a boy."

In "A Hill," memory echoes, reproducing what purports to be a personal experience in order to serve the dramatic needs of the poem's subject, which is the horror of alienation and physical iso-lation—the cold that goes with being utterly alone. But the speak-er's disturbing déjà vu initially grows out of visual experience in wihch everything seen is "on sale":

> A clear fretwork of shadows
> From huge umbrellas littered the pavement and made
> A sort of lucent shallows in which was moored
> A small navy of carts. Books, coins, old maps,
> Cheap landscapes and ugly religious prints
> Were all on sale. The colors and noise
> Like the flying hands were gestures of exultation,
> So that even the bargaining
> Rose to the ear like a voluble godliness.
> And then, when it happened, the noises suddenly stopped,
> And it got darker; pushcarts and people dissolved
> And even the great Farnese Palace itself
> Was gone, for all its marble; in its place
> Was a hill, mole-colored and bare.

The before and after of experience are turned by echo, shading, reflection. They contribute to a baroque world that Hecht builds out of oppositions in diction, description, allusion, and rhetoric. Here, the richness of experience occasions its opposite, which somehow has never left the speaker. The latent opposite to any experience seems always a possibility. The warm, shadowed, gladelike world of an Italian marketplace has its opposite waiting. A cold, featureless hill is on the other side of the convex market, waiting like a shape turned inside out. This sort of reversal of the features one finds in a landscape is a familiar event in Hecht's poetry. The reversal occurs variously and, as in "The Feast of Stephen," frequently winds up with an isolated individual catching a contrast such as "a brief glimpse of bloodied hair . . . an unintelligible prayer."

The dynamic oppositions of Hecht's baroqueness are related to a kind of symptomatology—the announcements and contradictions between what people ought to do, what they are capable of doing, what they say they will do, and their actual performance— writ large, between history and morality. Hecht has commented that what he saw in the death camps in Germany was "beyond language." When his poetry is read with this remark in mind, his reversals (for example, in " 'More Light! More Light!' " or "Behold the Lilies of the Field") appear to operate as figures for that part of human experience which reason and language so often fail to capture.

The echo of Hugh Latimer's martyrdom in the opening of " 'More Light! More Light!' " is, we realize upon rereading, figurative, because despite the cruelty and violence of his martyrdom, it represents the world shaped opposite to what the Nazi with a Lüger represents. In addition to echoing Latimer's fate, the poem's rhetoric and diction operate figuratively. As discussed in chapter three, the opening stanzas remind us of a more optimistic use of language: " 'I implore my God to witness that I have made no crime.' " Latimer can "implore" his "God," who will be present as a "witness." Language unites rather than divides. The rest of the poem depicts a more skeptical vision of martyrdom, as does "The Feast of Stephen," in which the first martyr becomes only the latest martyr, and one without reason. The hope that makes martyrdom meaningful is turned away from us, as we are forced to confront our own inhumanity. Here, the traditional beliefs invoked by echo remind us of the absence of meaning in the modern events described.

The title of "Green: An Epistle" suggests both distance and the drive to span it. Usually, epistles are exchanged by people who are apart. But the distance here is within the poet. The gap between appearance and the thing represented exists internally. Thus "Green: An Epistle" opens and divides a dislocated self in order, finally, to reunite that self. Again, echo plays a role. Hecht's rhetorical arrangements are capable of recalling Auden's voice, especially as it sounds in "In Praise of Limestone," a poem Hecht discusses in *Obbligati*. At one point in " 'Dichtung und Wahrheit,' " he quotes Auden's poem: "We, 'the inconstant ones.' " But in "Green: An Epistle," what we hear at times is something more generally like Auden's voice, which is re-created in several ways—repeated rhetorical patterns, a deflating wit, and complete ease in moving back and forth between learned echo and physical description—such that the poem reads the tradition and the landscape simultaneously. First, a few lines from "In Praise of Limestone":

> Mark these rounded slopes
> With their surface fragrance of thyme and beneath
> A secret system of caves and conduits; hear these springs
> That spurt out everywhere with a chuckle,
> Each filling a private pool for its fish and carving
> Its own little ravine whose cliffs entertain
> The butterfly and the lizard; examine this region
> of short distances and definite places.

We are led ahead by "Mark," "hear," and "examine." This is an excerpt from "Green: An Epistle."

> Think of the droughts, the shifts of wind and
> weather,
> The many seeds washed to some salt conclusion
> Or brought to rest at last on barren ground.
> Think of some inching tendrils worming down
> In hope of water, blind and white as death.
> Think of the strange mutations life requires.
> Only the toughest endured, themselves much
> altered,
> Trained in the cripple's careful sciences
> Of mute accommodation.

Hecht's repetition of "Think" matches Auden's three-part directions for the reader's attention. Hecht's wry, cautionary conclusion
is not that different from Auden's, which is " 'soft as the earth is
mankind and both / Need to be altered.' / (Intendant Caesars rose
and / Left, slamming the door.)"

I do not mean to suggest that the echoes of Auden and others
are derivative badges. They are some of the furnishings of Hecht's
well-read imagination. In "The Lull," which is dedicated to Tate,
again we are invited to move through shadows, "Through a loose
camouflage / Of maples bowing gravely to everyone / In the neighborhood," a description not only of light and shadow but also, by
figuration, an echo of Tate's formal and sometimes formidable
manners. This kind of echo, or shading, unites setting and character. It is a means for using the past to populate the present. And
the present can be something personal, such as the friendship Hecht
and Tate shared.

Whereas Justice often employs parataxis, Hecht tends toward
hypotaxis. Here is only one example, again from "Green: An Epistle," of Hecht's use of hypotactic arrangement.

> I write at last of the one forbidden topic
> We, by a truce, have never touched upon:
> Resentment, malice, hatred so inwrought
> With moral inhibitions, so at odds with
> The home-movie of yourself as patience, kindness,
> And Charlton Heston playing Socrates,
> That almost all of us were taken in,
> Yourself not least, as to a giant Roxy,
> Where the lights dimmed and the famous allegory
> Of Good and Evil, clearly identified
> By the unshaven surliness of the Bad Guys,
> The virginal meekness of the ingénue,
> Seduced us straight into that perfect world
> Of Justice under God. . . .

The turns made here are like those of a screw driven beneath
the surface. They are, in part, the realizations of Hecht's generation, after the events of the war, about the problematical ways we
arrive at the truth. But the comparisons made finally do not reach

outward so much as they burrow in. Hecht's practice dramatizes the movement of a mind attempting to approximate its subject, which here is itself. A similar movement is made by Hecht elsewhere—"Apprehensions," "The Venetian Vespers," and, in a slightly different way, "Behold the Lilies of the Field." Hypotaxis goes hand in hand with Hecht's baroque monologues. One clause or phrase spiralling down from another, as Hecht circles through his subject. His method is a mind's cycling through its subject in a way that, on a dramatic level, stalls movement for the sake of closer investigation. Hecht's monologues are a means for magnification. So is his diction.

Through the diction of his monologues, Hecht frequently writes a poetry of personal impersonalism. He creates a double character who speaks to us with the resonance of two voices: someone speaking personally but doing so from a broad range of cultural experience. In Hecht's poetry there is often a persona whose ruminations dramatize the play between the normative thought we employ to explain ourselves, which is thought rich with echoes, and the fiercely unique sense each individual has of his or her own life. We are taught to understand our lives in certain ways; but we experience our lives in much less structured ways. A major concern in Hecht's poetry is the angularity created by the differences between these two views. He is a master at balancing the faith in meaning of modernist impersonalism with the skepticism of late-modern personalism—reservations about the self and about authority. Hecht counterpoises the impersonal self created by one diction with a personal self created by another. The Socratic "Heston" in "The home-movie of [the] self" plays against a welter of suppressed feelings in a simile-like pattern that insures each perspective is balanced by an opposing view.

V

In Mona Van Duyn's poetry, the play of similitude appears in various ways. In addition to her uses of simile and metaphor with slippage, Van Duyn creates simile-like patterns by using humor, the rhetorical question, the conditional tense, metonymy by catalog, mimicry, and even titles and epigraphs. Often Van Duyn

gathers the particulars of experience into a strophe that stands metonymically for a larger, if fleeting, vision of wholeness. With each
of these techniques she is pursuing what her poem "An Essay on
Criticism" calls "a likeness proved out of difference." However,
proof here is nothing like scientific claims for certitude. It is more
a matter of the poet's belief and the reader's assent, "a poem . . .
by consent." And this is because the only "world" we have is "the
one we believe to be, / that we touch and are touched by in af-
fections, conceptions, and body." By "working through otherness
to recognition," as well as by the use of "abstraction," "the see-
saw poise of the metaphor," "the imperfect urgency of rhetoric,"
and "unearned, inglorious similarity," Van Duyn sees poetry moving "in time" as "time moves" to what in "To My Godson, on His
Christening" she summarizes as "fresh possibilities." As she makes
clear elsewhere in this poem, these are "possibilities" ferreted out
of similitude, and they are not meant for anything utilitarian:

> I've thought that the dream of the world is to bring, and again
>   bring
> out of a chaos of same, the irreplaceable thing,
> so, when it dies, we may clap for that brilliant wasting.

Possibility is a major theme in Van Duyn's poetry. She looks
for it through similitude. The "merciful / disguise of metaphor,"
especially metaphor with slippage, and the "chaos of same" are
played into "fresh possibilities." The title of her collected poems,
Merciful Disguises (1973), suggests the concern with similitude
her poetry demonstrates. It follows the constitutive path it does
because, as she says in the concluding poem of *Merciful Disguises,*
"Walking the Dog: A Diatribe," she moves through "a dark /
where there are no forms"—no forms except the likenesses we
make, for example, in "To My Godson, on His Christening," "A
lexicon, contrived for the time," or, earlier in the same poem,
"deeds like the little poet's metaphors . . . good only in brave
approximations."

One way she examines her "brave approximations" is by humor, which begins with incongruity. "Leda" starts with an epigraph from W. B. Yeats's well-traveled version of the story: "Did
she put on his knowledge with his power / Before the indifferent
beak could let her drop?" Here is Van Duyn's answer:

Not even for a moment. He knew, for one thing, what he was.
When he saw the swan in her eyes he could let her drop.
In the first look of love men find their great disguise,
and collecting these rare pictures of himself was his life.

Her body became the consequence of his juice,
while her mind closed on a bird and went to sleep.
Later, with the children in school, she opened her eyes
and saw her own openness, and felt relief.

In men's stories her life ended with his loss.
She stiffened under the storm of his wings to a glassy shape,
stricken and mysterious and immortal. But the fact is,
she was not, for such an ending, abstract enough.

She tried for a while to understand what it was
that had happened, and then decided to let it drop.
She married a smaller man with a beaky nose,
and melted away in the storm of everyday life.

Hidden in, but nevertheless represented by, the poem's humor
is a question about the problematical means we have for gaining
the truth of a situation. Is myth reliable? Or is common sense?
Van Duyn plays this query through the pattern of the *as if*. The
"unheard equation" is the identity of Leda, the same figure then
as now. The "unheard condition" is Leda *then* from the male
point of view, matched against Leda *now* from the female one.
The new Leda lets the event drop much the way she has been
dropped. Her "openness" is the answer to Yeats's question. Her
life goes on and with it the lives of her children. They represent
futurity, and the continuity of things is the result of possibilities
that Van Duyn wishes to remind us continue to be ours. The contrast between Yeats's insistence on his brand of high seriousness
and Van Duyn's responding turn to playfulness is the first way
she opens her subject. Van Duyn gives us the incongruity between
the mythic world of meaning dear to some of her modernist elders
and the quotidian world in which she finds herself and in which
a contemporary Leda would have to live. The lessening of altitude
here stems from the same skeptical attitude that gives preference
to less denotative tropes. Of course, another important contrast is
the reversal of point of view. Leda gets to have her say, and what

we receive is a comically deflating story. Knowledge cannot carry us beyond our very real human limits. Marrying "a smaller man with a beaky nose" is Leda's fair approximation of the truth, mythic or otherwise.

Another source for trope is the rhetorical question, a technique by which Van Duyn plays a proposed equation against the question mark's doubting conclusion. Here is "Addendum to Any Day, Any Poem," the first part of "Two Poems, with Birds":

> Assume, in a bird's eye, the world as a dainty bulge—
> is the problem of definition greater, or less?
> In that chipper bubbleful much would be diminished
> by restriction, much would mount up to massiveness.
> No state of affairs then, but a thousand Affairs of State.
> Is this simpler? Or harder? Texture turns into form
> if one strolls the hilly bark, or through grassfields, on ground
> all mined and thumping with life, hunts bug or stalks worm.
>
> When we eye it, not one bird's worth at a time
> but with eyes like zeppelins, it may be the vista bests us,
> for what crowds quietly even through snow fence metaphors
> is the unexamined life, shifting and lustrous,
> and lands may mellow or chill in that weight of particulars.
> If our largeness of view leaks, does it let out more
> than we mean to waste, minute encounters, tucking,
> tipping the day into an imperceptible contour?
> Do selves go thin for the fat idea of man,
> and think in sackfuls while they drop and scatter
> pips, seed, nutmeats, kernels and cores
> enough for many a pigeon's simple supper?

The implied answer to both these concluding questions is "maybe so, maybe not so." By ending this way, Van Duyn draws us into the dynamics with which she is wrestling, which is finally a question of perspective. It is a linguistic perspective. Although we are taken on a flight, and the details of what we are given are defined by the physical attributes of flying, what we are really asked to consider is how any of us mean. Mean in two ways: mean anything to others, and intend our own meanings. At the encompassing altitude of our mental flights, do we "go thin for the fat idea

of man"? Does "the vista best us" with "the unexamined life"?
Yes. Our metaphors are "snow fence metaphors," with gaps between the boards; they stop the snow but otherwise stop nothing.
And no. The "pips, seed, nutmeats, kernels and cores" get scattered around well enough for further life, "a pigeon's simple sup-
per"—that is, an ordinary bird, a young girl (the subject of the
second poem), and someone who is easily fooled and thus will fall
for the give-and-take playfulness of the poem's questioning. Instead of the *as if* formulation for trope, we have a *maybe yes,
maybe no* arrangement.

Van Duyn creates a figure with the conditional tense by reversing the *as if,* so that the reader finds things balanced in terms of *if
as.* Here is the opening of "From Yellow Lake: An Interval":

> Now in this evening land of fire and shadow,
> a swallow world, a fallow world, of lake and meadow,
> where the mud turtle flops from his log, flat as our fate,
> but the green-headed flies swarm up, so furious is our delight,
> and down the red roadway that the sun has gone,
> a penitential sparrow drops his dung,
> I would peel off my mildewed body like a skin,
> but keep my heart, a freshening bloom.
> Form upon form, creation seems so near
> that separateness fades from the shy vacationer.

The conditional tense's *if,* "I would peel off my mildewed body
like a skin," is balanced against the *as* of being a member of the
world described here. Van Duyn then says that "nature suspects
this homecoming, and tries / the soft prodigal with his own analogies," by which we bite on one resolution or another:

> in dusk the angler stands and sends from shore,
> sweeter than worm or bug, the barbed lure.
> Perilously it drops down the deep lake,
> where, prismed, moves with watery grace the pike,
> who rises, clasps with fangs, his fierce faith,
> and drowns in air, his mythos in his mouth;
> and questionless bloats out his vacant golden eye,
> but his body beats out in carnival agony:
> "Fisherman, fisherman, is the love you give
> my luck, or is your marvelous luck my love?"

The answer to this closing simile-by-question is that both things are true. All her "questions swell" the "monstrous craw" of "a final crow," while in the woods around her an "owl" functions as a "clumsy oracle," hooting "at the sound of rain, a sleepy miracle." The world is "mythos" if we liken it so. One more gesture of likening and differentiation appears in the concluding stanza of "From Yellow Lake: An Interval," which begins by repeating the opening stanza of the poem:

> Now, in this evening land of fire and shadow,
> a swallow world, a fallow world, of lake and meadow,
> where the mud turtle flops from his log, flat as our fate,
> but the green-headed flies swarm up, so furious is our delight,
> in my body I would be sleek and dumb
> as those white worms, blossoming under their stone—
> then, warmed, put on my human clothing and report
> back for the wintry work of living, our flawed art,
> and conspire in the nailing, brutal and indoors,
> that pounds to the poem's shape a summer's metaphors.

Introducing her conclusion with her beginning, Van Duyn turns our perspective by comparing the sameness of the two sets of four lines with the different connotations those lines have when beginning the poem and when introducing its conclusion. By its end, the poem has used the conditional tense to move its *if as* consideration of things from the wishful entertainment of sameness with one's surroundings to a recognition of the at times awful difference that goes with "human clothing," in which one nevertheless "pounds . . . a summer's metaphors." That is, poetry as a mode of thought, "the poem's shape," is the "flawed art" by which we liken the world enough to be able to live in it. As it is handled here, the conditional trope is an initial step toward something new in that world. It is a vehicle for Van Duyn's probing possibility, just as metaphor and simile are.

"The Pietà, Rhenish, 14th C., The Cloisters," is another poem that uses the conditional tense to establish the *if as*. Remarking on the contrast in size between Christ and Mary, Van Duyn tells us that Mary is "like an upended cot smoothed neatly" with "a tight, girlish bolster / of breasts," which appears "queer / to them both, as if no one had ever rested / upon it." Having opened by means of "like" and "as if," the poem then shifts into a more extended trope, which is set up by an *if could as* arrangement that begins in the fifth stanza:

> It is a face that, if he could see
> as we are forced to see, and if he
> knew, as we cannot help but know, that
> his dead, dangling, featureless, granite
>
> feet would again have to touch the ground,
> would make him go mad, would make his hand,
> whose hard palm is the same size
> as one of his mother's tearless eyes,
>
> hit it, since nothing in life can cure
> pain of this proportion.

The poem continues through a series of variations, in which Christ at one point regards in horror the way he and Mary have turned out disproportionate and fixed so in stone. Mary conditionally replies:

> "My darling, it was not
> I who belittled you, but love
> itself, whose nature you came to believe
>
> was pure possibility, though you came through
> its bloody straits. And not you,
> but love itself, has made me swell
> above you, gross and virginal
>
> at once. I touch what's left on my knee
> with the tips of my fingers—it is an ugly,
> cold corrugation. Here on my lap,
> close in my arms, I wanted to keep
>
> both the handsome, male load of your whole
> body and the insupportable,
> complete weightlessness of your loss.
> The holy and incestuous

met and merged in my love, and meet
in every love, and love is great.
But unmanned spirit or unfleshed man
I cannot cradle. Child, no one can."

I have quoted this poem at length to give some sense of the complexity that Van Duyn generates. Based on a familiar sculpture, the poem begins by likening a likening. Within that doubled structure, it then uses tropes in order to take various perspectives toward its subject, which is finally the way love at once holds us in one place and transforms us into something wholly other than what we were—the strangeness of sameness, or the way identity comes from outside.

Van Duyn uses metonymy-by-catalog in many poems, including "Recovery," "In the Cold Condition," "Letters from a Father" (the title poem of *Letters from a Father and Other Poems* [1982]), "Photographs," "Ringling Brothers, Barnum and Bailey," "Cinderella's Story," and "The Vision Test." The details in her catalog share enough in common that they have the force and direction of a strophe. "In the Cold Kingdom" opens:

Poised upside down on its duncecap,
a shrunken purple head,
True Blueberry,
enters its tightening frame of orange lip,
and the cream of a child's cheek is daubed with
Zanzibar Cocoa, while
    Here at the Martha Washington
    Ice Cream Store
    we outdo the Symbolistes.
a fine green trickle—
Pistachio? Mint Julep?
    Words have colors,
    and colors are tasty.
sweetens his chin.
In front of me Licorice teeters like a lump of coal
on its pinkish base of Pumpkin.
    A Rauschenberg tongue
    fondles this rich donnée,
    then begins to erase it.

The exotic and richly varied pleasures of an ice-cream parlor are listed in order to stand metonymically for the equally exotic and rich offerings of the world. The humor and exaggeration of the one substitute for the strangeness of the other. Because the world we inhabit is for us a condition made up of an infinite variety of particulars that define that condition, Van Duyn must use the condition of an ice-cream parlor—its many offerings *"Swilling in language"*—to represent the many ways we live. The one "Cold Kingdom" stands collectively for another. Instead of saying the conscious and unconscious possibilities of our lives are *like* those of a wide selection of desserts, or saying that we venture forth *as if* our futures were such an offering, Van Duyn abjures generalization or summary for catalog. The benefit she gains from this is twofold. The first benefit is that the incongruity of having too many things from which to choose results in the poem's humor. We laugh at what the speaker describes and then laugh at ourselves. The second benefit of cataloging details that appeal to *"the bloated imagination"* is the dramatic element introduced by requiring the reader to go through such a long list. Having done so, the reader concludes with a summarization that, taken as a whole, then works metonymically.

This structure of metonymy, characteristics standing for a subject, appears frequently in Van Duyn's poetry as a catalog. That is, because they characterize it, objects or events are listed for the thing she has in mind. She works this way because she has a collective name in mind. And, while language arranges semblance sequentially, semblance may just as well cluster as it may unreel. In "Marriage, with Beasts" two people bring their "love to the zoo to see what species / it is." Holding their heads "up to cages," they find that "what happens . . . is as informal / as disease" and that they, "like lust, are serious / about making sense of a strange, entire surface." What follows is a list of the various animals to which the husband and wife compare themselves in a series of rapid, unspoken mimicries which they make without contact, merely by looking such that the animals they study are turned into humorous reflections of human attributes. Animals are described as "big bruisers . . . in tap-shoes," who are "like football players ready to butt or shove." Once the similarities are established, they make possible the differences: these beings "neither marry nor burn, being as couplers / wholly impersonal." With a humorous allusion to Dylan Thomas's "The Force that through the Green Fuse Drives the Flower," the speaker addresses her threatened and threatening mate:

> A murderous rage is the force that through the green fuses
> drives the daisies of love. Why yes, sweet mate,
> your face and dress are dearer than anyone else's.
> Why yes, life's light, we could kill each other with pillows.

The poem continues with the two looking "at the birds" in order to "tease" their "remarkable hearts / with flocks of bright little resemblances." The couple carry their "heads" or "head-bowls . . . not of straw, but metaphors" as they make their tour, watching the animals, each a " 'watched spectator.' " They are "Headstrong" as they meet various members of the zoo, some of whom recall "Nemerov sparrows." ("A mountain lion" reminds her of Jeffers and Dickey.) What they discover are approximations of the gap between the animal world and a human one. That gap and a metaphysical gap recalled in "how we've raised our own eyes from the ground" and may be only able to "tuck our heads in a wing" are the poem's combined question. The husband and wife carry their heads around the zoo in a comical effort to understand their problem. But "Marriage, with Beasts" concludes with the speaker losing her head and then getting "it back on" as she concentrates directly on an incongruity that previously has driven the poem's comedy only indirectly, a "lion" that "discounts his mate, / coming up to see" the speaker at an uncomfortably close range. She gazes into his gaze, which is nothing more than a "slit," and finds a disturbing question looking back at her:

> No god is there. I feel nothing Ledean.
> What can it be that comes without images?
> An eye, nothing in it but what he is,
> the word, then,
>
>   after all this,
>
>   not love but
>
> LION?

Lion "ceases / to be a word." His "slit" of a gaze "widens" to something "Illiterate. / Perfect . . . without adjective" until "it ceases / to be a word." The lion's gaze is "without adjective" because it exists in a world without qualitative distinctions. The poem ends with the disturbed speaker's disturbing summary. Shaking, she says:

> Now take what you've seen of me home, and let's
> go on with our heady life. And treat me, my pet,
> forever after as what I seem; for it seems,
> and it is, impossible for me to receive,
> under the cagey wedlock of your eyes,
> what I make it impossible for you to give.

The lion cannot be likened. Things are disguised. The meaning of the lion turns into something nonanthropomorphic. Yet it is symptomatic of a human problem. In terms of strangeness or otherness, marriage is not that different a matter from the staring contest described here. "Heady," "cagey," and "wedlock" pun on various forms of entrapment which marriage combines under an order that only "seems." Here, similitude is most accurately represented by a strophe in which the speaker catalogs as many characteristics of "wedlock" as possible. This is because the condition Van Duyn addresses never lends itself to being either true or false but instead is a myriad of facts and qualifications which defies reduction. Similitude results from aggregating details.

"Growing Up Askew," from *Letters from a Father and Other Poems,* is an example of the way Van Duyn regards mimicry.

> They had the Boston Bull before I was born,
> and Mother liked her far more than she liked me.
> We both had a trick. When Mother shaved one forefinger
> with the other and said, "Shame, *sha-a-me!*" Peewee
> would growl and snap most amusingly right on cue.
> I, when shamed in the same manner, would cry.
> I see my error now, but what good does it do?

Van Duyn's poem mimics mimicry. Her humor rises to an ironical turn, but the irony is local. "Growing Up Askew" is governed by matching the dog and the mother, the dog and the child, the past and the present. The dog mimics the mother's actions; the daughter should have mimicked the dog's humorous behavior in order to protect herself from the mother. Finally, the daughter should have mimicked the mother in order to join her by reflecting her disapproval. Such a deflection would have enabled the daughter to stand in line with, rather than outside and against, the power the mother has to enforce "proper" behavior. What Van Duyn mimics, however, is not the daughter stepping into line and avoiding difference but her standing outside in a self-defining act of withholding which is both painful and differentiating. Given by her mimicry the option of either likening or differentiating, she opts for the latter in a swerve away from hierarchy—here a track for obedience which perpetuates an arrangement through further obedience.

The truth claims for "Growing Up Askew" are based in part on personal experience (rather than allusion to one or another part of the tradition), but they rest even more on the similitude found in Van Duyn's past experience, during a moment of reflection. The poem is taken from the speaker's life and spoken in the first person, but it is objectified by the pairing of the Boston Bull's behavior with that of the daughter, which turns out to be a contrast between the dumb animal's defiance and the human being's docility. The taut relationship between a mother and her daughter, which is a recurrent theme in Van Duyn's poetry, leaves the daughter less free in her response than the household pet is in her diminutive way. The poem is governed by a recognition of how an earlier mimicry of the animal's defiance would have saved the pain implicit in the later poetic mimicry that Van Duyn offers for the entire situation. Had the speaker acted as the dog did, her response would have been (as the poem is now) to mimic a mimicry, to imitate the dog's "growl and snap," which, however comical, was itself a mirroring deflection of the mother's scolding. "Growing Up Askew" is about entrapment, but the likening and differentiating that Van Duyn performs here open up choices, rather than precluding them. The similitude created by mimicry makes difference possible. It creates a distancing safety.

The two ideas of mimicry stand in comparison to each other by means of an unspoken simile that is presented in the negative value of turning away: the speaker's response to her mother's saying "shame" was *not* like the dog's; what the speaker would do now is *not* as she once did. The problem was different from what appearance made it seem. And now reflecting each other, both the past and present appear skewed. To *skew* is "to move in an oblique direction"—"to swerve," "to distort." The speaker tells us she grew up skewed, askew; she also tells us that the proper response to this would have been to skew the world and her mother in return, which was what the dog did and, in the incongruity of her action, was why she was considered funny. Had Van Duyn deflected the mother by one mimicry or another, she would have answered one torsion with another and thus shielded herself. As an adult, Van Duyn knows how to deflect, but now the object of her gesture is time rather than a scolding.

Van Duyn also introduces the play of similitude with epigraphs and titles. Just as Magritte uses the titles of his paintings to create tautologies, Van Duyn lets an epigraph introducing a poem stand as a normative summary in order that the poem, in its play of sameness and difference, may violate that summary with something complex and contradictory. Tautology opens up discourse by placing two apparently identical things side by side. Once they are that close together, differences emerge. The epigraph from Yeats used in "Leda" immediately brings the same mythical characters onto the stage. Leda and Zeus stand before us dressed out as Yeats would have had them. They are the same figures. And this gives Van Duyn the opportunity to make them contemporary, which turns them into quite different figures. The simile-like play here is created mainly out of changes in the context within which Leda and Zeus are viewed.

In "The Vision Test," Van Duyn's first figure starts with her title, which puns on physical and intellectual "Vision." The speaker describes a comical moment that occurs while she is renewing her driver's license. Giving her "profession" as "Poet," she derails the "kindly priestess" of normative thought who measures each applicant against her own version of "a highway language of shape, squiggle and sign." Once the "vanilla pudding, baked-apple-and-spice / face in continual smiles" has ceased her "Oh, ha ha ha ha ha hee hee," "She resettles her glasses, pulls herself together, / pats her waves. The others listen and watch."

"And what are we going to call the color of your hair?"
she asks me warily. Perhaps it's turned white
on the instant, or green is the color poets declare,
or perhaps I've merely made her distrust her sight.

"Up to now it's always been brown." Her pencil trembles,
then with an almost comically obvious show
of reluctance she lets me look in her box of symbols
for normal people who know where they want to go.

A "Vision Test" can be an optical test, and of course it also can
be an intellectual test. Because these two meanings are held together by the poem's title, they begin as likened. Indeed, one meaning originates from the other. The literal eye test becomes a figure
for a test of mental capabilities. These two meanings play off each
other during the poem's narrative. The popular attitude that a poet
must be a blind fool is matched by the need of the "priestess" to
ask what color someone's hair is when that person is standing right
before her. We are given the tautology of "symbols" out of the
tautology of the "Vision Test." The repetition of the test, first
physical and then intellectual, is matched by the repetition in the
"symbols." Just as the test occurs on two levels, the symbols exist
on two levels. Or they once did. If we are "fallen from / The symboled world," as Nemerov tells us we are, then the second level on
which symbols once operated may no longer exist and the poet's
status appears worthy of laughter after all, but only if we forget
that tropes are constitutive and do not have to be read deductively
from some larger order. Van Duyn's speaker knows this. Her ex-
aminer does not.

"The Hermit of Hudson Pond" plays the normative epigraph
with which it opens against the aberrant behavior of the hermit,
who explains his rationale in a suicide letter. The hermit's cabin
is " 'immaculately neat.' " The epigraph tells us that "Like most
of the hermits in the area [he] obeyed to the letter the Fish and
Game Laws." But the poem takes this scrupulousness and in its
own pursuit of similitude turns it inside out:

"I killed myself because I had to kill
my baby dog for chasing deer. I threw

my pistol into the lake after I shot
baby dog. I didn't have nerve enough
to shoot myself. I didn't have to shoot
my dog. No one knew she was chasing deer
but me. I want to suffer because I think
it was a crime to shoot my baby dog.
If you find this, Ray, I'm all done living. I'm on
the bottom of the lake beside my dog."

Van Duyn concludes by telling us this story was taken from Anne Howe's "Hermits of the Moosehead Region" in *Moosehead, Maine Bicentennial Booklet* (1976). This plays the normative character of "Fish and Game Laws" plus a bicentennial celebration against the aberrant actions of a hermit who here violates one normative pattern by adhering too strictly to another one. It plays the character of hermits, who are considered different anyway, against the sorrowful extreme of one hermit.

In many other instances Van Duyn uses the play that results from tautologies between title and poem, or between epigraph and poem. In "A Kind of Music," a quotation from George Santayana is played against the behavior of a young puppy, whose actions are comically irrelevant—"runs off when he's called, when petted is liable to pee, / cowers at a twig and barks at his shadow or a tree," and so forth. There is "No justification" for "his actions." But "when it comes to loving . . . all responses are reasons and no reason is necessary." The quotation from Santayana runs in part: "When consciousness begins to add diversity to its intensity, its value is no longer absolute and inexpressible . . . life [is] a kind of music made by all the senses together." Scatterbrained as the dog is, he is, in his affection for those around him, as valently sound as a moving piece of music.

"Placet Experiri" begins with this epigraph: "A 96-year-old woman was granted an interlocutory decree of divorce yesterday and said, 'I'll never trust another man as long as I live.'" This contrasts with the poem's conclusion—a woman who is "Ninety-six years, and the world's / never opened its shell before, oyster without pearls, / insane, obscene, as pink and soft as a girl's."

The epigraph of "The Gardener to His God," taken from *The*

Flower Grower, is " 'Amazing research proves simple prayer makes flowers grow many times faster, stronger, larger.' " The poem concludes:

> For in every place but love the imagination lies
> in its limits. Even poems draw back from images
> of that one country, on top of whose lunatic stemming
> whoever finds himself there must sway and cling
> until the high cold God takes pity, and it all dies
> down, down into the great world's flowering.

The oppositional and mutually defining relation between titles or epigraphs and the poems they precede is a common mode of thought in Van Duyn's poetry. It is one of the many "disguises" by which things present themselves, either turning toward us or away. Figures allow Van Duyn at once to examine the world around her and to avoid becoming one of "the self-examined / who've killed the self." For her, as for the other poets discussed here, similitude is the way "The world blooms and we all bend and bring / from ground and sea and mind its handsome harvests."

VI

To Elizabeth Bishop the world was often close to escaping likeness. Based on the childhood experience described by "In the Waiting Room," and the conclusion of "The Country Mouse," Bishop seems to have operated out of an intellectual reserve, a kind of diffidence, that she used similitude to control. Often her figures seem to have been selected for the strangeness they suggest rather than for semblance, matching the complications of relation and identity that troubled her more generally. The experience that Van Duyn describes in "Growing Up Askew" is strikingly similar to what Bishop describes in "The Country Mouse." Peewee and Beppo are both Boston Bulls, but the similarities are much more significant than this sort of coincidence suggests. As children, at least on certain salient occasions, both Van Duyn and Bishop seem to have seen themselves as having little more status than that of a house pet. However, Van Duyn says she sees her "error now," and Bishop records having said to herself, " 'You are not Beppo, or the chestnut tree, or Emma, you are *you* and you are going to be *you* forever.' " Sartre's tree aside, what the sadly comic uses made of two Boston Bulls tell us are the ways two children learned to understand themselves, here, by likening and differentiating in the humblest and most local terms, terms which obscured what they represented as much as they revealed those representations. In his introduction to Bishop's *Collected Prose,* Robert Giroux says that all of Bishop's "writing" is "precise and objective."[38] While on one level Bishop's work is just what Giroux says it is, on another level it is very much "askew," as Van Duyn means the term. The world faced by two little girls could never be approached directly. The sense of alienation implicit in these two anecdotes concerning pet dogs is a radically subjective, rather than an objective, condition. In each case the speaker's consciousness is located at the margins of power and authority for the world described. The precise objectivity of Bishop's descriptions gives her readers the feeling of close observation, but Bishop's close-ups come from a telescope.

The reason for the telescope, for the separation that the speaker maintains from the world, has to do with likening, or, as Bishop says, it has to do with "how 'unlikely' " identity is, insofar as it requires likening by pairs and multiples of pairs. To borrow from her "Gentleman of Shalott," for Bishop, looking in the mirror doubles the image, but for her, unlike her gentleman, " 'Half is [not] enough,' " at least not for a child figuring out who she is. The speaker of "In the Waiting Room," a very young Bishop, is almost seven years old. She is waiting for her aunt in the dentist's office, but she is also waiting for herself, for what amounts to reaching the age of reason. What occurs in the dentist's office is a concatenation of realizations made almost simultaneously. The *National Geographic* containing the article about the Johnsons is a means for self-location, location this time primarily in terms of mores rather than the geographer's spatial understanding. The cannibalism that the Johnsons have found and are studying is self-reflexive for them and for their readers, who while they may be shocked are also confirmed in the presuppositions of their culture. Habeas corpus never looked any better. The *National Geographic* seems to reffirm the integrity of national boundaries, especially those of the English-speaking world. And this is a particularly valuable service because a world war is in progress. Moral and geographic remoteness elsewhere produces feelings of cultural closeness and rightness at home. But what if a reader is not far enough along to be acculturated to the *askew,* to enjoy that cultural exchange in which a positive is gained from two negatives? What about a child of seven who is capable of independent thought but not prepared for the way violence and loss shock us and produce an odd kind of pleasurable self-confirmation? The aunt's painful tooth with its root canal feels like a tiny inverted version of the volcano pictured in the *National Geographic.* The two sources of pain, the tooth that hurts now but that can also tear flesh and the volcano that can burn flesh, have their threatening interiors. So do other things—the dentist's inner office, from which the *"oh!* of pain" comes, the people who because of pain wait for more pain in the expectation of a positive result, and Worcester, Massachusetts, which surrounds the entire scene but which with sundown becomes one of the dark interiors of World War I.

The article about the cannibals and their " 'Long Pig' " is, by implication, an article about anyone who reads it. The shock felt at the strangeness of "naked women with necks / wound round and round with wire / like the necks of light bulbs" is as powerful as it is because of the reader's shared humanity with people who are doing an inhuman thing. The child gives a "sidelong glance" to see the others in the waiting room in order to see herself in relation to them, and she asks herself: "How had I come to be here, / like them, and overhear / a cry of pain?" She has already given a sidelong glance to the cannibals and to their victim. And she has found she is like both—those who kill and eat, as well as the one who is killed and eaten. "How 'unlikely' " indeed; and also how totally likely, and therefore mirroring and self-distancing. The "similarities" that Bishop catalogs toward the end of the poem—the "boots, hands, the family voice . . . or even / the *National Geographic* / and those awful hanging breasts" are " 'unlikely' " yet hold people "together."

The play between things that turn toward us in recognizable likenesses and away from us in strangeness is dramatized in the mind of a formative Elizabeth Bishop but ends without any real reconciliation. The last two stanzas do not meld, but stand together and apart in a way that characterizes much of Bishop's work.

The diffidence with which they end the poem results from double vision. In one stanza, there is the surreal nightmare of one "black wave" after "another, and another." And in the following stanza, there is the very real nightmare of "The War" and the "night and slush and cold" of "Worcester, Massachusetts." The overpowering waves are on the subjective end of the telescope; Worcester, which we have been made to visit, stands in stark outline at the other end of Bishop's telescope. Matching two views, the one magnified the other reduced, of the same predicament this way produces a simile-like structure. Bishop has made "similarities" dissimilar and dissimilarities similar. For her, the slippage created by this process is, ultimately, a problem of identity.

Bishop's "Sestina" recounts a child's life in an "inscrutable house." What is "inscrutable," finally, is the way time displaces the relations that give us identity. After her father died and her mother was sent to a "sanatorium," Bishop lived with her mother's parents. The house described in "Sestina" recollects salient parts of the life she had in her grandmother Bulmer's house in Great Village, Nova Scotia, where Bishop lived for a while and where she started school. In her prose piece "Primer Class" Bishop records her life with her maternal grandparents. She learned her numbers "from the kitchen calendar and the clock in the sitting room, though [she] couldn't yet tell time." The family had "cups of tea," Bishop's being " 'cambric tea,' " and, for a while, every time she left the house and "said goodbye" to her grandmother, Bishop asked her "to promise . . . not to die before" she "came home." "Sestina" is about Bishop's dependence on her grandmother and about the way relation gives identity to a child. It also is about the other side of relation, in which people turn away into separation, because the grandmother is old and not likely to live long enough to see her grandchild to maturity. A second orphaning is pending, and the instruments for prediction and security, the "almanac" and the "Little Marvel Stove," are inadequate to either task, as the grandmother will prove to be inadequate because of her age, which she recognizes with "her equinoctial tears."

The house is presented in "failing light," where the weather brings rain and where "the old grandmother / sits in the kitchen with the child" near the "Marvel Stove, / reading the jokes from the almanac." Laughter and conversation are misleading symp-

toms that "hide" the grandmother's "tears." The incongruity of
the jokes matches the incongruity between the age of the granddaughter and that of the grandmother, both reasons why the grandmother turns "her tears" to laughter. The double negation is at
work again, as indeed the entire poem is a double negation in which
the combined loss of parents and then the grandmother is reiterated
in order to overcome loss. This exchange is kept alive throughout
the poem by words such as "foretold," "time," "mad," "clever,"
"rigid," "winding," as well as other words that are repeated, especially "tears," "Marvel," and "marvellous." Categorizing change the
way these words do makes it seem more intelligible than it really is,
and therefore bearable.

The "clever almanac" cleaves the days and months of the year
into discrete entities. As a source of prediction and wisdom (the
weather it tells one to expect and the maxims it hands out in the
form of jokes and sayings), the almanac raises the problem of
what the future will be like for the grandmother and her granddaughter. It also cleaves or turns things away in another sense,
by reminding us of its many inadequacies—the inaccuracies of its
weather predictions and the extremely limited usefulness of its
pithy sayings. In its concern for the future and its anecdotal wisdom, the almanac is like the grandmother. The two are also alike
in that they are very limited, though of course their limitations are
quite different. The one predictor operates on a general scale, the
weather everyone will experience, and therefore is impersonal; the
other, who says *"It's time for tea now,"* is quite personal.

The warmth and security of the house are played against a cold
and uncertain world outside. The stillness, almost the waiting, of
the granddaughter and the grandmother inside is set against the
inevitability of time and change that will take away what the two
of them have together. The examples of sameness, the details of
the poem given in the repeated words of the sestina, take their
particular significance here from the impending change that is the
poem's subject. Here sameness dramatizes change. Identity between
two generations will end in a separation that will take Bishop to
the other side of her family in Massachusetts, where she will be
adopted by Beppo, who, we are told in her prose piece "The
Country Mouse," punished *"himself"* for vomiting "in the con-
servatory," what Bishop calls "his peculiar Bostonian sense of

guilt." She was happier in the Nova Scotian house, before its "winding pathway" led her away and made her life there "rigid" because finished.

There is an economy implicit in "rigid" and "winding." Or perhaps Bishop would say there is an art, as she does in "One Art"— "The art of losing isn't hard to master" and, a little later, "Lose something everyday." Or elsewhere, in "The Moose":

> "Yes . . ." that peculiar
> affirmative. "Yes . . ."
> A sharp, indrawn breath,
> half groan, half acceptance,
> that means "Life's like that.
> We know *it* (also death)."

This is an exchange in which "rigid" is dependent on "winding" for its meaning. The "affirmative" understanding of life that Bishop finds in "Yes . . ." comes from the acceptance of a negative, death. Each condition mirrors its opposite, and, by accepting whichever one presents itself at a given time, we call its opposite into presence. We take what is linear, the movement from presence to absence, possession to loss, or life to death, and we give that perception an added dimension. By accepting the direction of these movements, we mirror the opposite direction. Performed frequently enough, an area is created in which things are ventured but not lost, retained in the play of similitude implicit in the "peculiar / affirmative. 'Yes'. . . . 'Life's like that.' "

In "The Fish," Bishop recounts her catching of a most unlikely fish, which in its oddness turns itself both toward and away from our expectations of what a fish might be, as it leads her to a vision of relation and similarity in which she says: "everything / was rainbow, rainbow, rainbow!" A spectrum's diversity is curved, given shape and relation, by careful description and narrative. The poem's lines tend to be short, and the momentum that is sacrificed by this seems at least partially offset by the way details are set apart, calling maximum attention to themselves. Along with this, a kind of locutionary change-up occurs from line to line, without mechanical intervention. Bishop counterbalances her diction, which shifts back and forth between things ugly and grotesque and things delicate, beautiful, and somehow worthy of respect. Thus the fish is "a grunting weight," yet he is "venerable." Or, more anatomically, he is "infested / with tiny white sea-lice," but the "barnacles" on his sides make "fine rosettes of lime." The fish is "homely"; his "brown skin" hangs in places "like ancient wallpaper." But, again, Bishop suggests that he has passed enough tests to be "venerable." He has fought the hook numerous times before now and won, and the "rosettes" he wears are badges for his campaigns and his endurance.

There are "the frightening gills, / fresh and crisp with blood / that can cut so badly." Three turns occur here. The gills start out as threatening, then become delicate, then return to being threatening, "frightening." This sort of alternation continues, as the fish is described in terms of "coarse white flesh / packed in like feathers." There are "the big bones and the little bones," and the "dramatic reds and blacks / of [the] shiny entrails." All of these details are given in one sentence, causing the reader to alternate between repulsion at what the fish looks like, inside and out, and a feeling for the sensitive edges of the fish's corporeal existence, the "fresh and crisp" gills. The sentence ends with "the pink swim-bladder" described as being "like a big peony," and we are once again restored to an acceptable likening. But not for long. There are the fish's large shallow eyes versus Bishop's, which, we realize by the end of the poem, "stare" with recognition. The fish's face is "sullen," and "the mechanism of his jaw" seems to reduce him to something less than the living. Then the "five big hooks" and "five old pieces of fish-line" are added to the fish's face, and he returns to being "venerable." Approximately half of the details attract us; the others are repulsive to us. But all are relational. The alternate ways we are led to regard the fish are echoed by the boat.

The boat's "pool of bilge" is unpleasant, but the "oil" that floats on its surface has "spread a rainbow." But this is "around the rusted engine," the "bailer rusted orange, / the sun-cracked thwarts." And so it goes. The poem is strung together by opposing details that sometimes disguise one another and that also work somewhat the way the "thwarts," which are transverse to the boat's "gunnels," work. A *thwart* is a transverse bar in a boat. It also is a "rower's seat." To *thwart* someone is "to oppose," "to baffle," "to block," "to defeat." The boat's "oarlocks" restrain the oars, which move against them the way the "gunnels" and "thwarts" oppose each other. But without oppositions, the boat would neither hold together nor move ahead when it is rowed, or when it is powered by its engine. That is, Bishop is talking about opposition and movement, and movement by opposition.

But the "victory" that fills "up / the little rented boat" is not oppositional. It is not Bishop's having landed a fish that heretofore had been the champion. Indeed, it is clear that the fish is either old and tired or not well, and that Bishop's catching it is not a physical victory. This is no longer the big one that heretofore got away but something else. Opposition between predator and prey is not the point. "Victory" usually means defeating an antagonist or achieving mastery over something or someone, but Bishop leaves us with a conclusion more complicated than that.

Given no regular rhyme scheme, the poem nevertheless ends with two foreshortened couplets: the rhymes "strings" / "everything" and "rainbow" / "go." The connections implied by "strings" are various—strings attached, tying things, linking one thing with another, finding one's way out of a maze and thus not only overcoming confusion but also recovering the past or a previous place. But "everything" goes beyond even the most complex understanding of and function for "strings." Relation is taken to a new dimension. As is the fish, the "rainbow" that Bishop sees is rich both for its physical suggestiveness and for its cultural baggage. The colors of the spectrum are contained in a rainbow, which works prismatically, and a rainbow provides the physical evidence that the sun is near. Rainbows are taken to represent the promise that there will be no more floods, and, less seriously, they point to the figurative pot of gold—one benefit or another. The bow that connects two points also connects the gestures Bishop makes toward the fish. She pulls it in, but she lets it "go." "Strings" attach opposing ends and in that sense are bipolar. They are inadequate in the face of what connects "everything." And "rainbows," which at once bridge two points and establish the separateness of those points, fan out into the spectrum, with gradations of color curving between their two ends. We are back to the workings of similitude. Or, in Bishop's words, we see how things that are in some way alike also can be so " 'unlikely.' "

The "victory" that Bishop enjoys briefly is the overcoming of her sense of separateness, a sense that seems to be related in part to her generation's move from symbol and allegory to simile-like tropes. No longer weighted symbolically, the fish is as unattractive as the cannibals found by the Johnsons. Letting the fish go is a gesture that overcomes the will's desire either to hold itself apart or to dominate. Also, the poem contains humor and high spirits. Bishop and her readers must face age, too. By letting the fish go, she implies she must let herself go. She ventures her will. Just as the oil in the bilge does not lose itself to the water but instead spreads into an unlikely rainbow, Bishop does not sink herself into the usual ways of regarding an old, ugly fish. She extends the spectrum of her regard, finding instead a rainbowlike beauty in the fish, which implies standards of likeness and possibilities of order that go beyond our usual concerns. Things that are " 'unlikely' " can be likened by a generous eye.

While Bishop was part of a generation that tended to exchange equivalence for likeness, that exchange was never fixed. As soon as it occurred, its opposite—or, more likely, its near opposite— began to happen, as part of a movement back and forth between covering over and uncovering. Heidegger speaks of our " 'destitute time.' " In the same discussion he argues that the "manifestness of Being within metaphysics" may equal "the extreme oblivion of Being."[39] What this suggests for contemporary poetry is that as soon as symbol is thrown out, as soon as the metaphysical understanding of "Being" is rejected, a return begins. Thus, dismissing symbol and allegory leads to the use of simile and simile-like structures, which work constitutively to reproject the first possibilities of the larger metaphysical structure that has been dismissed. The identification of the shift downward in figurative language describes only the first half of what is a continuous movement rather than a completed act. It is a movement in which we "come to learn what is unspoken."[40] Things are concomitant.

If he were presented with the movement in contemporary poetry from symbol and allegory to simile, mimicry, metonymy, and synecdoche, Heidegger would repeat what I have previously quoted him as saying in response to Sartre: "The reversal of a metaphysical phrase remains a metaphysical phrase." Or, in terms of the nonbeliever Bishop, her mostly like-minded friend Lowell, as well as others of her generation, the way we understand turning away from symbol, allegory, the tradition, and the presuppositions that accompany them is like the navigator's (or cartographer's) latest reference point, which is extremely important to his or her current position. The part of similitude that reveals unlikeness, therefore, is no more a turn *away* from something than it is *in reference to* it. As we conceive of it, the former proposition that a metaphysics is valid is not thrown away but retained, relationally, by its opposite, which is its constitutive likeness. Bishop's "The Gentleman of Shalott"—who takes "the indication / of a mirrored reflection" as an adequate if "economical design"—finds " 'Half is enough' " because it implies and likens the other half. Her "victory" in "The Fish" is Bishop's letting the fish go, her movement beyond the push-pull of the hook and line. And it is relational, an action that reflects one's movement from gathering to releasing. Or, more abstractly, it is the movement from utilitarian thought to poetic thought, one that parallels the way figurative language abjures causal reasoning, realism, and other prescriptive modes of thought in order to extend relations, rather than demonstrate what is already apprehended.

VII

Like misleading symptoms, lies present us with inaccessibility and unlikeness. What could be more inaccessible than the vacuum of a lie? At the same time, lies can name what is absent. In "Lying," Richard Wilbur begins with someone "at a dead party" who, amidst drinks, "the chuckling ice," and talk characterized by its "toxic zest," claims to have "spotted a grackle" when in fact he has not "of late." The details that the party is "dead" and that the speaker's remedy is to lie mirror each other. The action of lying matches the "dead" character of the party in a way that is central to what happens throughout the rest of the poem. Life and death, truth and falsity are at odds in the conversation of those attending the party, and what now is contingent will eventually become conclusive. The "faithful unto death" are matched against the "chill of severance," which results from Adam's role as namer and what happened to that role after the Fall, when "all things came / To take their scattering names." Telling a lie becomes the basis for a meditation on "the delicate web of human trust," in which Wilbur says "we invent nothing, merely bear witness" to what is "there before us" waiting "to be seen or not / By us, as by the bee's twelve thousand eyes, / According to our means and purposes." Here, seeing is re-cognition, a kind of likening, and it is constitutive. Eventually, the "web of human trust" is exemplified by "Roland, who to Charles his king / And to the dove that hatched the dove-tailed world / Was faithful unto death, and shamed the Devil." That is, Roland's faith, or vision, led to his action, which not only likened what was real but also, because it "shamed the Devil," refused what was not real.

Meanwhile, on the other side of things that exist, there remains what is nonexistent, the "nothing" of a lie. And related to this is "the arch-negator, sprung / From Hell to probe with intellectual sight." Along with the struggle of the opposing powers of darkness and light, something else is investigated in "Lying," our "intellectual sight," the modes of thought by which we grasp the truth or we lie. At our best, the tropes we use sustain our origins in "cognate splendor." Similitude overcomes "severance" and "scattering names." At less than our best, something else happens. The mind's analytical powers are equally capable of separating and dividing what finally ought to be left whole. In this poem Wilbur suggests that we always have the power to choose which direction to take but never have complete control over our means or the results of our choices.

Wilbur says, "Odd that a thing is most itself when likened," again suggesting not only that tropes are constitutive but also that *Being* is extensional rather than discrete. Describing the way Satan "drifted through the bar-like boles of Eden"—"pretending not to be," likening himself to nothing, and "moody with self-absorption"—Wilbur turns his attention to one form of likening. Here, it is seen in the way "the catbird's tail was made / To counterpoise, on the mock-orange spray, / Its light, up-tilted spine; or, lighter still," the way an onion's skin, "rocked by trifling currents, prints and prints / Its bright, ribbed shadow." To "counterpoise" is, here, to mirror and to liken, and thus to connect. Good and evil are counterpoised. Although we think of them as opposites, we also have to recognize that they are neighbors. "What," we are asked, "Finds pleasure in the cruellest simile? / It is something in us like the catbird's song," which comes "From neighbor bushes," is "harsh or sweet, and of its own accord, / Proclaims its many kin" and "is tributary / To the great lies [myths] told with the eyes half-shut / That have the truth in view." Negatives and positives are part of our fallen economy. Similitude is a major medium of exchange in that economy. Or, to return to the idea of neighbors, similitude is the point of comparison and thus common boundary shared by two things that are otherwise discrete. Boundaries join as much as they separate. And, as with myths, some lies tell a truth.

The progression of "Lying" can be traced in a kind of spiritual mapping summarized by the terms "toxic zest," "severance," "boredom," "strangeness," "nothing," "moody self-absorption," and "tormented"—and answered finally by actions such as Roland's and with "cognate splendor." In brief, the poem moves from a contemporary instance of acedia, "boredom," to a vision of heroic action informed by faith. Roland's story is, or can be, "cognate" to our own, his choice similar to those we make. The "dovetailed world," Wilbur tells us, remains a possibility, for those who are capable of faith and action. Or, if we choose, we can report false blackbirds and imitate "the deftest fraud," feeling "a chill of severance" as we hear "the shrug of unreal wings." But truth is not completely a matter of choice or intention. The mind itself proceeds by likening; thus it is not a completely independent agent. Instead, the mind is a combination of continuous synthesis and problematical circumstance. Here is "Mind":

> Mind in its purest play is like some bat
> That beats about in caverns all alone,
> Contriving by a kind of senseless wit
> Not to conclude against a wall of stone.
>
> It has no need to falter or explore;
> Darkly it knows what obstacles are there,
> And so may weave and flitter, dip and soar
> In perfect courses through the blackest air.
>
> And has this simile a like perfection?
> The mind is like a bat. Precisely. Save
> That in the very happiest intellection
> A graceful error may correct the cave.

"The mind" is neither "bat" nor "cave" but both. Or, perhaps more satisfactorily, it is the point of comparison or boundary along which "bat" and "cave" meet. In "Water Walker," Wilbur says, "Always alike and unlike." In "Mind," his simile sustains that principle. It compares (plays both similarities and differences) "mind" and "bat." The two are placed beside each other, but not too precisely so. They are not fused. Were they, the edge, or boundary, where the activity of thinking takes place would be dissolved, and the mind would retire into a kind of gridlock. Thinking requires a certain amount of slippage for new things to occur. It needs "A graceful error." Both simile and metaphor benefit from a certain amount of imprecision. The words "Save" and "graceful" suggest the mind's need for disruption made by something greater than the mind, for an intervention that keeps things moving. Simile is a paradigm for this kind of event. As Wilbur says in "Marginalia," "Things concentrate at the edges." Simile delineates edges and makes them dynamic.

An equally important thing the mind needs is relation, "bat" to "cave," or play to boundary. Edges always come between two things that, because of their proximity, are related. The "simile" in the poem doubles itself by doing what it says. It is not an equation but an occasion in which movement never ceases. Proximity is both spatial and temporal. It means both close and imminent. The "simile" in "Mind" brings the "bat" into the "cave" and lets it "weave and flitter, dip and soar," as thought must do in its attempt to unravel the "mind," while never being outside the mind. As Wilbur says in "Ceremony," which by its title announces a kind of occasion, "we are the woods we wander in." And later in the same poem, "What's lightly hid is deepest understood." All of these statements suggest a gap and slippage that accompany similitude. Or, as Wilbur says in "Grasse: The Olive Trees," "Even when seen from near, the olive shows / A hue of far away." This follows the statements that "Whatever moves moves with the slow complete / Gestures of statuary" and that "olives lie / Like clouds of doubt against the earth's array." The puns begin to multiply. Here "the earth's array" is both its order and its attire, what arranges and what covers over. And the "olives lie" in both a stationary sense, "against the earth's array," and in the sense of telling a lie. That is, they also arrange and cover over. Movement is characterized by its opposite, by "statu-ary," just as "lie" and "array" are made of internal opposites. Central to the whole balancing act is "doubt," what in itself is a neutral capacity of thought that causes the mind to ravel and unravel everything it encounters but that also always entails its op-posite, belief, and that entails some form of relation—self to other-ness or, in the Cartesian model, self to self. Our ability to doubt is part of the slippage we need to explore similitude. It is what the openness of the "cave" is to the "bat" moving through it.

The simile-like structures of thought continue. In "Fern-beds in Hampshire County," Wilbur says that "the whole wood conspires, by change of kind, / To break the purchase of the gathering mind." And, turning on a close relation to "kind," Wilbur uses "ken" to make a similar point in "In a Churchyard":

And the mind skips and dives beyond its ken,

Finding at once the wild supposed bloom,
Or in the imagined cave
Some pulse of crystal staving off the gloom
As covertly as phosphorus in a grave.

Yet if any contemporary poet has the ability to refuse the move-ment from symbol and allegory to simile-like structures it is Wil-bur. He appears to satisfy the opposing position, to sustain modes of correspondence and equivalence, finding himself frequently "called to praise" a higher order ("hills [that] are heavens"), as in "Praise in Summer" or, in the well-known "Love Calls Us to the Things of This World," to praise that moment when "The soul descends once more in bitter love / To accept the waking body." Wilbur has a dualist's vision in which readers might expect symbol and allegory to rule, but these tropes fail to dominate his poetry because for him *existence* is more verb than noun.

For Wilbur, we are verbal beings much more than we are nom-inative ones. His poems are active rather than static, suggesting that he would appreciate Heidegger's remark that "only the leap into the river tells us what is called swimming."[41] Heidegger says this as a preface to the question that lends its title to his book *What Is Called Thinking?* Wilbur's thinking is figurative, and his figures rarely stand still. His allegiance seems to be given to the proposition that God is immanent in the world, and because of this Wilbur's figurative thought is constitutive and requires its own portion of simile-like structures. Rather than read God deductively from heaven, Wilbur would like to reflect upward.

The source of Wilbur's energy is not a fixed point. Speaking of Noah's ability to "bear / To see the towns like coral under the keel, / And the fields so dismal deep," in "Still, Citizen Sparrow," Wilbur says: "Forgive the hero, you who would have died / Gladly with all you knew; he rode that tide / To Ararat; all men are Noah's sons." Viewed from a modern perspective, Noah is a somewhat Nietzschean character capable of "crossing-over," as Heidegger would say.[42] He is the figure for "a man who passes across," who serves as the bridge between "the lastman" and "the superman" in that he endures "the bedlam hours," builds his boat, and has "heart to make an end, keep nature new."[43] His are "bedlam hours" because what he does defies accepted understanding. Noah's actions do not parse, because they do not appeal to the practical judgment shared by his neighbors, those who "died / Gladly with all [they] knew."

Put slightly differently, in Wilbur's "For Dudley," "All that we do / Is touched with ocean, yet we remain / On the shore of what we know." Our "common sense" is "what we know," Heidegger would say, and it keeps us from thinking "through anything from its source." It is like a "fish" that has been "dragged on the dry sand," where "it can only wriggle, twitch, and die" because, when put "On the shore," it lacks "the depths and expanses of its waters." Heidegger's "image" for the "multiplicity of meanings" is the fish in water, which requires "the currents and quiet pools, warm and cold layers [that] are the element of its multiple mobility." Here, "element" is singular because meaning is not divided but exists in a liquid environment characterized by its continuous modification. The "currents," the "pools," and the "warm and cold" are all part of one thing. As Heidegger lists them, our first inclination is to read them as opposites, but that reading misses his point. The way we bridge beyond "the shore of what we know" is not by rehearsing what we can analyze or what we already understand (stand under). We move into new territories by similitude, through which we think new relations, which may incorporate things that oppose each other but which nevertheless are projections into the complex surroundings that Heidegger uses water to characterize.[44]

In "Walking to Sleep," Wilbur says that "what you project / Is what you will perceive." This sounds like intentionality as Husserl describes it, but Wilbur goes further, saying that "what you perceive / With any passion, be it love or terror, / May take on whims and powers of its own." Thus projection may obtain something akin to immanence, although prior to it Wilbur has urged stepping "off assuredly into the blank of [the] mind." What Wilbur applauds is seen clearly in "My Father Paints the Summer." During a cold and rainy July that for most people spoiled the summer, Wilbur's father chose otherwise:

> But up in his room by artificial light
> My father paints the summer, and his brush
> Tricks into sight
> The prosperous sleep, the girdling stir and clear steep hush
> Of a summer never seen,
> A granted green.

Summarizing, Wilbur says:

> Caught Summer is always an imagined time.
> Time gave it, yes, but time out of any mind.
> There must be prime
> In the heart to beget that season, to reach past rain and find
> Riding the palest days
> Its perfect blaze.

The painting is made "by artificial light," just as Wilbur's poems are made by poetic artifice, or Noah's boat was made by handicraft. But the words "granted" and "prime" are the keys to what Wilbur's father achieved with his painting, and, by implication, what Wilbur himself believes he can achieve with his poetry. The "granted green," the fecundity of "a summer never seen," is something the painter provides for those who have missed the season. It also is an agreed-upon green, as in, Let us simply agree the world *is* green and dismiss this temporary gray. Also the green is agreed upon in the way that works of art appeal for our assent.

Having gained our assent, the true weather—or, more accurately, the literal weather—does not matter. And, of course, *grant* means "give," "bestow," so what the father has done is to give to others, and his son especially it seems, what the summer could not provide. And this is a particularly powerful idea, because it not only counters one reality with another but also entails a measure of freedom, the exercise of a freedom that similitude makes possible.

In addition to these contemporary meanings for *grant* there are some obsolete ones—"acknowledge," "confess," "admit," "concede." Wilbur seems never to have forgotten the family tree for any word he uses. Here, older meanings are revived, and, when contrasted with the apparent accuracy of realism, or "common sense," of most contemporary poetry, those meanings make a further point, which is that poems do not argue to win but propose to find what nevertheless they can only acknowledge, confess, admit, concede. That is, to the degree that poetry is limited to realism, and the causal processes that support realism, it is not as free in its modes of thought as it might be. In "Walking to Sleep," Wilbur says that "what you project / Is what you will perceive." A world understood in terms of realism or some other system of thought becomes a projection itself, and a systematized projection can determine perception. The difference between discovery and redundancy is in how projection is handled, whether it repeats accepted perceptions or, through new figures for likening, torsions experience in order to uncover new objects.

The other key word in the passage quoted from "My Father Paints the Summer" is "prime," which has meanings that range from the anatomical to the abstract. The heart is a pump, and pumps need to be primed, filled. Thus, the heart must be full to "beget" a "season," or a child. Or, taking the word as a verb, for the poem ends with the word "blaze," "prime" connotes a powder charge. Because the poem is about painting, "prime" reminds us of the first layer of paint applied to a wall or canvas. And because a son is talking about his father, "prime" suggests coaching, or preparing someone, such as a son, ready for whatever the future holds. And the connotations go on—"to harvest," "to stimulate." And one archaic meaning that provides its own interesting harmonic—"to assume precedence."

Nominative meanings for "prime" are the initial daytime ca-

nonical hour, the first stage of something, spring, the most invigo-
rated stage of something, the foremost member of a group, a prime
number (which is not divisible by anything greater than *one* or
the number itself), a defensive move made in fencing, the initial or
tonic note on a scale, a symbol used to differentiate one character
from a related one. In some cases the nouns seem to contain the
verbs. For example, someone may be in his "prime" because he
has been primed, or the heart may be full and capable because it
has been primed. The most characteristic thing about Wilbur's poetry is the way that action winds up close to the permanence of a
name—the way the world's activity winds up reiterated rather than
lost.

Line for line, Wilbur is one of the most rewarding poets of the
twentieth century. Beneath the very real gracefulness that gives his
poetry the appearance of an achieved stasis and calm, however,
there is a world as turbulent as any seen during this century. References to World War II and the holocaust are frequent, if characteristically muted. If one reads Wilbur closely and lives with his
poems, one begins to sense that he possesses not only clarity of
mind and goodness but also (as he says of his subject in "John
Chrysostom") the "wildness to rejoice." And he does so with
words characterized by action—a diction that in its own way is a
kind of "wildness," in the sense that it is never quite domesticated
and that its meanings are never found quietly resting in one place.

Wilbur opens "An Event" by saying, "As if a cast of grain
leapt back into the hand," and we are off into a world of dynamic changes and reversals, in which the birds, to which the
"cast of grain" is compared, "fly" the speaker "still, and steal [his]
thoughts away." The words "cast," "fly," "still," and "steal" repeat the give-and-take that runs continuously throughout Wilbur's
poetry. But, as I hope my discussion of "Year's End" in chapter
three and the discussions of various poems here demonstrate, there
is always present in Wilbur's poetry a different but equally active
form of give-and-take, and that is the way his diction makes use
of secondary meanings, archaic meanings, and earlier contexts.
For Wilbur, language exists in a large building, or context, that
constantly produces echoes. These echoes give the dimensions of
that building or, to return to "Lying," are able to remind us of
a cocktail party, of Eden, and of Roland's heroic action, thus re-

flecting the dimensions of a temporally extensive context that is summarized here as "the garden where we" forgot "Out of what cognate splendor all things came / To take their scattering names."

VIII

One form of similitude that occupies John Hollander's attention is echo. Of course, the punishment Hera gave Echo was repetition. For the poet, echo entails not only hearing what already has been said and serving as the audience for another poet, but also repeating what was said. In part, this is any *contemporary* poet's plight of belatedness. But in Hollander's view echo is not a negative for poets so much as it is both a kind of litmus test (by which new poems meet the measures of their predecessors) and a source; besides, the *contemporary* does always get the last word, even if it is only a passing one. Viewed as an agent for intertextual readings, echo is not diminishment but, in its temporal way, is a constitutive agent for poetry. And recognizing this saves poets from the slavish pursuit of novelty, which itself becomes a kind of imitation. In his preface to *Vision and Resonance* (1975), Hollander describes his interest "in the idea of tradition and the way it operates in the poet's decisions about matters of form."[45] In *The Figure of Echo: A Mode of Allusion in Milton and After* (1981), he argues that "texts are haunted by echoes."[46] For poets, the literary past continually modifies the present tense of new poetry, as much as any other source of experience and understanding does; thus poets "deal with diachronic trope all the time."[47]

In his poems Hollander frequently refers to trope, echo, and text, alluding to these devices so as to hold them at arm's length and, in proper Cartesian manner, inspect his means for inspection. Hollander is fond of invoking the structures of his chromatic thought in order to tilt his figurative mirrors and deflect a little added area for himself. But before investigating the signed paths of echo in Hollander's poetry, we should consider the way echo itself operates as a trope.

Hollander calls the chapters of his *The Figure of Echo* "Echo Acoustical," "Echo Allegorical," "Echo Schematic," "Echo Meta-

phorical," and "Echo Metaleptic." None of these chapters, including "Echo Allegorical" and "Echo Schematic," treats echo as a
means for correspondence, or equivalence. Instead, echo is valued
for its power to modify things. One chapter will serve here, "Echo
Metaphorical," in which Hollander's discussion ranges from the
echo of Shelley made by Williams in "Spring and All," discussed
earlier, to complexly interwoven echoes made by Stevens, Tate,
and numerous other poets.

The point to be gained from "Echo Metaphorical" concerns
slippage. If echo is metaphorical, the metaphor is more a vehicle for similitude than it is one for equivalence. In the similitude of
echo there is the play of a continued sound, the lasting vibration,
which remains the trace of its original sound but which steadily
changes. Or, as Hollander says of the readings that echo leads him to
make, there are "regions of resonance."[48] There are mountains
and caves that return voices. Most interesting, there is "concavity,"
an earlier voice emanating from somewhere farther back in the
"cave."[49] In less figurative terms, Hollander says that "in the very
rhetoric of returning only *part* of an utterance, there is something of
trope always implicit" (italics mine). He goes on to acknowledge
debate over the ways metonymy and synecdoche handle "the representation of wholes by parts," adding that "competing views" on
this subject are not his concern.[50]

What I wish to extract from these comments is that, in addition
to the slippage created by echoes that work metaphorically, there
is another kind of slippage created when "wholes" are represented
by their "parts." Then a simile-like structure of likening informs
what happens. It is true that echo "represents or substitutes for allusion as allusion does for quotation."[51] But the use of echo does
not require that the poet return to the sometimes modernist appeal
to a higher structure of meaning read deductively. The salient point
here is the movement traced by Hollander's description itself. Equivalence comes most close to occurring with quotation, where it nevertheless fails to come about because the quotation is always heard in
contexts different from that of the original circumstance. Allusion is
still less precise a reproduction. And echo is the least precise, with
all its problematics—its ability to only "return fragments of speech"
and the fact that "serial echoes" become fainter as they continue.[52]
These limitations are attributed to echo, because it is an acoustical

phenomenon, but they have their figurative applications to literary echo.

Echo is important because of what is lacking. It begins with disjunction and exists over a gap. The constitutive role of echo resembles sonar. It identifies silent structures. It may revise the past by returning only fragments, but it makes the past proximate and thus modifies the context of the present. At the same time, fragments may be metonymic or synecdochic, especially because, once outside the cave, Platonic or otherwise, echo is directional. Working diachronically, the voice must be aimed properly in order to get a return. Because echo uncovers something that time has obscured, it contributes to situations even as it is the manifestation of disjunction and a generation's belatedness. Like simile, echo is the dynamic play of similarities and differences, but with echo these exist in an utterance made at two different times. The ideas provided by echo are similar because the words that return are identical; at the same time the ideas are different because the two contexts within which the words are understood, then and now, are different.

In *The Figure of Echo* Hollander describes the way Frost's "The Most of It" actually "recalls Thoreau's reinvestiture of Echo as the consort of Pan."[53] Then in his poem "To Elizabeth Bishop," which appears in *Harp Lake* (1988), Hollander twines Frost's buck with Bishop's moose. Having begun with his misreading of *moose* in French as "original" and later finding it to be "orignal," Hollander questions the meaning of his having found "a hidden, seeing 'I' / In *'orignal'* ":

> A kind of lie
>
> Against French verity? a vision
> Of lyric truth caught in collision
> Between two consonants? Misprision
>
> (As someone else has put it) of
> The letter, so that we may love
> The figure, flying high above?
>
> Perhaps the "I" was a decree:
> "In all Originality
> Where once God was, let ego be."

Or was it that I overheard
—Or thought I did—an antlered word
Of Frost's: not one about a bird

But in this case, about a male
Buck, crashing out once through frail
Underbrush to frame a tale

Of "counter-love, original
Response" (he thus meant echo, full
Of later sound, accountable

As much to what it makes of what
It's given, as to that it's not
The first voice, from the prior spot.)

But then, I must have been in doubt
As to what echoes are about:
If a buck answers to a shout

So a she-moose can make response
To echoing buck, for wisdom wants
Nothing called up just for the nonce.

So now, although I couldn't quite
Hope to put the whole matter right
I've burned the extra "i" for light.

A Bloomian "misprision" of "The letter" makes the figure possible all over again, but in a richer context, with the "resonance"
of previous uses (Thoreau's and Frost's) called back into presence in a sort of intellectual rhyming (for example, "doubt" and
"about"), of which the poem's rhyme scheme reminds us. The
play between what echo gives and what it cannot give—between
the way it is "accountable / As much to what it makes of what /
It's given, as to that it's not / The first voice, from the prior
spot"—is the way it becomes a source for meaning. This play
calls the context of "prior spot" into the present situation. Similar
yet different, one frame implicitly questions, or "doubt[s]," and
thus qualifies another. With several frames evoked at once, depth
of field is created, in which different frames inscribe one another
with their various shadows and shades of meaning.

It is helpful at this point again to recall Gadamer's idea of limits, such as those imposed on games, serving as the occasions for meaningful free play; thus restrictions (such as boundaries, time limits, and a certain number of players) make it possible for play to become meaning, momentarily for a player to become a hero. But by understanding echo as bringing two or more contexts, which provide limit and restraint, into proximity, Hollander's idea makes the structures of two or more games play against each other, rather than appealing to one structure so that play occurs only within it. As Hollander remarks in the opening poem of *Harp Lake,* "Kinneret," "Resemblance [trope, echo, a reexamined text] turns our language inside-out."

Companion poems follow "Kinneret": "From the Old City" and "From the Inner City." In both of these perspective is informed by and restricted to *from.* The understanding behind both poems is derived from different views of a city that is lived in in several ways at once. The city is composed of two Jerusalems. The first one, which is subject to "a high romance of / Resolution," war, is more like "a Djinn" that might "fling" everything "to Gehenna." But this city also is a place informed by modern science, as well as by ancient myth, where one senses the disturbing multiplicity of our origins:

The illimitable grains,
Idols themselves of golden
Specks gathered across worlds of
Darkness, from deserted stars.

The second city is more contemporary, a "metropolis" subject to the ironies of a war done in "six days' work, that . . . was / Good" but had to be abandoned, when the seventh day was due, to "the jackals of peace."

"From the Old City" states that "truth that was and / Is now and ever shall be" is "Figured, not builded of stone." As an echoed figure, "The wanderer . . . comes / Upon" such figures as "the rock and the sky," as well as "the past of sand" with "truth lying in spaces" that are "Too small for anything but / Trope," through which figuration enables the speaker to find things "Afresh." "From the Old City" presents the tradition embodied as a city with a "hollow Sepulchre, and / That allusive Rock from which / The Prophet was plucked skyward / And father Isaac was not." The city is "Mortared with / Dropped zealousness and muddied / Blood." Its "high domes" are "set / On cylinders and banded / With squinting eyes turned every / Which way—these have claimed the day"; the day is ruled by those who fail to read the figures before them. They are willing to "hold the tent, the robe or / Whatever it is of blue / Overhead." They "fly the flag / Of whatever the weather." And so goes the city's old pragmatism, denying likeness, the "dark commonality / Of rock and sky," a figure of sameness and obliteration that defies anthropomorphic time.

"From the Inner City," in contrast, provides swatches of a modern world that evades the "hollow Sepulchre" still informing the character of the "Old City." Instead, the "Inner City" is a world that matches subjectivity with technology:

> All this recent rubble,
> Too young to have been ruined
> So soon, before the laughing
> Series of sunlit ages
> Fills the vacancy of lots
> Of destruction with meaning.
> Then broken building-shells will
> Be overgrown with the green
> Of history; then lessons
> About burning will have long
> Been learnt, and long forgotten.

"From the Inner City" in part surveys a romantic city built on technology and lacking the test of an objectifying laughter. Here, "the metropolis" lies "Within, unhappier far / Beyond dilapidation." We see "Not the heart of the city / But its blasted fistula, / Hard by the river of cars." Speculating from an understanding "beyond the cars and roads / Of water, resting in a / State of grass," the speaker recalls something permanent. Neither quite in grace nor happy with America's romantic grass, the speaker returns to "the old / City that is the inward / Place of wisdom." It is not Auden's "City without Walls," a city lacking the limits necessary for meaning; it is a place *with* constitutive walls, that are subject neither to "enterprise" nor to "fire" but make possible "the place of thought," which

> May yet flourish in their midst.
> There, where stone brings forth figures
> And words arise from chimneys
> In the airy mornings, light
> Itself watches—not without
> Amazement—what it has wrought.

Stones work figuratively; "words" climb from "chimneys" in a metaphorical "light" that admires its own creation. So go trope, echo, and text in the play of similitude.

In "With Regards to an Old Notebook," a long prose meditation that constitutes "In Between," the second section of *In Time and Place* (1986), Hollander says: "We who keep our fingers dry can only employ those touching tropes of contact—looking, considering, picturing, describing, invoking—so that in the continually unruffled surface the figures of depth will remain strong." The second section is positioned *between* the sections "In Time" and "In Place." And, as a figure for past and present given place, the house to which the speaker returns in this piece provides its own resonant walls, resonant as any "Old City" or "Inner City." It is his "watchtower." And, "Being figurative, its walls are neither here nor there; its windows are the eyes of the space within it. Like all watchtowers," it "is also a beacon, sweeping the horizon, or the nearby trees, with the beam of awareness." The limits of the house provide a necessary "beam," because "Outdoors has no meaning until it has first been read through windows from within." Or, as Hollander says in "Green," in *Spectral Emanations: New and Selected Poems* (1978), "all significant shapes" represent "the attention that regards" them. Like echoes outside, they are directional. And "what lies behind the eye perceives itself in the depths and surfaces of the smallest spill of water on a black tabletop, or in the profoundest pool set in a cup of mountain."

The inner echoes, which are the echoing walls of the house that serves as a "watchtower" in "With Regards to an Old Notebook," complicate and round out the "attention" that looks outside and delimits meaning. The house, both literal and figurative, needs something more. One needs "To see the world through the spectacles of text" yet "Not to be blinded by frozen language to the light of what" that language "designates." And one needs not "to learn *of,* or *about,* as if that were to encounter" meaning, because "Experience itself is indeed a word." The echoing complexities of being between objects and times leads Hollander to quote Thoreau: "I know not whether I am sitting on the ruins of a wall, or the material which is to compose a new one." The principle of echo suggests that both propositions are true, just as "syntax, our headlong flight from subject through predicate, leaves its terrible traces of commitment," because "every word we write must look back warily—if not in outright fear—at the syntactic demands made on it by What Has Gone Before." In Hollander's hands, trope, echo, and text bring the past and the present together in order to torsion possibilities for the future.

In *Blue Wine and Other Poems* (1979), Hollander gives specific attention to similitude, here in the guise of "trope." Here is "Atropos":

> A Trope? There are no tropes where the thread is
> Cut there is no turning of strands, no twist
> Of the literal line of cord. And then
> Even the literal unravels: that
> Is when we most need the intertwining,
> The turning, the making taught, in order
> That the rope lie right. But neither the pure
> Straight nor the twisted straight are there any
> More: here are only frayed fibers, as if
> Gone back to an original dead grass.

This is as clear a statement of the constitutive powers of trope as anyone could desire. Just as "There are no tropes where the thread is / Cut"—that is, no figurations—there also is no "literal" world. The part of the world we commonly think of as plainly factual rather than imaginary, as denotative rather than connotative, or as strictly "literal" rather than wanderingly literary, needs its opposite in order to exist, in order not to become "dead grass." Thing and thought are mutually constitutive. The paradox is that "the pure / Straight" needs "the twisted straight."

Utilitarian thought generally formulates such dependency in the reverse order.

"First Echo" states that "These echoes were recorded here / In another time." A catalog of other times follows. Then the question is asked whether it is "truth they tell? / Or are they truthful to this place, / Merely, and very old?" This is the familiar question as to whether text or context has primacy, the place being the context. The implied answer is that both have primacy. No echoes occur without sound, and none occurs without the flat surface that limits that sound, bouncing it back into the play of our hearing.

"Last Echo" follows:

> Echo has the last word,
> But she loses the rest,
> Giving in to silence
> After too little time.
> And, after all, what is
> A last word, then? After
> All the truth has been told—
> No more than a cold rhyme.

The "Echo" that is the "last word" lacks its context and thus comes after "the truth," though we usually think of the "last word" as *being* the truth, or passing for it. It is "a cold rhyme" because it sounds the same but does not really resound. It lacks the resonance of its previous surroundings. The opposite proposition is also true: most echoes are not "Last" ones but parts of the bridge that extends over the gap between utterance and listening. The final echo is no longer a trope likening what was meant before to what is understood now. Instead, it is the end of likening, a place where signs end and roads break off into unrestricted spaces that, because of their openness, are incapable of rounding anything back for auditors who may come later.

"What Was Happening Late at Night" is a poem that turns through a series of concerns—all related to similitude:

> He was searching all the pages by lamplight for himself
> But there was no speculum in the soft text, giving him
> His difficult, raw images. The pages held pictures of

Desire for error mirrored in the errors of desire.
Hard surfaces that give most of the light and take of none
Are far less generous than the dark, in which we perceive
What we are now verily, what all shall come to for us.

The roses of music had blown and blasted; from the cool
Unwithering summer dark, echoes of silences dressed
Into neat blocks sailed through air, the window near his chair, then
Entered his ear and built there walls of deafness surrounding
The empty city he would become, walls of dead echo,
The fingers of the wind slept across the pines; only from
The book's pale chords wild powers in the lamplight plucked a song.

Some trope, some turn or return, is needed, "But there [is] no speculum in the soft text," where the "Desire for error" is "mirrored in the errors of desire." "Hard surfaces" work as reliable reflectors. They "give most of the light and take of none." But the "dark" is "generous," even as, paradoxically, it absorbs the light. Inaccessibility, the unlikeness of dark, turns out to be a source. Absorbing rather than reflecting, the dark is the turning away from light, telling us "what all shall come to." The oxymoron "echoes of silences" works similarly: difference becomes the basis for similitude, just as likeness can be the stage that precedes differentiation. We realize that "all shall come to" not only dark but also silence. The same is the case with "walls of deafness" and the "city" with "walls of dead echo." Sound and silence create each other. And what silence teaches is loss, anticipated and then answered, here by text. Or, as Hollander says, "The book's pale chords wild powers in the lamplight plucked a song." And as he says at the end of "Piano Interlude," *"Song is not born in rooms emptied by fulfillment, / But only in long, cold halls, hollow with desire."* One desires that which one knows about but does not possess; thus absence—or one's inaccessibility to the object—initiates the recovery of that object.

The title poem of *Blue Wine and Other Poems* describes the way a wine that is " 'a profound red in the cask' " actually " 'reads as blue / In the only kind of light that we have to see it by.' " The idea of *text* is never far from Hollander's thought. The wine's text (made possible by its bottle, or cask) is part of the issue here. The wine is a figure for its own change, and for metamorphoses in general. It is at once unique in its blueness, where one expects it to be red, and it is "the wine / Of generality," the catalyst for larger relations. Reminiscent of a Stevens meditation such as "The Man with the Blue Guitar," it simultaneously provokes thought and modifies it on levels of consideration that reach the reader serially but that, after they are understood, exist as one event:

> There are those who will maintain that all this is a matter
> Of water—hopeful water, joyful water got into
> Cool bottles at the right instant of light, the organized
> Reflective blue of its body remembered once the sky
> Was gone, an answer outlasting its forgotten question.

And there are other possible answers, "the water . . . collapsed in glass / Into a blue swoon" or "the water colored in a blush of consciousness . . . when it first found that it could see out of itself." These answers are given by those "who remain happier / With transformations than with immensities like blue wine."

The wine, we are told, "was blue: reality is so Californian." Humor balances things. Or "reality" is "changed" in the wine the way it is "changed" when played on Stevens's "blue guitar." Hollander continues:

> Perhaps this is all some kind of figure—the thing contained
> For the container—and it is these green bottles themselves,
> Resembling ordinary ones, that are remarkable
> In that their shapes create the new wines—.

The play of similitude here is the interplay in figurative thought between "the thing contained" and the "container"—bottle and wine, word and thing. Such play goes to the heart of "Blue Wine" and the collection as a whole, in which trope, echo, and text are the occasions for turning. The "transformations" we desire out of some previous intellection, as well as "immensities like" the imaginative "blue wine," force us into a world of likenesses which is tropic because it constantly turns, twists, and changes. It is a world in which wine is at once itself and something other, what we have known but not as we have known it, thus something more than we understood before we likened it to other things. We use "the common inks of / Day and night" to "color the water" or to make "parodies of the famous labels," "parodies" being forms of deflected echoes, as all of our different strategies for exploring similitude require that we pivot and, like Echo, produce something that is partly new and partly a repetition.

IX

In Robert Pack's poetry, similitude often presents itself within the boundaries created by families. Relation is explored through one's relations. As he does in "Waking to My Name," discussed in chapter three, Pack suggests that we are extensive beings who find our identities by turning toward and away from one another. We are autobiographical and biographical selves, both subjective and objective entities. As much as we are the discrete selves we feel ourselves to be when turning inward, we are our relations—those complex others—toward whom we also turn. This is a view that makes simile-like play a matter not only of likeness and difference but also of extension. The self is an aggregation of selves, and naming the self is therefore an interpretive process that reconciles our various turns.

Faces in a Single Tree (1984), a series of monologues, names people who are parts of a family tree that has grafted knowledge to life. The play between the ways these people regard themselves and the ways they see one another dramatizes the various levels of accessibility and inaccessibility they have to one another—their different levels of understanding and the sense of connection that they feel or sometimes miss. Insofar as they are accessible, they are clearly relational. As members of the same tree, their inaccessibility to one another is also relational, but, like misleading symptoms, relations are sometimes unreliable.

In "Trillium," a daughter is told by her mother about her fears that her husband may be taking walks in the woods in order to see another woman, that he may have blithely walked into a love triangle. The husband tells his wife about one flower in particular, that "Everything about the trillium comes / in threes" . . . "petals, sepals, stigmas; / the ovate leaves." And he follows her around the house discussing the flowers he has seen on his long, supposedly solitary, walks in the woods. Addressing her daughter, she asks:

> Why should the fact a flower
> has suggestive names—like wake-robin,
> stinking benjamin, wet-dog trillium—
> be so significant to him, unless
> there's a confession in those names, hiding
> even from himself?

Or from herself.

Earlier in the poem, the mother has said that she wonders if the father is "having an affair," for he is "hiking in the woods, / just as he used to do when" the daughter was "born." Then she asks, "Why can't he take you sometimes on his walks?" and immediately says, "I figured you'd get angry if I spoke / what's really on my mind." She has spoken what is on her mind on two levels at once: the husband/father's possible infidelity twice over—the parallels between his behavior now and when the daughter was born, suggesting the mother's unacknowledged sense of rivalry with her daughter or with any other woman who might have become fond of walks.

As the poem proceeds, it focuses on the relationship between the mother and the daughter, which increasingly seems to have Electra playing the harmonics of the situation. The mother says, "No daughter ever loved herself unless / she loved her mother also." Recalling "how the two of" them "would bake" the husband/father's "birthday cake," the mother skips ahead to something more direct: "What has he said to you? / I think you're keeping something to yourself." She says "to yourself" when we might expect her to say *from me*. This hinting of an oblique charge suggests the mother's fear that the daughter may be keeping something *for* herself. The mother adds, "When you were in my womb, you'd press your head / against the pulsing of my artery." Getting her daughter to sleep was a difficulty overcome only by the daughter's "exhaustion," and it left the mother "stand[ing] there looking, baffled by such sleep." She rounds off her rivalry with a genial bite:

Is there a chance he'll leave me for this *girl?*
What do you think? We haven't talked like this
in years—about the birds and flowers, no less!
We make a funny triangle: husband,
wife, and trillium—till trillium do
us part. Thanks for the smile—I need it now,
and promise not to ask what else you know
about my rival, wet-dog trillium.

Here "trillium" stands figuratively not only for some possible "funny triangle" between the father, the mother, and *another woman* but also for the consonance and dissonance in the relationship that has developed among the mother, father, and daughter— who, being the third person to join the family, made a triangle of it. The mother is confiding in her daughter, and the two of them are on the same side. Yet in her figures, the mother also manages to turn away from time to time. Her likenings deflect things, with the very language she intends to turn toward her problem. When she says, "I think your father's having an affair," she seems to be suggesting a fourth party, avoiding her question, apparently unacknowledged to herself or anyone, about the possibility of the daughter's role in the father's distraction.

The mother directs her likening of the problem away by her humor—"this *girl,*" her talking "about the birds and flowers, no less," and "till trillium do / us part." Or, literally, the mother proceeds with an accusation that applies to the father and another woman. Later we see that the mother cannot point away without leaving a trace back to what she is asserting, denying, and attacking by turns. Both following them and refusing the intentions behind her language, the mother speaks to the rivalry she feels with her daughter mainly by making her figures oblique. She sews her line of reasoning on the bias. What she fears on a psychological level but disguises on a literal level is too close a problem eliciting too violent an emotion to be viewed directly. It is allowed to the surface only insofar as it slips to one side. She says, "We haven't talked like this / in years," suggesting that the daughter has outgrown such conversations and also implying a degree of separation. Then the mother domesticates any tension in her statement with humor, after a pause, by saying what they really have been talking "about" is "the birds and flowers, no less!" rather than bees. "No less" all over again. Her headlong line of reasoning continues: "We make a funny triangle: husband, / wife, and trillium— till trillium do / us part." Which "us"? Is the daughter a candidate for becoming her mother's rival? Is the figure of "trillium" (itself suggestive of *tri,* three) a recognition of the silliness of her fears, a domesticating name for a threat from outside the family, or a roundabout way to Electra? Pivoting again, the mother says, "Thanks for the smile—I need it now." Then, turning the implications of her speech once more, she gives her "promise not to ask what else" the daughter "know[s] / about" the mother's "rival, wet-dog trillium."

Why should the daughter know anything if she is not implicated in the triangle—at least not implicated in the mother's imagination? The mother's theory for the father's motive, for his walks and possible infidelity, is that he is growing older; but the source for her worries could just as easily be her own anxieties about aging.

The autobiographical self, burdened with death and the knowledge of death, is placed among family relations, which work additively, sometimes absurdly or comically, to create a biographical self whose end is determined by his or her family's fate rather than individual fate. The mother's aging may be projected toward the father and daughter, for example. This is part of a mutually constitutive play of likeness and difference, here among family members. Suggested by the title *Faces in a Single Tree,* the controlling figure that likens, the family tree, also entails differentiation. It is the tree of life, as well as the tree of knowledge, or doubt. Either way, the tree remains relational. Here is another approach to thinking about similitude.

The guilt and anger felt by us toward someone close, such as a family member, who has died works psychologically in a way similar to figurative turns. As we grieve, we recollect the years we have spent with the person who has died. Often, a feature of our recollection is the things that have caused disappointments, which usually occur between people close for a long time. One turn, therefore, is that anger will accompany some memories of the person who has died, then guilt for feeling angry over something trivial compared to the absence that death imposes—guilt as though our anger wished the death because that is the bad outcome that currently attends the anger. This sort of evolution of emotions involves turning toward the source of grief, then away in anger, then away in another direction in guilt. But each turn is related to the others though, like a symptom, it may be either accurate or misleading.

In *Faces in a Single Tree,* the subjective voice that begins each poem is quickly taken beyond itself into a world of obligations, a world of objective meaning, as husband speaks to wife, wife to husband, father to son, daughter to mother, and so on. The series of poems defines the self by relation first, introspection second. Subjective experience is less important than the torsions individuals apply to one another as they move between the freedom and restraint implicit in their relationships. In "Trying to Separate," for example, a wife tells her husband that he relies on the harsh Vermont winter to give him a sense of himself; he needs to feel that "each day is hard." Her awareness of his need—and how it differs from hers—takes us beyond either person's isolated experience. In the companion poem, "Trying to Reconcile," the same or an equivalent husband says, "choose something or we're all just whirling stars, / just snow the blind wind heaps upon the snow." This is the poem's conclusion. Previously, the husband has said to his wife, during their talk about having a baby, that he wants "a child to free something in [him] more generous than sex." The obverse to the self's isolation is choosing to build something that reaches beyond one's sense of personal emptiness. The expected child will present itself as a physical fact, perhaps in some ways as taxing as the Vermont winter. Ultimately, its birth will define those who feel they must attend to it. Separate as their conversation shows them to be, they will be named by the relation they recognize and accept.

The fusion of antinomies is, in Pack's view, an important part of the way similitude works among family members. With Pack, sometimes antinomies represent the need for trust set against distrust, but more generally they are part of the way Pack sees order set against disorder. There is always the opportunity for choice. Perhaps this is seen most clearly in "Inheritance," in which a father responds to his son's indebtedness to him by saying, "sons can't pay their fathers back / unless they give the same love to their sons":

> Some day you'll feel your own life flowing in
> your son, and then your debt will be redeemed.
> One cool October afternoon, when he
> is splitting wood with you, and you
> are resting on a stump beside the sumac
> blazing in the last warmth of the sun,
> he'll take his T-shirt off, and as the axe
> descends, you'll watch his shoulder muscles flex
> and then release beneath his flawless skin.
> A waterfall, you'll flow out of yourself.

Pack's treatment of the father-son relationship here is a refreshing departure from the Oedipal paradigm of antagonism—though regarded either way, whether a son turns toward his father or turns on him, relation is the governing principle. When the son wishes to borrow money, the father explains—alluding to Abraham, and thus indirectly to Isaac—that they are beyond money, which is a medium for power used to bridge a gap wider than familial ties. Because the relation is so close, a son's debt can never be repaid, only "redeemed." The father "flows" outside himself by desiring for his son what the son most desires.

Another means by which Pack explores similitude is through humor, which he uses to modify perspective on a subject. Pack knows that laughter is judgmental. We not only agree on a joke's closure by laughing at the end, we also agree in more complex ways—about incongruity and the means for resolution. Humor is based on incongruity, and laughter is one means for resolving what is incongruous in our experience. Laughter is another form of the play between likeness and difference. A symptom of disjunction, laughter is the other side of our desire for relation. But unlike symptoms, which we expect to point to a problem, laughter seems to correct or modify the problems it identifies, at least temporarily.

Clayfeld Rejoices, Clayfeld Laments (1987) consists of another sequence of poems, this time devoted to a partly Adamic, partly picaresque character tellingly named Clayfeld, who is equipped with compulsions and enthusiasms, such as his baseball cap, women whose names begin with *M,* a microscope, his duck Ishmael, playing the role of Mephistopheles in *Faust,* and bad puns. Clayfeld teeters and rollicks along between rising and declining fortunes, making points about all of his relations as he proceeds.

In "Clayfeld's Daughter Reveals Her Plans" we see first the turning away of relation when Clayfeld's daughter tells him she is marrying a son of the landed gentry of Maryland. She has brought him a present, a hunting horn that he is to use to start the hunt planned for " 'Two days before the wedding.' " Later, using this horn, he will turn again, but his first response is negative.

> ". . . George Washington loved fox hunting,
> and Thomas Jefferson, and . . ." "Fox hunting!"
>   flushed Clayfeld bellowed out,
> "a fucking fox hunt thought up by some sterile,
>   Syphilitic, lisping English earl
> to titillate himself, and you want me
>   parading on their lawn
> in Mr. Mincing Blueblood's scarlet britches
>   and my yarmulke—
> or maybe I should wear my baseball cap?—
>   tooting my brains away?"

So goes the play occasioned by familial ties and boundaries. The marriage of his daughter will to some degree liken Clayfeld to his in-laws, but, true to character, he will continue to turn and oscillate between competing forces—his daughter's happiness versus the world of the fox hunt, or, more peacefully, his "yarmulke" versus his "baseball cap." Although Clayfeld enjoys a generous comic range, many of the encounters that relation entails are anything but funny.

"Replacing the Elegy" ends with Clayfeld's ruminations on one of his loves, Marina, and her account of when she was a little girl and her mother left her on a rock beside a lake at night, swimming out in order to commit suicide while her daughter waited. "Clayfeld imagines that / her mother heard the murmuring waves, / like wordless lips / as if *her* mother's voice still summoned her." Later, Marina's father tells her they " 'have to go home now,' " and,

still later, after the mother is gone, Clayfeld imagines the child being served breakfast by her father:

> And now Clayfeld can hear Marina's father ask
>   at breakfast in the hazy light,
> "Do you want raisins, peaches, blueberries?"
>   Among the windless leaves,
> Still out of sight, an oriole begins to sing,
>   and she tells Clayfeld, "Yes,"
> that she remembers she replied, "I'd like
>   a little bowl of everything."

Marina's mother listens to *her* mother; Marina recalls her mother's
choice to die, as well as her father's taking care of her; she has
Clayfeld to understand her. And Clayfeld becomes, in part, a com-
posite of all these people, regarding them from various angles of relation.

In "Clayfeld's Anniversary Song" the play of likeness and difference operates on another scale—our wish to anthropomorphize
everything, turning the world to our own purposes, when in the
evolutionary long run the world's relation to us appears to be turned
away from us and our concerns. Thus we liken our concerns to those
of God and seek to see the world we inhabit as being an extension of
human values. Viewed this way, time should produce anniversaries
that celebrate our presence, rather than evolutionary change that entails our disappearance. Our recognition of the incongruity between
human finitude and the infinite is a source of despair in the Kierkegaardian scheme of things, but the Darwinian version explored here
answers despair with comic objectification. The poem begins with an
epigraph that quotes the remark of the biologist J.B.S. Haldane that
Creation shows God's " 'inordinate fondness for beetles.' " Pack
continues:

> There's no accounting for
> one's taste in love, my dear, even with God.
>   Some 85 percent
> of all animal species comprise insects,
>   with an inscrutable

preponderance of beetles! Although they seem
   grotesque to you and me
(stag males can kill with their huge mandibles
   or seize their choiceless mates)
yet there they are, Nature's elect display,
   with such variety
embellishing a single theme great Bach's
   imagination pales
by comparison. Having invaded
   on water, land, and air,
adorers of decay, some woo their mates
   by rubbing their own wings
to rough out strains of ragged melody,
   while some display their fire
(protected by an inner layer of cells
   so they won't burn themselves)
delighting in each other with abandon
   we can't emulate.
A quibble in the cosmic scheme of things,
   not doubt: Nature is not
concerned with individuals, even
   species are cast away—
tonnage of dinosaurs with just a little
   climate shift. Yet, life alone
is what God seems to care about—only
   ongoing life, trying
new forms for His vast, slapdash enterprise
   of changing things. Against
such precedent divine, what arrogance
   is human constancy—
rebellion in the most unnatural
   and prideful way of love
seeking to preserve the past. No wonder
   we're appalled by death,
ashamed of our own sweat, and endlessly
   examining ourselves.
What parents ever wished their child would be
   an evolutionary

breakthrough, rendering us obsolete?
　　The quintessential prayer
that dwells in every human heart repeats:
　　O Lord, keep things the same;
let me be me again in paradise,
　　reading in my old chair
or strolling through a grove of evergreens.
　　I fear that we'll be viewed
by Him as undeserving of the life
　　we've got, and punished, yet
no differently than other creatures are—
　　we'll be forgotten too,
beetles and all. Who knows—perhaps someday
　　He'll tire: "Enough!" He'll cry,
and start a list of everything He's done.
　　And when He gets way back
to counting us, and pictures you again,
　　just as I see you now—
watering the wilted fuchsia hanging
　　beside the limestone wall,
plucking the dead leaves from the zinnias—
　　He'll think: "It's not their fault
they measured time in anniversaries
　　as if their need for meaning
made me manifest in *their* intent;
　　I burdened them with an
excessive will to live. But by my beard,
　　my beetles were magnificent!"

The poem concludes with the locutionary ball on God's side of
the net, as he takes his own turn at likening and differentiating.
What we are as a species remains in his purview, but we are recalled as secondary or, worse, to some rather deflating company—
beetles. A problem of similitude exists between God and humanity. If God is so fond of the varieties of his beetles, just how
much credence can we put in the idea that we are made in his
image, especially when God's response to our desire for "anniversaries" is to say, "as if their need for meaning / made me
manifest in *their* intent"? If we were made in his likeness, would

he carry on at such length about "Some 85 percent / of all animal species," as well as the multiple images displayed by beetles, and turn us such a deflating regard? Apparently, the "grotesque" appearance of beetles is "inscrutable" only from our perspective. We would like to view beetles as misleading symptoms, rather than God's ideal inventions, or "Nature's elect display." But they are seen here, in their "variety," as being just as relational to any first cause or prime mover as we are—in fact more so, because they possess a power of variation and adaptation that we, in the dearness of ourselves, seem to lack, or do not want. Their capacity for variation indicates that they are close to our origins in ways we do not like to accept. The idea that we are made in God's image is made comic by the beetles' "ragged melody" and "fire." Anthropomorphism has been turned into the proposition that we are made not as "individuals" but in God's "vast slapdash enterprise / of changing things," a mode in which beetles have proven themselves not only accomplished but also superior. The humorous articulation of a major source of despair for human beings objectifies and deflects it, for a while. Our laughter makes us feel we are outside the contradiction that makes us laugh.

"Clayfeld's Anniversary Song" is a poem that addresses what probably remains the primary basis for skepticism among contemporary poets. Setting aside for a moment what at least in terms of scale are the unprecedented horrors of the twentieth century, we plead to "keep things the same; / let me be me again." But our understanding of time and process leads us to see ourselves as fairly early instances in "everything [God's] done." At the end of creation, when he gets around to recounting all he did, he will come to us only when he "gets way back."

Before It Vanishes (1989) is a sequence of poems written in response to the physicist Heinz R. Pagels. Quoting from Pagels's *Perfect Symmetry* and *The Cosmic Code* prior to each poem, the collection has the form of a dialogue in which Pagels presents a physicist's descriptions of the physical world and Pack turns those descriptions into figures for human concerns. The detached and bemused attitude ascribed to God in "Clayfeld's Anniversary Song," a central poem that originally helped get the Clayfeld sequence under way, continues in this collection, but this time with what formerly was God's long view located in physicists' models. As Pagels is quoted as saying at the beginning of "Proton Decay," "We will have lots of time to explore the universe before it vanishes." Pack adds:

> death in our minds
>
> outlives our life, it's part of us,
> it's always what our wakeful searching finds,
>
> and every flowered star we love
> is brief as azure nightfall on this hill,
> brief as companionable breath that lengthens into words
> and then goes still.

With Pagels, accuracy of description is the main concern, whereas with Pack, though accepting of what Pagels tells him, the human scale of significance is a constant countertheme—one that in "Place" urges him to "laugh out loud" on learning there is "no special place" in the universe "because / just being . . . there alive with time to pause / and words upon [his] tongue" allows him "to fabricate that pause as such / and thus possess [his] pausing self." His "privilege" is "invented freedom from fixed circumstance / through laughing words, through music / patterned beyond randomness and chance."

Pagels's description of the physical world is so important for Pack because he knows that we grasp things by similitude. The "Big Bang" followed by "entropy increase" are newly usable figures for our old myths of Creation and the Fall into time. They enable us to think figuratively about human structures without the hierarchies of tradition and traditional faiths. They let Pack liken rather than equate, bestow order rather than deduce it from above. Where figures are concerned, both physicists and humanists are equally larcenous. Here, figures enable Pack and Pagels to try their hands at mythography. As Pack says in "Neanderthal Poem Ah Number One," "Words are a lake / in which we look, Professor Pagels, partner, at / ourselves, reflecting what we make." What Pack's figures, and his words for figures, allow him is "difference from identity," his version of the play of similitude in order to explore relation—sometimes with humor. In their "indeterminacy," "electrons" are "like" the variables of a "wife" first present then retained in memory. When she is present, is she an *"observer-*

tunnel by tunnel, building related arteries. Language is our richest resource. The poets whose gifts with language have been the greatest have been the ones who have been not only the most innovative but also the most successful. But, if not lost completely in a mole-like obscurity, they have mostly lived very quietly, while the census takers have surveyed experimentation, revolution, whatever was new. But also, by the same definition, whatever grows old.

The more newsworthy but ultimately less successful responses to modernism made by postwar poets were good examples of Harold Bloom's Oedipal paradigm, which places poets in a position relative to the tradition of either putting up or shutting up. Poets who wrote emaciated poems, for example, saw themselves as working at a far remove from the New Critics and modernism, but instead of enjoying real freedom and maintaining a real distance, they repeated what they sought to displace. The syntactical disruption created by their foreshortened lines was a smaller version of the hallmark virtues of the New Criticism. Disruption turned out to be a mechanical substitution for irony, paradox, and ambiguity.

A more successful response to what for some poets was the modernist hangover was poetry that employed speech or song or both. Poems that speak and poems that sing can be differentiated along the borders between realistic detail, which speech can achieve, and lyrical projection, to which song aspires. Another way to distinguish between the intentions that produce these two very different poetic utterances is to consider the question asked by Martin Heidegger's essay "What Are Poets For?" (*Poetry, Language, Thought*), in which he separates "the will to power," which employs utilitarian language and settles for the probabilities of a realistic world of achievable ends, from "the will as venture," which uses poetic language to occasion new possibilities of relation.

Provided one is not too put off by the implications of Heidegger's teleological title, which seems to imply that poets do not always exist for human purposes, the question of "wholeness" may be thought of in terms of "the will as venture," of which melody is a good example, because it is an occasion for a self-ablative will to resolve, absolve, and dissolve itself. But why the ablative's sense of separation from source? Behind poems that sing there is the desire for a kind of "wholeness" in the relation between the physical world and a metaphysical one, or a phenomenal world and a transcendent one. Desire is barometric. We desire what is absent but what we nevertheless somehow know. What poets lack but desire they try to make—in this case, sing what they miss.

In contrast to the projection of wholeness made by poems that sing, poems that speak acknowledge the steady presence of skepticism, which appears as a kind of realism achieved through plain diction, the enumeration of detail, the avoidance of lyricism. Poems that speak operate by an economy of minimal implication. The self that feels drawn into question turns that question on his or her surroundings, enumerating the particulars of a situation in order to question it in return. But neither speech nor song need stand alone. Often they function side by side in the same poem, registering changes in attitude toward the poem's subject. Taken together, both types of poetry are related to postwar skepticism, which led to the split between poems that liken and poems that use symbol and allegory for correspondence.

Howard Nemerov uses as many different tropes as any contemporary poet, and often he does so to explore the discrepancy he finds between today's world and an earlier "symboled" one. Nemerov also employs what in his hands is a unique kind of trope, mimicry. One way he matches and mimics is through humor. He also mimics, mirrors, and deflects through descriptive meditative passages, in which he shields himself from what he fears by reflecting it back on itself. Thus, in "View from an Attic Window," Nemerov tells us he "cried . . . because [he] had to die." But by the time this is said, he has extricated himself from what initially was a direct and terrifying realization. The articulation of his poem holds a more primitive realization at arm's length and turns it away. It deflects what was seen and allows us to see something no longer paired with us and threatening directly but rounded in its implications, as if we were safe, which allows us to study what nevertheless is still a threatening situation.

The work of poets discussed in chapter five provides a number of accomplished examples of the way, in the absence of a metaphysics that would validate symbol and allegory, the less extensional tropes have worked constitutively in contemporary poetry. Justice's remark in "The Sunset Maker" is *"As if . . .* but everything there is is that." This is a succinct statement of the central

strain in our best contemporary poetry. The emphasis has shifted
to likening in place of equating because in a process-minded era,
one in which Justice tells us "The clocks are sorry, the clocks are
very sad," it is easier to believe in similarities that are not dis-
proved by slippage or a certain amount of imprecision than it is
to believe in the more precise concept of symbol and correspondence, a concept in which the clocks are unbelievably precise and
in which one can imagine the clocks being absolutely correct and
therefore incapable of sorrow. Instead, time is localized, made
personal. In the poem from which the latter quotation is taken,
"Psalm and Lament," Justice ends by saying: "Sometimes a sad
moon comes and waters the roof tiles. / But the years are gone.
There are no more years." Time is understood in terms of grief
and nostalgia. There is no larger structure, insofar as this poem
is concerned, within which to understand time some other way.
We experience it as a

> long desolation of flower-bordered sidewalks
>
> That runs to the corner, turns, and goes on,
> That disappears and goes on
>
> Into the black oblivion of a neighborhood and a world
> Without billboards or yesterdays.

Viewed skeptically, our experience of time is always discrete.
There are no "yesterdays" because there is no history, no narrative
to set things in order, to relate one event to another. The view
toward time held by "Psalm and Lament" is first of all an expression of grief. After that it is an articulation of skepticism. The understanding Justice offers is a familiar one. For Justice, as for so many
of his contemporaries, doubt serves as a condition for thought.

Justice says in "Nostalgia of the Lakefronts" that "It rains perhaps on the other side of the heart." The "lakefront disappears /
Into" a few "stubborn verses . . . Or a few gifted sketches." The
rain brings back a concatenation of earlier scenes: "Nostalgia
comes with the smell of rain, you know." And "you know" it
severally—as an experience you have with rain, as what you
"know" from the past that rain recalls for you, and "you know"
in the sense that you are being told. Those points at which the

emotional tenor of Justice's sense of time crosses with his skepticism reveal what is not only new but also good about contemporary poetry. The new good thing that Justice and other contemporary poets have done is to articulate what they lack, which in a way is nothing new at all. Lacking the arrangements of logic, faith, metaphysics, and tradition as reliable bases for judging experience, Justice's generation has characterized itself by making guarded assessments of experience. But the strongest poetry that this generation has produced has not precluded the possibility of more finished arrangements. Possibility is the other side of doubt. Holding what is lacked in question, in play, keeps the thing missed from being lost. The tropes that liken are the means for exploring similitude. They are also the preliminaries for greater certainty, maybe, on occasion, even consensus, however problematical that kind of certainty remains, and probably ought to remain.

Notes

CHAPTER 1

1. Randall Jarrell, *Poetry and the Age* (New York: Octagon Books, 1972), p. 216. Previously published: Randall Jarrell, *Poetry and the Age* (New York: Alfred A. Knopf, 1953), p. 216. Also available: Randall Jarrell, "From the Kingdom of Necessity," in *Robert Lowell: A Collection of Critical Essays*, ed. Thomas Parkinson (Englewood Cliffs, N.J.: Prentice-Hall, 1968), p. 45.

2. Etienne Gilson, *The Mystical Theology of Saint Bernard* (New York: Sheed & Ward, 1940), p. 208.

3. C. S. Lewis, *The Allegory of Love: A Study in Medieval Tradition* (New York: Oxford University Press, 1958), p. 46.

4. Gilson, *The Mystical Theology of Saint Bernard*, p. 212.

5. Ibid., p. 214.

6. Friedrich Nietzsche, *The Birth of Tragedy and The Case of Wagner*, trans. Walter Kaufmann (New York: Random House, 1967), p. 106.

7. Lewis, *The Allegory of Love*, pp. 44–48.

8. Julian N. Hartt, *The Lost Image of Man* (Baton Rouge: Louisiana State University Press, 1963), p. 10. See also Julian N. Hartt, "The Theological Situation after Fifty Years," *Yale Review* 51 (Autumn 1961): 75ff.

9. Hartt, *The Lost Image of Man*, p. 17.

10. Marjorie G. Perloff, *The Poetic Art of Robert Lowell* (Ithaca, N.Y.: Cornell University Press, 1973), p. 164.

11. Robert Lowell, *Robert Lowell: Collected Prose* (New York: Farrar, Straus & Giroux, 1987), p. 30.

12. "Where the Rainbow Ends" and "Waking Early Sunday Morning" are published in *Robert Lowell: Selected Poems* (New York: Farrar, Straus & Giroux, 1977). Hereafter I shall annotate poems only if they are not readily available in anthologies or individual collections.

13. Vereen M. Bell, *Robert Lowell: Nihilist as Hero* (Cambridge: Harvard University Press, 1983), p. 4.

14. Nietzsche, *The Birth of Tragedy,* p. 136.

15. Ian Hamilton, *Robert Lowell: A Biography* (New York: Random House, 1982), p. 96.

16. Steven Gould Axelrod, *Robert Lowell: Life and Art* (Princeton, N.J.: Princeton University Press, 1978), p. 81.

17. Hamilton, *Robert Lowell,* pp. 138ff.

18. Jean Stafford, "A Country Love Story," in *The Collected Stories of Jean Stafford* (New York: Farrar, Straus & Giroux, 1969), pp. 133–45. See also Jean Stafford, "An Influx of Poets," *The New Yorker,* 6 November 1978, 43–60.

19. Flannery O'Connor, *The Habit of Being: Letters of Flannery O'Connor,* ed. Sally Fitzgerald (New York: Farrar, Straus & Giroux, 1978), p. 71.

20. Immanuel Kant, *Critique of Pure Reason,* trans. Norman Kemp Smith (New York: St. Martin's Press, 1965), p. 225.

21. Dudley Fitts, "A Review of *The Mills of the Kavanaughs,*" *Furioso* 6 (1951): 77.

22. Irvin Ehrenpreis, "The Age of Lowell," in *Robert Lowell: A Collection of Critical Essays,* ed. Thomas Parkinson (Englewood Cliffs, N.J.: Prentice-Hall, 1968), p. 89.

23. T. S. Eliot, "Ulysses, Order and Myth," in *Selected Prose of T. S. Eliot,* ed. Frank Kermode (New York: Farrar, Straus & Giroux/ Harcourt Brace Jovanovich, 1975), pp. 177–78.

24. Jacques Maritain, *Art and Scholasticism,* trans. J. F. Scanlan (Freeport, N.Y.: Books for Libraries Press, 1930), p. 71.

25. Helen Vendler, *Part of Nature, Part of Us: Modern American Poets* (Cambridge: Harvard University Press, 1980), p. 157.

26. Edmund Husserl, *Cartesian Meditations: An Introduction to Phenomenology,* trans. Dorion Cairns (The Hague: Martinus Nijhoff, 1973), p. 2.

27. Ibid., pp. 18–21.

28. Ibid., p. 22.

29. Ibid., p. 107.

30. Ibid., pp. 107–8.

31. Stephen Yenser, *Circle to Circle: The Poetry of Robert Lowell* (Berkeley and Los Angeles: University of California Press, 1975), p. 87.

32. O'Connor, *The Habit of Being,* p. 152.

33. Husserl, *Cartesian Meditations,* pp. 114–15.

34. Martin Heidegger, *Poetry, Language, Thought* (New York: Harper & Row, 1971), p. 91.

35. Nietzsche, *The Birth of Tragedy,* p. 136.

CHAPTER 2

1. Various points have been made concerning the differences between modern and contemporary poetry. The most useful discussions of the changes between modern poetry and postmodern or late-modern poetry are in James E. B. Breslin's *From Modern to Contemporary: American Poetry, 1945–1965* (Chicago: University of Chicago Press, 1984), Paul Breslin's "How to Read the New Contemporary Poem," *American Scholar* 47 (Summer 1978): 357–70, Christopher Clausen's *Place of Poetry* (Lexington: University Press of Kentucky, 1981), Robert von Hallberg's *American Poetry and Culture, 1945–1980* (Cambridge: Harvard University Press, 1985), Robert Pinsky's *Situation of Poetry* (Princeton: Princeton University Press, 1976), and Alan Williamson's *Introspection and Contemporary Poetry* (Cambridge: Harvard University Press, 1984).

2. I first made this argument in "Emaciated Poetry" (*Sewanee Review* 93 [Winter 1985]: 78–94), the basis for this chapter, in order to demonstrate the arbitrariness of what have become certain free-verse conventions, as well as to demonstrate the way those conventions generally obscure the rhythms that continue to characterize American language. Dana Gioia has made interesting use of this line of reasoning in "Notes on the New Formalism," *Hudson Review* 40 (Autumn 1987): 395–408.

3. Yvor Winters, "Poets and Others," in *Yvor Winters: Uncollected Essays and Reviews,* ed. Francis Murphy (Chicago: Swallow Press, 1973), p. 113.

4. Lionel Johnson, "A Note upon the Practice and Theory of Verse at the Present Time Obtaining in France," *Century Guild Hobby Horse* 6 (1891): 65.

5. T. S. Eliot, "Ulysses, Order and Myth," in *Selected Prose of T. S. Eliot,* ed. Frank Kermode (New York: Farrar, Straus & Giroux/ Harcourt Brace Jovanovich, 1975), pp. 177–78.

6. C. Hugh Holman and William Harmon, eds., *A Handbook to Literature* (New York: Macmillan, 1986), p. 530.

7. Pinsky, *The Situation of Poetry,* pp. 6, 134, 175.

CHAPTER 3

1. Martin Heidegger, *On the Way to Language* (New York: Harper & Row, 1971), pp. 89–90.
2. Julian N. Hartt, *The Lost Image of Man* (Baton Rouge: Louisiana State University Press, 1963), p. 10.
3. Heidegger, *On the Way to Language*, p. 107.
4. Ibid., p. 135.
5. Martin Heidegger, *Poetry, Language, Thought* (New York: Harper & Row, 1971). Quotations from Heidegger in this part of the discussion are taken from chapter three, "What Are Poets For?"
6. Carl G. Vaught, *The Quest for Wholeness* (Albany: State University of New York Press, 1982), p. 9.
7. Hans-Georg Gadamer, *Truth and Method* (New York: Seabury Press, 1975), p. 48.
8. Heidegger, *Poetry, Language, Thought*, pp. 99–103.
9. See A. Poulin, Jr., "Contemporary American Poetry: The Radical Tradition," in *Contemporary American Poetry* (Boston: Houghton Mifflin, 1985), pp. 685–703. For a thorough discussion of personalism, see Alan Williamson, *Introspection and Contemporary Poetry* (Cambridge: Harvard University Press, 1984). For an understanding of "culture poets," as opposed to those poets interested in personalism, see Robert von Hallberg, *American Poetry and Culture* (Cambridge: Harvard University Press, 1985), especially chapter one and the conclusion.
10. Eugen Kogon, *The Theory and Practice of Hell* (New York: Farrar, Straus, 1950), p. 97.
11. Heidegger, *Poetry, Language, Thought*, pp. 99–107.
12. Ibid., p. 104.

CHAPTER 4

1. James E. B. Breslin, *From Modern to Contemporary: American Poetry, 1945–1965* (Chicago: University of Chicago Press, 1984), pp. 2, 14, 257, 259.
2. Donald E. Stanford, *Revolution and Convention in Modern Poetry: Studies in Ezra Pound, T. S. Eliot, Wallace Stevens, Edwin Arlington Robinson, and Yvor Winters* (Newark: University of Delaware Press, 1983), p. 14. Here and elsewhere, Stanford makes the point that the first area of expertise for an English-speaking poet is the En-

glish language. In his criticism of Pound, Stanford demonstrates the limited usefulness of foreign borrowings, especially when fundamental resources from our own language are overlooked. This sort of emphasis given to the English/American tradition of poetry has characterized the attitudes of a group of younger poets, most of whom are in their thirties and forties, who have demonstrated a keen interest in questions about the way form delimits meaning. At the time of this writing, two journals have forthcoming issues devoted to the new formalism and to certain neoclassical principles: one is an issue of *Crosscurrents,* edited by Dick Allen, which is devoted to the new formalists; the other is *Hellas,* a new journal edited by Gerry Harnett and billed as a "journal of radical neo-classicism." These poets are not that opposed to foreign borrowings, but they match Stanford's interest in the English/American tradition.

3. Howard Nemerov, *Figures of Thought: Speculations on the Meaning of Poetry and Other Essays* (Boston: David R. Godine, 1978), pp. 57–70.

4. Hannah Arendt, *The Human Condition* (Chicago: University of Chicago Press, 1958), p. 4.

5. Nemerov, *Figures of Thought,* pp. 59–60.

6. Arendt, *The Human Condition,* p. 3.

7. Nemerov, *Figures of Thought,* pp. 68–69.

8. Neal Bowers and Charles L. P. Silet, "An Interview with Howard Nemerov," *Massachusetts Review* 22 (Spring 1981): 56.

9. Nemerov, *Figures of Thought,* p. 62.

10. Howard Nemerov, *New and Selected Essays* (Carbondale: Southern Illinois Press, 1985), p. 4.

11. Ibid., p. 14.

12. Ibid., pp. 4–5.

13. Bowers and Silet, "An Interview with Howard Nemerov," p. 44.

14. Harry Torczyner, *Magritte: Ideas and Images,* trans. Richard Miller (New York: Harry N. Abrams, 1979), p. 102.

15. Nemerov, *Figures of Thought,* p. 18.

16. M. H. Abrams, *The Mirror and the Lamp: Romantic Theory and the Critical Tradition* (Oxford: Oxford University Press, 1953), p. 31.

17. Nemerov, *New and Selected Essays,* p. 9.

18. Paul de Man, "The Rhetoric of Temporality," in *Critical Theory since 1965,* ed. Hazard Adams and Leroy Searle (Tallahassee: Florida State University Press, 1986), pp. 209–10.

19. Roger Cardinal, *Figures of Reality: A Perspective on the Poetic Imagination* (Totowa, N.J.: Barnes & Noble, 1981), p. 14.

20. Martin Heidegger, *Poetry, Language, Thought* (New York: Harper & Row, 1971), p. 99.

21. Ibid., p. 91.

22. Benjamin Jowett, trans., and Irwin Edman, ed., *The Works of Plato* (New York: Modern Library, 1956), p. 299.

23. Ibid., p. 290.

24. Yvor Winters, *In Defense of Reason* (Denver: Alan Swallow, 1937), pp. 431–34.

25. A. Walton Litz, *Introspective Voyager: The Poetic Development of Wallace Stevens* (New York: Oxford University Press, 1972), pp. 44–45.

26. Sören Kierkegaard, *Fear and Trembling and the Sickness unto Death* (Princeton: Princeton University Press, 1941), pp. 162, 166, 201–3.

27. Martin Heidegger, "Letter on Humanism," in *Phenomenology and Existentialism*, ed. Robert C. Solomon (New York: Harper & Row, 1972), p. 345.

28. Jowett and Edman, *Works of Plato*, pp. 284–91.

29. Ad de Vries, ed., *Dictionary of Symbols and Imagery* (Amsterdam: North-Holland Publishing, 1974), p. 377.

30. Ibid., pp. 449–50.

31. Roman Jakobson, "The Metaphoric and Metonymic Poles," in *Critical Theory since Plato*, ed. Hazard Adams (New York: Harcourt Brace Jovanovich, 1971), pp. 1113–16.

CHAPTER 5

1. Martin Heidegger, *Being and Time* (New York: Harper & Row, 1962), pp. 51–52.

2. Stephen A. Erickson, *Language and Being: An Analytic Phenomenology* (New Haven: Yale University Press, 1970), pp. 81–85.

3. John Hollander, *The Figure of Echo: A Mode of Allusion in Milton and After* (Berkeley and Los Angeles: University of California Press, 1981), pp. 64–65.

4. Heidegger, *Being and Time*, pp. 56–57.

5. Ibid., p. 43.

6. Ibid., p. 44.

7. Martin Heidegger, "A Letter on Humanism," in *Phenomenology and Existentialism*, ed. Robert C. Solomon (New York: Harper & Row, 1972), p. 343.

8. Ibid., p. 345.

9. Peter Fingesten, *The Eclipse of Symbolism* (Columbia: University of South Carolina Press, 1970), pp. 152–56.

10. Paul A. Bové, *Deconstructive Poetics: Heidegger and Modern American Poetry* (New York: Columbia University Press, 1980), p. 52.

11. Ibid., p. xi.

12. Ibid., pp. 5–7.

13. Ibid., p. 51.

14. Cleanth Brooks, "Irony as a Principle of Structure," in *Critical Theory since Plato,* ed. Hazard Adams (New York: Harcourt Brace Jovanovich, 1971), pp. 1043–44.

15. Heidegger, *Being and Time,* p. 265.

16. Ibid., p. 189.

17. Edmund Husserl, *Ideas: General Introduction to Pure Phenomenology* (New York: Collier Books, 1962), p. 291.

18. Jacqueline Vaught Brogan, *Stevens and Simile: A Theory of Language* (Princeton: Princeton University Press, 1986), pp. 125, 126.

19. Hans Vaihinger, *The Philosophy of "As If": A System of the Theoretical, Practical and Religious Fictions of Mankind* (New York: Methuen, 1984).

20. Brogan, *Stevens and Simile,* pp. 132–33.

21. Ibid., pp. 133–41.

22. Ibid., p. 179.

23. Ibid., pp. 182–83.

24. Martin Heidegger, *On the Way to Language* (New York: Harper & Row, 1971), p. 93.

25. Ibid., p. 107.

26. Ibid., p. 102.

27. Ibid., p. 105.

28. Donald Justice, *Platonic Scripts* (Ann Arbor: University of Michigan Press, 1984), pp. 86–87.

29. Ibid., p. 138.

30. Ibid., p. 104.

31. Ibid., pp. 74–75.

32. Ibid., pp. 104–5.

33. Ibid., p. 95.

34. Ibid., pp. 9, 16, 36, 59.

35. Anthony Hecht, *Obbligati: Essays in Criticism* (New York: Atheneum, 1986), p. vii.

36. Hollander, *The Figure of Echo,* p. 114.

37. Ibid., p. ix.

38. Elizabeth Bishop, *The Collected Prose* (New York: Farrar, Straus & Giroux, 1984), p. xi.

39. Martin Heidegger, *Poetry, Language, Thought* (New York: Harper & Row, 1971), pp. 91, 95.

40. Ibid., p. 96.

41. Martin Heidegger, *What Is Called Thinking?* (New York: Harper & Row, 1968), p. 21.

42. Ibid., pp. 71–72.

43. Ibid., pp. 62–63.

44. Ibid., pp. 71–72.

45. John Hollander, *Vision and Resonance: Two Senses of Poetic Form* (New Haven: Yale University Press, 1975), p. ix.

46. Hollander, *The Figure of Echo,* p. 23.

47. Ibid., p. 114.

48. Ibid., p. 58.

49. Ibid., pp. 2, 95.

50. Ibid., p. 60.

51. Ibid., p. 64.

52. Ibid., p. 1.

53. Ibid., p. 20.

54. Robert Pinsky, *Poetry and the World* (New York: Ecco Press, 1988), pp. 61–64.

55. Ibid., pp. 91–92.

56. Ibid., pp. 176ff.

57. Ibid., pp. 144ff.

58. Ibid., p. 180.

59. Ibid., p. 144.

Index

Index